Law and Visual Jurisprudence

Volume 8

Stefan Huygebaert, Ghent University, Ghent, Belgium
Miklós Könczöl, Pázmány Péter Catholic University, Budapest, Hungary
Magdalena Łągiewska, University of Gdańsk, Gdańsk, Poland
Anita Lam, York University, Toronto, Canada
Massimo Leone, University of Turin, Turin, Italy
David Machin, Zhejiang University, Hangzhou, China
Samantha Majic, City University of New York, New York, USA
Danilo Mandic, University of Westminster, London, UK
Francesco Mangiapane, University of Palermo, Palermo, Italy
Aleksandra Matulewska, Adam Mickiewicz University, Poznan, Poland
Renisa Mawani, University of British Columbia, Vancouver, Canada
Rostam J. Neuwirth, University of Macao, Taipa, Macao
Arnaud Paturet, Paris Nanterre University, Naterre, France
Andrea Pavoni, Lisbon University Institute, Lisbon, Portugal
Timothy D. Peters, University of Sunshine Coast, Sippy Downs, Australia
Andreas Philippopoulos-Mihalopoulos, University of Westminster, London, UK
Richard Powell, Nihon University, Tokyo, Japan
Kimala Price, San Diego State University, San Diego, USA
Alison Renteln, University of Southern California, Los Angeles, USA
Marco Ricca, University of Parma, Parma, Italy
Peter W. G. Robson, University of Strathclyde, Glasgow, UK
Austin Sarat, Amherst College, Amherst, USA
Cassandra Sharp, University of Wollongong, Wollongong, Australia
Julia J. A. Shaw, De Montfort University, Leicester, UK
Richard K. Sherwin, New York Law School, New York, USA
Lawrence M. Solan, Brooklyn Law School, New York, USA
Mateusz Stępień, Jagiellonian University, Cracow, Poland
Kieran Mark Tranter, Queensland University of Technology, Brisbane, Australia
Farid Samir Benavides Vanegas, Ramon Llull University, Barcelona, Spain
Denis Voinot, Lille University, Lille, France
Honni von Rijswijk, University of Technology Sydney, Ultimo, Australia
Marco Wan, University of Hong Kong, Hong Kong, Hong Kong
Oliver Watts, Australian Government Art Collection, Canberra, Australia
Xu Youping, Guangdong University of Foreign Studies, Guangzhou, China

Jan M. Broekman

Knowledge in Change

The Semiotics of Cognition and Conversion

Springer

Jan M. Broekman
Faculty of Law and Higher Institute of Philosophy
KU Leuven
Leuven, Belgium

ISSN 2662-4532 ISSN 2662-4540 (electronic)
Law and Visual Jurisprudence
ISBN 978-3-031-23000-4 ISBN 978-3-031-23001-1 (eBook)
https://doi.org/10.1007/978-3-031-23001-1

This Springer imprint is published by the registered company Springer Nature Switzerland AG
The registered company address is: Gewerbestrasse 11, 6330 Cham, Switzerland

Preface

No, my knowledge is not my private and personal possession. On the contrary, the doors to the treasures of knowing are complicated instruments—and one of them is their dependence on cultural patterns which change their masters and participants. It seems difficult today to peacefully connect our traditional Ego with a modern Self. We have wonderful remembrances about the first but are hardly able to match them with the latter. Such memories accompany uneasy feelings of losing control over the steering wheel without any notion what to do. And they profile our precious assessments concerning our knowledge! The possessive pronoun changes amidst all other components and just registers the relativity of what we call knowledge. No epistemology is fixated or independent from its settings—this also makes visible how necessary a thinking about knowledge is! Relations with the relevant components of cognition are, on the one hand, fragmentary and dependent on their context and, on the other, fundamental and observable if not challenging.

A reliable epistemology seems missing in any worldview based on recent combinations of analog, digital, AI and Quantum thought patterns about human reality. Meaning and sense of social symbols are today perhaps related to social or political issues but seldom to any foundational cognition. The reason is that actual semiotics became rapidly covered by the digital culture, which replaces the traditional cognition processes by an all-round grip in the sense of conversion. This process, and with it the observations concerning the Subject of such a new form of knowledge formation, is the basic idea of this book. So, one might read about the Subject being transformed into a Self, and the latter into a Selfie as the actual form replacing the traditional Subject position. The fascinating dynamics of the Selfie, which are much wider than the Selfie-picture, are essential for every actual semiotic observation; they are in this book for the first time determined in a position named the 'Self-E' which determines the Self in the context of our digital culture. Conversion, once used by the technical empowerments to transfer analog into digital action and thought formation, gradually upholds the traditional concept of cognition in the last decades of the twentieth century. The interweaving of cognition and conversion became central in the twenty-first century, and the Self-E became the key to understand this change. A major task of conversion was namely to create an appropriate 'fit' to the world of analog ideas, concepts, languages and knowledge, and this task extended in our days the notion of our terrestrial roots, as the last pages of this book on 'climate change' explain.

The *decentering of the subject's polar position* became a fundamental process in the second half of the twentieth century, and it changed the world-wide structure of human cognition since those days. No wonder, because a possible 'decenterment' of the subject with the 'I and the Body' or the 'I and the Mind', on the one hand, and the 'Subject and its Object', on the other, differentiates the character of signs and complicates the sources of dynamics, in particular the features of the semiotic Self. Indeed, the key question remains: 'what is a human being without the capability to position itself as 'subjectivity'?' That capability changes with the world in which the word has to be understood and spoken. Looking back at the last century implies that this idea mirrors the power of insights in *analog* language. The latter remark specifies and broadens our approach to questionable ideas which are represented here.

Three aspects of this context are to review.

First, there is the actual situation that each consideration of language or lingual expressiveness is—in contrast to the studies in the preceding century—tied to a specific *type* of language. That requires much deeper insight in a typology of language and its relevance at every lingual occasion.

Second, there is today always a differentiation between *analog, digital* and *quantum* types of language in the background. Their relations are an important issue, not unlike their definition.

Third, we are confronted with a constantly *flowing* understanding that focuses on the numerous sub-relations between the distinguished language types. Who talks about language thus talks about *intertwinements* of lingual elements.

We must study and master these aspects: there is a task ahead expressed in the slogan concerning the decenterment of the subject. A triad 'Subject–Self–Self-E' took therefore its central place which once was totally captured by the 'I', and functions in the form of a continuously changing dynamics. Because of that process obtains cognition a different position in the heart and mind of every human being. That leads to the formulation of a newly conceived challenge, which eventually concerns law, social sciences, politics as well as communication studies. Leading are here the fixations sustained by *grammar structures*, the hitherto unclear boundaries between *language types* and their *flow of intertwining,* as well as the fascinating *global features* of expressions, for instance in digital translations of analog languages. So, the position of the subject became an issue of *intertwining language types* and not of simple translations resp. transitions. This clarifies how translations are never a matter of words only but always include the worlds in which words function, which represent *all* intertwining components of lingual articulation.

The reader who pays attention to the connections between cognition and conversion will continuously be in the grip of various forcefully mirroring C's. *Cognition* of facts and life relate namely to a process of *conversion* in which signs play a role.

That remains mostly in the dark. An all-embracing process of continuous *conversion* provides nevertheless *knowledge* on and about life and planet. Both are the product of mirroring, one discovers surprisingly. What power has this move of the mind, and at what issue is it focused? A provisory answer is given, when the consideration is accepted that every *meaning* activates its *sign functions*, so that *mirroring* appears to be *semiotically* relevant. No wonder that the idea of a general *visual semiotics* is active. It has a wider relevance than when visual objects are just concerned as a sign, and it shows a deep modernization of knowledge. The latter became during the last decades more and more in the grip of conversion processes, which causes the integration of two expressivities embraced by the human mind, namely *language* and the *digital*. The two form a unique background for a visual semiotics. It seems a rare phenomenon that the power of mirroring constitutes forms of knowledge that are related with changes understood as processes of conversion.

Conversion is a central concept that should provide an appropriate understanding of knowledge in digital worlds. What the term 'epistemology' in the analog world meant is going to be replaced and intensified by what 'conversion' means in the digital world—far beyond a 'translation' from one field of meaning into another. The many analyses and descriptions of the DACs and the ADCs are widely spread and even philosophically extended. Conversion seems therefore to be the most recent and encompassing coordinate of episteme since the second half of the twentieth century. It is indeed an important element of our knowledge which contributes to our understanding of the many forms of conversion.

Notice that any 'bio-', 'noo-' or 'logo-' does *not* explain how *a single Self* could cause and create forms of life. The latter are indeed never without a well-designed subject but, on the other hand, never fully determined by it. The term *Semiosphere* which is introduced on the following pages is therefore not in the first place focused on '*semiotic*' dimensions but on the '*sphere*' which characterizes the social and psychological features of a 'Self'. So, we should in effect interface with our own thoughts, experiences and ideas! It seems interesting that in this case the human body seems to be understood as the birthplace of this interface—in other words: as a carrier of extra-sensorial awareness—since it combines *sensorial* and *artificial* awareness. Is that insight important in locating human cognition in the range of insights produced by the human mind?

That question is essential for understanding why this book focuses in its final pages on law in general and 'climate change' in particular. They concentrate on the latter issue as the representation of an appropriate and most general human Self-understanding! They read like a renewed explanation of human origin. Its basic insight is that the terrestrial character of a knowledgeable human being cannot remain limited to strictly terrestrial features but is only understandable in wider, even planetary, dimensions. Problems of climate change confirm that attitude and challenge any human being to accept, understand and practice it. That is the perhaps greatest challenge human cognition ever faced. There is no construction on earth that does not claim: perceive me in my life's flow of meaning which honours the terrestrial as a feature of planetary influences and insights.

Indeed: your existence is richer than everyday subjectivity suggests! Its dimensions are embedded in terrestrial contexts which appear to be determined by spatial insights and discoveries of the human mind, embracing the most recent digital, AI and Quantum thought patterns and techniques. Cognition is their sticker—these pages should assist all of us to read them correctly!

Leuven, Belgium Jan M. Broekman

Contents

Chapter 1
Minds, Moons and Cognition

'As a result of efficient cooperative labor, four moons would illuminate the earthly night, the ice would recede from the poles, sea water would no longer taste salty, and beasts of prey would do man's bidding.'

Was there a dream told? What are such words, what do they mean, who has formulated them in what context? Are they from a fairy tale, or a book for teens, or any TV show? Did they sprout from the thoughts of a painter, who wanted to create a tableau of the planetary context of human life? Are they meant to be a stimulus to reconsider climate conditions caused by humans, their statal as well as industrial forms of labor included?

No, they are of the eighteenth-century French philosopher Charles Fourier describing human labor and its effects in the context of planetary occurrence.[1] And, most remarkably, were the same words a century later quoted by Walter Benjamin in his Parisian Passages and his notes on the Concept of History.[2] What is more: still another century later one discovers the same view in ideas and experiences of climate change being for instance formulated in papers and viewpoints of the IPCC. So, the view that planetary phenomena are not at all distanced from human needs and activities, survived at least during the last three decades. They underlined that human labor should be considered in a framework of planetary character. In other words, according to these philosophical and socially relevant ideas did labor, sciences, philosophy as well as the arts co-form the planet. How can that be, how has that to be understood and how should we refer to such ideas? What

[1] Fourier (1808). Fourier gave a specific meaning to the concept of *labor* which is remarkably near to Marx' concept of *Arbeit* which was initiated in the same eighteenth century. Both used the term 'work' as well as 'labor'. Important is their inner totality: labor cq. *Arbeit* embraces all creative activity including industry, craft, agriculture, etc. which arises from a truly liberated passion—this is his famous theory of 'attractive labor.' See furthermore Chap. 9, Sect. 9.5.

[2] Benjamin (1982), pp. 45–79, 1041–1060 and: 'Ueber den Begriff der Geschichte', in *Gesammelte Schriften,* Band I,2, pp. 693–704; these pages contain the quoted lines of Fourier. See also: Lindner (2011), p. 280: 'Fourier und der Fourierismus'.

J. M. Broekman, *Knowledge in Change*, Law and Visual Jurisprudence 8,

essential insight, especially about our knowledge and our self, must we accept today? The question raises again: was there a new reality articulated when Fourier spoke about the moons, the planet, the climate? Or did he speak about himself, the human being, its dreams, the freedom, and the importance of related thought formations?

1.1 The Ego of the New Plural

That question focuses more than ever on the actual field of semiotics. It tells us, that not only what we mean and know, but also what we envision plays a central role in our continuous unfolding of knowledge. The study of sign and signification are folded in an encompassing process which Edmund Husserl already characterized as an exploration of ego-positions and their power of reducing—i.e., mastering—meaning. This opened a dynamic view on the genesis of human knowledge, with the knowing subject in all its powerful variations and positions. Observation and lingual articulation of reality form the overarching dynamics in that field. It is important to underline the coherence of visual and lingual approaches in view of their sign-relevance, which tends to be linked to traditional forms of understanding the genesis of knowledge. The latter was traditionally understood as a subject which was a center of specific activities that creates a stable and manageable pattern of thoughts, ideas, issues and even data.

About the coherence of those patterns is more to say than ever before! Emphasis is on the fact, that lingual expressivities do not know any standstill. Human speech (even the speech clearly produced by a recognizable and understandable subject) is never a matter of standstill acts but always of acts in shared events. The issue of *socialization* is based on this fact, hence Fourier's emphasis on *cooperation*. There is always the *presence of the o/Other* which plays the dominant constitutive role in life. Levinas repeatedly underlined that this role is axial in the genesis of any self-consciousness. One must thus intensify the vision on the role of *an alter* in the frame of understanding *a subject.* This is essential for the relevance of visual semiotics although the epistemological components remained in the dark. Mannoury articulated that insight in his contributions to the *Amsterdam Signific Circle*, as did Eco and Sebeok in later publications.[3] They touched problems of visual semiotics without exploring the closely related concept of cognition. Missing epistemological dimensions appear to be central in our days.[4] A virtual semiology was in the minds of those who focused on the study of signs, but where do we find access towards a deeper understanding of that actual issue? An answer might surprise. We find it in the traditional underpinning of *the Subject as a Self*—which, of course, is a primary

---

[3] Mannoury (1949), Eco (1979), and Sebeok (1978, 2001).

[4] See Broekman (2019), pp. 298 f.

power of the Self in itself! Mutual recognition is constitutive, even if it should be discovered in the structures of the Self, which are also a matter of dynamics.[5]

These structures concern two processes: the first is named '*cognition*' and the second '*conversion*'. The essence of their togetherness is, that those two are merging in the beginnings of the third millennium and realize two different enduring structures (often named 'ages') of Occidental, even Mundial life and culture. Knowledge without digital components does no longer exist. Human activities without being part of the worldwide datafication became unthinkable. Even a human who does not read or write is subjected to these processes. He or she is involved in datafication and his or her activities are registered despite the variant approaches at hand.

So, the quoted words of Fourier still fascinate, his ideas remain admirable, and his thoughts appeal to the level of renewed considerations that focus on the remarkable unity of 'human self and planet'. Is our intelligence and cognition indeed connected with moonlight and sea streams in a more concrete and less imaginary manner than our linguistic expressiveness suggests? The question challenges in many dimensions. Fourier's use of the term 'socialism' focused on communal and autarchic forms of social life in broadly conceived patterns of cohesion, as expressions like 'familistères' and 'phalanstères' indicated. It is important to understand how they were already in his days marked by the constitutive character of human relations expressed via 'I' and 'You'—long before Martin Buber's 'dialogic' philosophy in the twenties of the twentieth century was exposed.[6] The latter would in the spirit of Fourier determine our socially constitutive character by means of focusing on the other or another person on the one hand (the world of I and You) and the 'it', the 'Es' (the world of issues and things) on the other. The dialogue between You and I thus confirmed the dualism of his approach. Those forms of dualist cognition are indeed dominant in the recent days of philosophy. And, more absolutely formulated, each denial of duality would embrace a new dualism: that was the case in earlier days as well as in our recent periods of thought patterning. This forms an enormous challenge to the human mind: how 'is', how 'exists' that mind, where or what is 'its origin'? Does there not exist the continuous facticity that human existence is ultimately to be expressed as a cosmic item? These questions do imply the insight that every 'I/You- duality' challenges all eventual dualist positionings. But those positions do confirm the reality of the human Self in their pluralities and their patterns of thought and knowledge.

This leads to a most remarkable insight, which relates to semiotics: an understanding and exploration of the Human Self does form the basis for *any* unfolding of

---

[5]There is a fascinating line in Continental Philosophy since Immanuel Kant's *Kritik der reinen Vernunft* (1781) and his thoughts about the 'Split Ego' [B.37, 303; A. XI], which leads to Edmund Husserl and his foundational works on Phenomenology (1913) [Husserliana Bd. VII] and underlines the dynamics of the Subject and its formations of an Ego. The German expression 'Ich-Spaltung' indicates a process and not an unmovable fact. Kant formulated in his *Opus Posthumum* [Ak. Ausgabe Kant Werke Vol. XX, p. 31] that the human being differentiates himself from animals because he is a 'sense-Being that knows itself' ['ein sich selbst erkennendes Sinnenwesen'].

[6]Buber (1923).

cognition. This is far more than a simple call for insight in a human being. It was already mentioned that there is an important, stable, and continuous development in Occidental philosophy from Kant to Husserl, a line which represents the power and appeal of *the relation of the Subject with- and within itself.*[7] Power and appeal are determined by the dominant cultural patterns of their ages between the years 1780–2000. Our thesis is, that this (more or less) unbroken line teared down in the last years of the twentieth and the first of the twenty-first century. One of the most important elements of that breach is indicated as the transition *from analog to digital reality.*[8] The latter determines inner changes in the subject and therefore also newly to be conceived dynamics of the Self. These are founded in a concept of the Self that is already unfolded in the philosophy of Immanuel Kant and presented in modern terms and relevance by Edmund Husserl's phenomenology which was initiated in the first half of the twentieth century. The central naming was via the concept of the Kantian 'Ich-Spaltung' as well as during later centuries for instance in the Husserlian 'Split I'. This concerns in fact a provoking lingual determination: we qualify and experience the deepest and perhaps most central function of a human life as *a being split*! *This 'being split' grounds the riddle of our modernity*. It enables—broadly and exemplarily formulated—the transition from analog towards digital Self-experiences. The unfolding of that split remains important even after Husserl's reductive analyses of ego positions.[9] It fascinates that a proper understanding of a twenty-first century's Ego (or Subject) strongly relates to insights unfolded in the seventeenth century, for instance in the works of Immanuel Kant.

Husserl interpreted the *plural* character of each subject, each 'I', each Self. That character seems determined by all possible connections with fields and structures of a human existence—such as consciousness, speech, temporality, time, or respect. None of them is without plurality, and all are based on the plural formed by the 'I' and the 'Self'. There is no philosophy nor any knowledge, no intersubjectivity or any ethics beyond that plural. In other words: human existence is founded in this basic plurality, and plurality generates knowledge in all regards. In his 1788 *Kritik der praktischen Vernunft* explains Kant how any human being is designed to create and receive *respect* (German: *Achtung*). This position constitutes the sign that a human person is responsive to moralities. Responsiveness is thus a moment of human self-consciousness. Heidegger formulated how it is an overture to insight in foundational structures of a human Self.[10] Morality is fundamental for each human act in whatever cultural setting wherever on the planet. Respect is one of the very few forms of human life that are generally accepted. It is clear, that in the sentiment of respect the sensitive 'I' itself creates an opening of the Self towards itself. The

[7] See Footnote 4.

[8] An *analog* signal is officially a continuous signal which represents physical measurements. Digital signals are discrete time signals generated by digital modulation. See:<https://www.google.be/search?>.

[9] See Chap. 4 of this book.

[10] Heidegger (1929).

sensibility of this fact and the complexity of this insight lead to the statement, that 'respect', which never touches material elements but always touches the human self as a person, is radically embedded in patterns of intersubjectivity. In the latter occurs the unfolding of my own Self—nowhere else, Kant and Husserl concluded.

This leads to an important next step in the unfolding insight in cognition and the foundation of knowledge. The 'split ego' leads in our days to the closing of what has been evident for the millennia since Kant and earlier thinkers: *subjectivity is no longer a detectable and manageable concept in the way it unfolded in analog cognition.* Indeed, that characterization is no longer relevant or correct. But there is no reason nor a technique to fully integrate *analog* and *digital* expressivities. And there is also no convincing argument for the suggestion that conversion processes create *forms of mutuality* in that regard. Such an impression already proved to be inadequate when functions of the DAC and the ADC were analyzed. No, not any *new duality* (of analog and digital features) makes the actual situation clear! One should on the contrary understand *the new plurality* which dominates cognition as well as conversion today. In other, rather absolute words one must conclude: *the digital is not the new form caused by the split of the split ego.* But one could nevertheless suggest that the digital is the *other Otherness* which creates intersubjectivity and thus the social dimensions of life on the planet. This other Otherness is therefore *a New Plurality*, which in our days embraces digital thought patterns and techniques as well as those of Artificial Intelligence and ultimately also Quantum techniques and thought patterns.[11]

In relation with this new understanding of cognition, a *fascinating change of sign* can be registered. In the predominantly analog world indicates the term '*Ego*' or '*I*' the Subject, but today's digital world embraces the term *Self* for it! In other words: the *Self* entered a world in which the digital dominates the New Plural. It poses itself as the major object of its inner experience. The possibility of a renewed self-affection comes to the fore. The Self needs this affection—it must be affected by itself to be a Self or an 'I'.

Exploring this thought patterning concerns the dynamics of the Self in the context of the New Plural; it thus focuses in the first place on the digital world-plurality. An invitation embraced by those newly conceived dynamics of the Self could be formulated. A simple 'be invited for a walk in the woods' could unfold such a challenge. After a few steps does the hand of the walker show its smartphone and an 'oops' formulated by him confirms that the walk is in the right direction. The gesture shows that we not only realize a www, a walk in the woods, but also and at the same time a walk in the www, the world wide web. Our steps are of the New Plural; they are digital in every move. The walk is unique: *a Self was invited, and a Selfie walks with us*! A first glance at the smartphone was already an act of great semiotic importance: the Self was mirrored in the picture of the walking route (named

[11] Human intelligence works beyond any analog/digital divide, and thus denies the idea of the digital being a new form of cognition and creating a dualism with the analog patterning. See Grier (2020), pp. 293 ff and 300 f.

'map'), and no wonder that the Self will soon be in the photo picture of the walking Self! The invited Self became a walking Selfie. *The Selfie transformed in the Self-E belongs to the new Subject in the New Plural.* His or her existence and cognition are in that New Plural not an issue of *knowledgeable, virtual,* but definitively of *perceptional, visual* semiotics, created and sustained by an infinite process of mirroring.

Once more, we repeat: the *Self* became the *Selfie* and then the *Self-E* in the New Plural, which is dominated by digital thought patterns. It functions like the *Subject* in earlier centuries of cognition but now in the form of a *Selfie* resp. *Self-E.* The latter is much more than an incidental picture in the hand of a smartphone: it is one's digital point of orientation in the third millennium's life which really changes the Self! This apparent change in the self-understanding of the self determines the inner structures of knowledge.[12] It thus starts an age in which the New Plural must be embraced to understand knowledge and reality.

1.2 Mirroring

Mirroring seems one of the most powerful metaphors in the dynamics that encircle cognition—both as an act and as a datum. And if the latter is indeed a component factor of knowledge, then it is also determinative for the concept and reality of history, Walter Benjamin suggested already in the middle of the twentieth century. The mirror images of man on the planet and on man in the cosmos represented a long tradition in the process of understanding human knowledge; they are in the soul of the actual Self-E. Its epistemological power became for that reason a truly specific mirror.[13] The latter is much more than a doubling (or a post factum unfolding) of images that contribute to delineate human life and consciousness. That view became for instance clear in Spinoza's thoughts on nature, but it also determined Fourier's view on human society; it formed a century later a guide in Buber's considerations of the 'Du' and became in that same century constitutive in structuralist views as well as in those of a human discourse which was broader and more meaningful than a pure ensemble of words.

Benjamin characterized Paris in the nineteenth-century as a 'Spiegelstadt', a Mirror-Town! Human history and its social life do represent in that light a unique

[12]The complexity of the New Plural in this age is difficult to oversee and to manage, as the Self-E introduced in this book indicates. The individual components are hardly determined: what are exactly the outlines of traditional analog language, of digital expressivities or of quantum insights on essential particles? In any case is no analog relation anymore without links to digital terms and vice versa. The subject's positioning is therefore closely linked with the behavioral possibilities provided by those two, with for instance AI and Quantum possibilities at their side. Those various influences enforce the Self to control and be itself through the form, format, and effect of the Self-E and its constitutive mirroring.

[13]The Greek *episteme* = knowledge.

moment of the dynamic togetherness of nature and knowledge! His famous 1939 essay on *The Concept of History* embraced the unfolding of human life as well as nature. Theology might in that text provide a thinly shining at the horizon, but in his mind do chessboards, tables and mirrors guarantee a secured success of cognition and self-presence—a mirroring that seems self-evident and knows nothing but continuity. That would be underlined nearly a century later when conversion became the partner of cognition. He already understood such perspectives of a future socio-cultural development which became visible in that twenty-first century. The proximity of these thoughts to our actual digital understanding of cosmos and planet is bewildering. No wonder that mirror and the mirroring belonged for Benjamin to the foundations of a knowledge-producing human mind which revitalizes the recognition of otherness as an occurrence colored by cosmic views. One should in this light read his notes ensembled under the title 'Passagen' which provide access to all his notes and remarks on this object.[14] He mentioned the importance of their imaginary structure as the major reason to pay attention to the *Parisian Passages* in his days which function as a forceful combination of name and image at the borderlines of an economy of wares. The names of the commodities in the mirrors of the Passages seemed precursor of the data in the next century's public life! That is the case in his famous notes when they regard the panes in the Passages, the window dressings, the shopping populations, the twinkles in their eyes which altogether format the relations between selves and others when walking what once were streets of the town. Note, that Benjamin and his walks through Paris did not yet have any notion of the Selfies who would follow him there in a later age!

Indeed: the great value of human life is based upon the discovery of the fact that cosmic dimensions enable an individual, an 'I', to value his or her 'You'. Buber mentioned here the 'Du-Sinn des Menschen' (the sense of a You in everyone) which guides and reinforces the life of any individual. Every occurrence of a human relation is a position in which the 'mirror' plays a role. One's presence is apparently valuated by this special feature of one's experience. If this occurs, Buber formulated, 'the individual will bless all cells that harbored him, as well as all in which he or she will arrive. This finding is not the end of its activity but rather its eternal central position'.[15] That finding is impossible without the mirror experience, which represents the tensions between an 'I' and a 'You'. Those tensions seem fundamental and constitutive. They do intrinsically belong to our understanding of the triads which are basic to key-words—like history, labor, or climate—and their interweaving as a constitutive process. But is this position final and definitive?

This most fascinating insight of all positions mentioned does indeed relate to the epistemological value of human mirroring. That value is also difficult to articulate, since the mirroring seems to articulate a process of acquiring knowledge which is also confronted with the no - thing, with the Nothing or with Nothingness, the Nihil,

[14] Benjamin (1982), Band V, 2, pp. 666 f.

[15] Idem, p. 94: 'Er segnet alle Zellen, die ihn geherbergt haben, und alle, in denen er noch einkehren wird. Denn dieses Finden ist nicht ein Ende des Wegs, sondern seine ewige Mitte.'

and its meaning in an awareness beyond any specific fragment of culture or form of cognition. But important for an insight in the tensions between philosophically designed dualisms and dual features of human existence is the fact that the no - thing is never nothing. On the contrary, a well-understood No - thing is a deeply engraved experience of historical features, of changing attitudes, of the presence and absence of existential features which confront a human mind with its cosmic flows.

This understanding validates the mirroring concept which received attention during the last centuries. It has been characterized as the most important and fascinating facet of human knowledge: human cognition as fundamentally and constitutively related to No - thing. The 'I-You duality' is not constitutive dualistic because of its continuous and multiplying relationships with nature, cosmos, or planet. It means: the 'I-You' relation must be understood in the light of a constantly changing context regarding those three, which is in the many understandings of the term intersubjectivity. The latter are fundamentally involved in that context. Where an 'I' is, is the existence of the 'You' a givenness as foundational factor.

That is the case with the phenomenon we call shadow; the latter plays a surprising role in the constitutive powers of intersubjectivity. Shadows are visible: they are most often visible thanks to my posture; they accompany me although I perceive them only in an almost unnatural and often extreme reflective position. But as a shadow, I am separated from you and at the same time identical with you in an order of naturalness which we call 'we'. It is most remarkable that in such positions the power of the negative is at least equal to the power of the positive.

It means in a philosophical perspective, that the introduction of a dialectics does not change anything in these circumstances. As a shadow of my Self, I am free from you but also next to You in an order of evidence we both did not create. This adumbration annihilates the contours of the 'me' for 'me' although they are clear for 'you'. Is that clarity the result of the fact, do that contours not differentiate? Your shadow is clearly never identical with mine, and so are our contours. The negations and our contours: do they not in an undetectable manner unfold their origin? Both are inconvertibly 'I' and 'Non-I': that is: 'You'! That view is foundational for 'cognition' as well as 'conversion'—despite their different Occidental context and culture. Why? We do live continuously with the desire to completely pay off any negation or other negativity in our relationship with the other. But we tend to forget that the total negation would become identical with the absolute positive in such a situation so that both would no longer realize their character of processing and realization. In other words: the possibility and history of any well-understood togetherness of an 'I' and a 'You' would be lost. The question arises how human cognition can constitutively relate to the No - thing, where every cognitive act seems to focus on an Any - thing.

1.3 To Grasp, to Fit

The two basic terms of this text—cognition and conversion—live from the dynamics and constitutive powers of their balances between the positive and the negative embedded in intersubjectivity. That observation forms the basis of a necessary insight into life during a period in which the structures of human knowledge change fundamentally. The coherence of the two mentioned expressions is an important sign of those dynamics at issue. They are by no means incidental factors of their changing color or profile. On the contrary: they are signs of changes concerning the multiple cosmic dimensions and patterns of accelerating diversification in the realm of human thoughts. The two terms indicate the unique and forceful pattern of change in all regards, and they concern the entire globe, its nature and its humanity included. In other words, they indicated a deeply unfolding change of features of humanity, culture, and cosmic conditions. Moreover, philosophy itself has changed! With those changes occurred important diversifications of linguistic concepts and the appreciation of languages and meanings. To give just one example: who in modern philosophy focuses on transcendental determinations, or is prepared to discuss reductions of meanings that colored keywords in earlier centuries? Indeed, languages changed, and meanings differentiated so that the question in what type of world we live today, seems inappropriate. Is there a common view about our living in a world which can be determined by linguistic expressions, by languages? No, that is no longer possible. In a world of data, sending and receiving are these views just technical questions which cannot resolved by social and/or philosophical considerations! Where are the data on which such a philosophy would be grounded? That unanswerable question only creates a disquieting and threatening silence.[16]

The proximity of thinking and partitioning in a world delineated by intersubjectivity is lost in continuously revised coherences of data and techniques which are in essence digital. The unity of human body and soul, once a basic property of humans, became a technically comprehensive issue in the digital world for which specific terminologies are leading our analytic thoughts. The partition of body and soul, once emphasizing the wholeness of a human being, became in actual digital changes, which are not an enhancement of analog features, a psycho-technical issue and thus a subject for specialists to study at distance from the experience of life itself. That technology relegates any eccentricity of the self: *philosophy became a networked form of intersubjectivity*. 'To be human' became an expression of the simulation of what once was named 'the human' and seems constructed beyond eccentricity and its rationalization.

The basic terms which form the center of our observation and though patterning thus are *cognition*, (i.e., acquiring by thought, experience, and the senses as grounded in selective capacities), and *conversion*, (i.e., the change or the causing to change from one form to another). They seem grounded in the complexity of adaptation and forms of identity in thought patterns of the human mind. Thanks to

[16] See Broekman (2019), pp. 283f.; Broekman and Fleerackers (2020), pp. 28, 62f.

the complexity of their socio-cultural relations are both a matter of a differentiation related to their enforcement of contouring and mutual shadowing. These powerful dynamic processes are often disregarded—even when such simple terms like 'to know', or 'to grasp' are used on the one hand and 'to fit' on the other.[17]

This embraces a fascinating problem. Every fragment and phase of intersubjectivity is confronted with a specific thought formation concerning the other in his or her desire to set itself free from the 'no' which seems to be constitutive of the 'non - I'. This appears to be one of the major issues in each thought formation about intersubjectivity. How does a theory of intersubjectivity touch a double no, a double negation that is constitutive in one and the same foundational experience of the other? Hegel's *Logic* suggests that the only issue which contributes to the growth of our scientific insight is the fact that '*the Negative is also Positive*'. It means, that any logical contradiction can be understood as a specifically defined negation.[18]

One must understand that a philosophy of the *no* or the *nothing* and its many different postures should envision any location between the 'no' and 'being' (or 'essence') that is *a well-determined* 'no' and 'being'. This is the case when such basic acts like 'to grasp' (in the case of cognition) or 'to fit (in the case of conversion) are at stake. In both A fundamental desire should be recognized in both, and that leads to the foundational structure of the experienced moment. The 'not yet' in the 'no' characterize such a moment, and the same determines each realization of intersubjectivity. 'Cognition' as well as 'conversion' are such moments if the intersubjective reality which can be simply indicated as 'life' functions. But on the other hand, do not forget: this understanding of life does pertain to our 'life in the cosmos'.

It was already suggested that there are 'signs of changes that show cosmic dimensions and patterns of accelerating diversification' in the realm of human thoughts, understanding and appreciating the human Self. This observation forms a background for the insight that such changes find their expression in a global transition of the basic features that determine human knowledge: *from cognition into conversion*. Indeed: to grasp something difficult or mysterious is always different from getting them fit. But this duality is dying. There is no 'something' anymore that is not already constituted by the power and insight of 'conversion', which means 'fit' in this case. 'Knowledge' in its traditional and philosophical sense does not exist anymore. The more dynamic realm of the digital reigns; the latter is determinable as knowledge at a completely different level of human experience and intellect in the case of conversion. In other words, there is no knowledge recognized in today's world without being marked as conversion. That implies a unique revolution of the character of culture—and not of one or another specific sector of it.

One must conclude how there are today, in our third millennium, two terms and indications concerning knowledge (in its traditional sense) which create meaning in the flow of human cognition. Analog and digital meaning color each other. It is

[17] See Broekman (2016), pp. 206 f.

[18] Hegel (1812), pp. 35f.

remarkable how a grip of digital thinking and operating, masters the flow of human thought formation only after first international ideas concerning climate and climate changes came to the fore. Digitality and climate change seem interdependent. *The 1972 United Nations Conference on the Environment* proposed in Stockholm to support three categories which are important in this context: (a) the Global Environmental Assessment Program, (b) the relevant Environmental management activities, and (c) International measures to support assessment and management activities carried out at the national and international levels.

We must underline, that none of these categories was determined as a special region of exercising any specific form of knowledge. Nobody could even think of conversion as an important element of the cognition at stake in the days during which these three categories were studied and applied. There was no mention of any digital thought or reality. The economy concerned in those conferences was not yet based on information technology. But access to the digital world only begun to unfold in days after the 1972 *Conference*: the first Macintosh Portable *laptop* became available in 1989 whilst the first computer to use at home, the Epson HX20, was already developed around 1981! A digital expressivity (a language to be applied in sciences or philosophy, in economy, politics, behavioral sciences or related disciplines) became refined only in the last decade of the millennium. That was also the case with thought patterns concerning the essence and presence of human individuals—even 'individuality' was a normal and in the Western world generally accepted expression. All this changed fundamentally: it is as if Jespersen's observation formulated in 1922 becomes true in those final days of the twentieth century. He stated that we created the feeling about a mysterious universal grammar influencing our daily languages and communication.[19] And, in contrast to Jespersen, we know the name of this recently effective grammar: *the digital*. We do experience daily one of the most comprehensive examples of the digital interpretation of an 'I–You' relationship. It was normal to speak of a 'Speaker–Hearer' relation in the days of the first global attention for climate change (1972). Today is that relation characterized as a 'Sender–Receiver' connection. Indeed: the digital expressivity changed the soul of humans in their contexts, emotions and experiencing social relations. In the computer language, which is fundamentally digital, are we no longer a hearer of words but the consumer, resp. receiver of messages. Information became defined as a sharing data between computer systems, not between human individuals. And economy became the model of intersubjective relations so that it changed our daily language!

The closeness of digital thinking and operating on the one hand and human behavior on the other makes us experience our body and mind as a very different part of a universal scale. The latter unfolds with the smartphone in our hands and the computer technologies in our mind. All this occurs as a new embodiment which is independent from the specific language we speak or spoke or the family of languages

[19] Jespersen (1922). See also, under the heading 'computer architecture': <https://en.wikipedia.org/wiki/Word_(computer_architecture)>.

to which our words belong, the mother tongue. A word is defined in computer architecture as *the natural unit of data used by a particular processor design*. Note, that the number of bits in a word (its size, width, length etc.) characterizes this basic element of spoken, written or conceived language. This characterization leads, surprisingly enough, to a new plural feature of language. Any word embodies analog meaning (the seme) together with basic features of digital character (the digit). The two embrace a variety of levels in which seme and digit are closely interwoven. Their continuous transition characterizes in today's mind the basics of language. This concept is named conversion and forms the foundation for the actual power of digitalization of the human mind, its observation, its cognition and inter–subjectivity.

1.4 No - thing and Nothingness

To understand the structure and embracement of the effects produced by an analogic expressivity integrated with a digital grip on life and language, one must go back to the inner structures of No - thing and Nothingness. One of the most fascinating suggestions concerning this issue in European mysticism, religion and philosophy was generated around 1492 by the Jewish mystic Isaak Luria, who is even today widely considered as the father of modern Kabbalah. It was the year of the downfall of the Moorish culture in Spain and the first oceanic expedition of Columbus. These events required an understanding influenced by the positive as well as by the negative because of their multidimensional meanings. The Divine Creation was marked by philosophers and mystics as a Creatio ex Nihilo.

Luria underlined that the Creation which happened in God Self was in principle a polar occurrence. The Divine Self was approached as a polarity which existed because the negativity was a necessary condition for becoming factual. In other words, the Highest is never without the 'No - thing'; without negation is not anything to perceive or to detect. Philosophy is not able to deny this insight. On the contrary: philosophy lives and endures her actuality through recognizing and maintaining her own mysteriousness. Of essence is the indelible fact of duality beyond dualism. In the 'I - Thou' relation reigns the same mysteriousness as in the Divine Creation—the two do mirror! One seems to be the shadow of the Other—a basic insight embraced in many cultures on the globe. A contracting of Oneself in a Self is a secret that constitutes the basis and the rationality, i.e., the sanity of otherness. The latter forms a duality far beyond any dualism: mirroring creates much more than a pure conjunctive existence. Each contraction allows a cohabitation: each one with a Self is in essence a being with an Other. That conjunction appears to be the foundational mode of human existence and reaches far beyond any coordination of a dualist nature—the reach is created by the 'No - thing'.

In other words: *the flow of constitutive mirroring leads to a new and forceful appreciation of the 'No - thing'*. There is no mirroring if the Self has not created an Other through its mirroring. If an 'I' is completely self-sufficient and beyond relations, then there is no cognition possible. It must exclude itself as identical with cosmos and reality. That is the secret of the No - thing which opens to Divine- as well as to human reality. That Openness relates in an almost mysterious manner to the 'No' of the No - thing.

Scholem explains is his 1957 publication dedicated to Walter Benjamin,[20] how Luria brought the idea to the fore that God performed in His Creation not a step outside His Divine Self but a step inward. It concerned an 'inner folding of Itself out of in Itself'. That *Folding Deus Absconditus* creates a necessary tangibility of the Impersonal in the inner sphere of the Divine Impersonality. The Impersonal (Home of the No - thing), Luria underlines, transforms in the Divine Personal only through this Act. A Divine Exile in His Self thus marks the essence of the Creation.[21] The negation plays in all this an important role. It is present in the observation of God, it is fundamental in each act of His Creation, it counts for every human relation to the other person. It is remarkable how also in human love, understood as the most intense form of sociability, the shadow of the negative is perceivable. In his *Philosophy of Law* Hegel wrote: 'Love is the most incredible contradiction which cannot be solved by the human brain because there is nothing harsher than this punctuality of the self-consciousness, which will be ignored but which I want to affirm. Love creates and at the same time solves contrarian feelings . . .'[22]

One of such essential moments in which the awareness of this complexity was formulated in an understandable language arose when the philosopher Spinoza wrote in the Dutch village named Voorburg[23] about the difference between the nature-concept in form of a '*natura naturans*' and another in form of a '*natura naturata*'. In his 1675 *Ethics* he tried to name the ties of the planet with the cosmos, which created a background for understanding nature as implying human cognition. The *natura naturans* indicates the planet's life in its infinite unchangeability. The latter makes the Cosmos independent from its Creator and its User: in terms of Spinoza's days understood as: independent from God and human beings. Those two terms remain an all-embracing conditional power only in their togetherness, Spinoza's *Ethics* underline. That relationship has been understood as the basics of knowledge in the naturata-cosmos.

The comparison with human relations has been outlined in all ages. An experience of such comparisons is often in words like: 'I see my Self in your eyes, I hear my Self in your words; without them I would not be able to be a Self that knows you and can live at the level of a common understanding'. However, the striving to adhere to the naturans-cosmos remains vividly present. Immanuel Kant tried with passion to embrace the existence of a 'Ding an Sich' and thus to mirror the naturata. And all of us do so—it's an observation that dominates our history. No wonder, that

[20] See Scholem (1957), pp. 285 f.

[21] Scholem (1957), pp. 13, 19, 234, 286, 297 f.

[22] G. W. F. Hegel: Werke, Gesamtausgabe (1832-45) Ed. 1986, Bd III, p. 222.

[23] Voorburg is a village in the western 'Netherlands'—and already by the Romans qualified as 'Forum Hadriani'. See de Spinoza (1996).

the 'mirror-experience' was described as one of the essential components of human knowledge and the humane condition in general. But: take care! What is behind the mirror? Who is the one that looks behind that mirror we cherish? That question relates to fairy tales and other stories known in nearly all languages! But the question pertains, surprisingly indeed, to touch the position of human cognition in cosmic coherences.

The latter embraces in essence the problem of the No - thing. In philosophy it seems to be represented by the supremacy of the so-called constitutive ego. Hegel qualified that supremacy as 'the punctuality of self-consciousness'. We are hardly able to imagine any alternative of that specific constitutive moment. No wonder, because most attempts to understand intersubjectivity embrace either the 'I' or the 'You' as a unique point of departure. Such exit points are considered as normal, whereas the 'No - thing' or the 'No - where' seems unacceptable. No wonder: the power of intentionality is no longer experienced as evidence when the answer becomes more important than the appeal. But be aware: at the same time will the 'No' or the 'No - thing' loose its traditionally threatening character. The 'I' that always seemed to be trusted to found cognition and the social, became fundamentally mistrusted during the foundation of cognition.[24] Only when the trust could embrace the negative, seemed the 'I' acceptable. In other words: only in a rich and sound distrust could the 'I' be accepted as a formative power. The role of negativity and its function in a social and cognitive unfolding of inter-subjectivity is extremely central. Hegel is most progressive in his experiences whilst looking behind the mirror. Philosophy should be serious 'in appreciating otherness and alienation as well as the conquering of this alienation' is his warning in the 1807 *Phenomenology of the Spirit.*[25] It means, not the *annihilation of the negation* but the *coalescent power of the negation* should be recognized by the philosopher! The greatness of philosophy will become visible in the functions of the negative at all possible and relevant levels: the vision of the Divinity, the Creation as well as the Fellowman.

This viewpoint, which is embraced by most philosophers in the twentieth century, includes the acceptance and clarity of difference and contra-diction. It is the Being itself that brings the 'No - thing' to the light as a major determination. For that reason, one should not bring the 'No - thing', the 'No' and the 'Negation' simply together in the field of thesis and anti-thesis. The negation is a cause of continuous tension and creates the decisive moments in the 'dualism versus duality' relationships. The Nihil is transitoriness, multiplicity, negation, and impediment behind the mirror.

[24] P. Valery: '... il faut entrer en soi-meme armé jusqu'aux dents'.

[25] Hegel (1949), pp. 20f.

1.5 Intersubjectivity

Understanding intersubjectivity in the Self of 'Oneself as a figure of the 'No - thing'' creates astonishment, because this leads to a different and above all a broader view on the 'I - You' relationship, far beyond the ideas of Buber or Rosenzweig.[26] That view contrasts also with the general and popular opinion that any encounter between an 'I' and a 'You' solves problems and enriches human life. That opinion might even unveil the basics of Love! It would therefore be completely understandable to suggest that the relation between an 'I' and a 'You', in other words: intersubjectivity, bans all negativity and all forms of nihilism—especially in social relations.

Reviewing the role of the *Nihil* resp. the *Negative* in the *inter-subject* relationship is for that reason a disputable but precious venture: it concerns ultimately the position of *the Self related with another Self in one's proper Self*! That is the theme to research, although authors like Levinas and Bakhtin already mentioned it as deeply dialogic.[27] In other words: we need renewed attention to the idea that any relationship with an Other should destroy the negative and thus create appropriate forms of inter-subjectivity as the basis for all social life. Is that destruction of the 'No - thing' correct, and therefore so important that it colors life and love? Can we never accept any negativity being constitutive in relations among subjects? That is a very special and seldom noticed question which nevertheless constitutes intersubjectivity.

The issue thus concerns the role of the 'No - ' in relation to the Other. That is to be interpreted as: the 'No - ' in the Self. The general feeling is, that intersubjectivity is most valuable when negations disappeared in all networks of human relations. But that is only façade. The 'No– 'appears to be a decisive factor and source of energy in every exploration of the Self. It could thus create astonishment to consider that intersubjectivity itself must be understood in the field of social relations including possible forms of negation. Those features and power become visible when the Other is characterized as the non-I in daily life. This characterization includes the difference between the specific determination of time and location of myself compared to other times or places. Both are not interchangeable—each lawyer would underline this in every variant system of law. In Hegel's view is the No or Nihil in the first place a matter of differentiation and sometimes also of contradiction. He argues that the Being as such[28] brings the Nihil as its own negative determination. It is for that reason difficult, if not impossible, to place the No - thing and its negative determination in the frame of Thesis and Antithesis. It is clear for him: the negative and the negation create the dynamics of all elements belonging to the dialectical process. Their succession is the most important issue. Not the dialectics as such but the sequences of the composing elements form the central point of Hegel's thoughts.

[26] See one of the classics on the theme: Theunissen (1966), pp. 243–277, see p. 258: 'In methodischer Hinsicht bleiben Buber und mit ihm alle Dialogisten weit hinter Sartre, aber auch hinter Husserl und Heidegger zurück.' Also see his § 48, pp. 259 ff.

[27] Bakhtin (1981, 1984). See also: Levinas (1987). See also: Ponzio (2012), pp. 21–25.

[28] In his original German expressivity: *das Sein selbst*.

For that reason, he characterizes the continuous attention for the negative as an important task for philosophy in its entirety.[29] The Negative is not a Beginning or a Final stage—it is a continuous and central occurrence. The 'No– ', the 'No–thing', the Nihil is in a central position when it takes the form of a transitoriness, plurality and unity, negation, or difficulty! In understanding this form is the riddle of grasping the real and most subtle essence of intersubjectivity in philosophy, Hegel's formulations demonstrated!

Any attention for the negative is to take seriously in our days of threatening climate changes determining many modern thought patterns.

The climate changes make us think of the cosmos in every act we pursue with a power that was in earlier centuries characterized as a Divine Power. It is as if we perceive this today in an encompassing picture: the power and dynamics of two polar regions—a Northern and a Southern—seem curtailed and this curtailment might in the end become an omnipresent annihilation. One should be aware that all conversations and actions about a climate crisis are in essence a negation or even an undefinable curtailment. No wonder, that we must recognize the epistemological dimensions in this problem, in other words: the dimensions that are characteristic for our thought formation and the acquisition of knowledge in general. The roles of nature and culture are difficult to determine. But it is clear, that both are relevant for cosmic and socio-cultural human life. It thus follows, that each position of myself regarding someone else is not to understand exclusively as a dualism. There are more complex factors involved, so that dualities might not be what they seem. The latter are basically triadic: each human life (also with regard to another) is complex because of its existential pattern composed of an 'I', a 'You' and the 'Cosmos' whereby the latter is not only a matter of 'nature' but also of one or more "I' and a 'You" s. To understand the composition of our words with regard to Cosmos and Self is difficult; their variations (often politically determined) seem decisive concerning all components of social life. The use of the word 'intersubjectivity' is in that regard an often-misused privacy device.

1.6 Conversion

The existential situation of a human individual depends—beyond others—on qualities of intersubjective patterns. These are marked by uncertainty, ambiguity, ambivalence and a forceful inner need to communication and community.

Two forceful drives characterize the human personality: the need to search for and discover the intimacy of life, and at the same time an irresistible drive outwards towards society and its other humans. Those two tendencies, the quest for knowledgeable components of personality and the sharing and fulfillment of life's meaning and significance, are foundational and neither contradictory nor identical. Man in

[29] 'Dieses Verweilen ist die Zauberkraft, die es ins Sein umkehrt'. See Hegel (1949), pp. 30f.

general thus embraces the power of re-constituting ideals and insights so that he can reconsider his motives and (for better or worse) embrace a new life. To become another or new person through the espousal of new, or at least very different, values and norms is in fact one of the basic properties of man. This is *the primordial power of conversion* which enrichens life with new themes and multiple disclosures of existential dimensions. It should be underlined how one encounters here the mysterious, often paradoxical and tragic power of freedom to change attitude, which Husserl has explored and presented as the basics of his *Phenomenology*. It focuses on the human being which can and should encounter its proper operative power to be, act and (to some extent) fulfill a unique dimension of freedom to change. That operative power was already named *metanoia* in Occidental philosophy's Greek tradition. The tensions between human freedom and social pressure originate in this inexhaustible source of reflection. They show the qualities of the free spiritual center of the human individual which can only unfold in social contexts. The latter are at issue in the word *conversion* which exists in multiple forms and languages already for thousands of years.

One should keep in mind how that term *conversion* indicated a unique change of position and functioning. It dominated human patterns of thought and knowledge for many ages and made an individual positioning possible via the human mind and social functions. The word thus relates to the act, process, or state of being engaged in an individual, social, or spiritual change—for instance from one of indifference, disbelief, or antagonism to one of acceptance, faith, or enthusiastic support. It is important to notice, that the word can also concern a physical transformation from one material or state to another.[30] That makes it even more interesting for the modern mind, which embraced the *analog* as well as the *digital* type of language as specific ways of expression in human life.

How became the term '*Conversion*' recognized and modernized? Any attempt to answer this precarious question relates to a fundamental issue. It became slowly visible but remained hardly understandable within the patterns of life at the beginning of the third millennium. A seldom experienced complexing factor came to the fore: how can it be that climate developments and their often-disastrous effects relate to patterns of human cognition and thus of specific patterns of cognition? These experiences suggest a relation between climate phenomena and forms of human cognition in which the patterning of language has a major role to fulfill. Could that lingual activity be determined by a natural phenomenon on the one hand (climate) and human knowledge (language as a non-natural issue) on the other?

One cannot proceed this form of thinking without taking the concept of 'history' seriously in consideration. The notion of history changed fundamentally since the beginning of the twentieth century. It was no longer solely related to certain regions and conditions of the planet and their levels of population. On the contrary, it developed an all-embracing consciousness about humans having existed and existing everywhere on the planet, including bacteria, plants, natural forces as well

[30] See <https://www.dictionary.com/browse/conversion>.

as animals or human feelings and existences in general. The 'past' of past times changed color and embraced the insight that there is no past without a future—an insight that includes the reverse, namely that there is no future without a past. What point of reverse between past, presence and future causes us to conceive a history? That became a major question when considering history in the days during which plurality seemed to master cognition.

It really fascinates how 'history' changed in function, sense and meaning during the third millennium's first centuries. It was no longer what it was in the preceding days: a matter of persons, groups, political and other communities which can geographically be delineated. It focused rather on diverse flows of times which became recapitulated in frames of human cognition belonging to various positions. The flows became presented as a 'theory', so that history in the third millennium's views became based upon new ways of understanding. The latter reached from gravity and electromagnetic powers to nuclear forces. No wonder that *the plural* begun to determine human thought and cognition. The 'sum' of histories according to the flow of theoretical insights and experimental outcomes was forged into cognition. The term 'history' became uniquely burdened, and its plural included all universes—among them the human universe.

Do not forget: 'history' fits to the word 'velocity', which indicates in this context the speed of thoughts and events. If the polar regions in the North allow ships a greater velocity than ever, they produce a meaningful complex of data, senses, and meanings. The word 'climate change' embraces such complexes in the beginnings of the third millennium, together with references to the worldwide spending of coal and CO_2. All dynamics implied belong together to a systematic observation and general knowledge that was indicated by terms like 'process' or 'system' produced by human understanding and construction. Never have terrestrial dimensions changed with such an intensity as in the third millennium. And it took many centuries and decades until these changes were recognized as being related to human cognition and its multiple gradations. Acknowledging the relevance of human knowledge became an issue after a long period of growing political and socio-economic annoyances. The latter started in the twenty-first century with debates at international conferences and broadened a world-wide digital communication at the level of its completion.

Each relation between *cognition*, including each relation between *knowledge* and *conversion* will soon be understood as a form of *conversion*. That maintains the dominance of thought formation in the many *digital* fragments of contemporary culture. This dominance characterizes the beginning of the globe's third millennium. Its geographical conditions are still an expression of relations between knowledge and expertness, but those between cognition and conversion appear to be dominant. The latter embraces forms and faces of artificiality, which were impossible during decades before their actuality today. It becomes visible that expertise and management do not know any barrier in the spheres of artificiality. Everything is possible, but what changes, lost its specific color and odor because *conversion* became its essence and power. The 'C' s changed and became powers of change during the decennia. Do not forget, that history changes continuously under the influence of the climate. The latter has an enormous and all-influential power!

As was said before: it really fascinates how 'history' changed in function, sense and meaning. But that is not all there is to consider! An additional key in our further understanding of the importance of *conversion* as related to the acquiring of *knowledge* understood as *cognition,* will be discovered in the understanding and uses of *language*. This is extremely important, because the understanding of our *Life* and our *Selves* is closely related to our understanding and exploration of *language*, in particular our *linguistic expressiveness.* That touches the intimate fact that any disordering of knowledge—primarily about our Selves in the context of our language—challenges the conception of our Self as well as our ideas about truth and reliability in human context. Our knowledge will, just as like body, always be kept in suspension whether it has the task to function as an object. And what is more important for maintaining our Self: we must accept that each fragment of our knowledge will be confronted with our self-justification. That tendency, which is implied in this position, seems directed towards *a recognition of the subject as our epistemological anchor.* Now becomes modernity's vital question to the fore: how can cognition in the New Plural be safeguarded when this anchor can no longer be trusted? That trust is not the product of the subject itself, or of any social relation—it is ultimately a cosmic fact. How do we read the structures of that fact? The question determines the ever-changing position of the subject, experienced in language, expressivity, and lingual understanding—in and beyond those relatively controllable domains.

This implies the possibility of an immediate disengagement of the subject–in–activity from any of its grammatical activities and foundations. In other words, the subject will no longer fulfill the role of the 'first-person-singular' in thought and expression. Any mention of 'the subject' in the expressivity of thinking and feeling, of a rational or emotional life, will be qualified as old fashioned, demoded, or irrelevant. It is repugnant to experience this as a lesson provided by our smart phone. This questionable position of the human subject and its subjectivity is a hitherto unknown and never ventured practice which came to life through the introduction and worldwide practices of digitality. These newly conceived practices and their special techniques brought a *conversion* that led to hitherto unknown forms of subjectivity. Dominant is today the subject as an element of structuring, functioning, or managing fields and flows of information and/or data. Keep in mind: *everything* can belong to these data; *nothing* can be excluded from that category!

The rule-giving and comparable constitutive prescriptive activities surround the subject in ways that were unimaginable for the earlier authority of the subject—a place and authority that is rather unimaginable for the actual philosopher. Speaking about a *transcendental subject* as occurred in earlier ages is today no longer understandable. That exemplary change in thoughts and speech is basic for the already often mentioned change from a dominant linguistic model named 'Speaker–Hearer Relation' into a 'Sender–Receiver Model'. The Speaker lost its dominant position, which was underlined and supported by grammatical rules. The Sender never received the same position or authority. He is just one of the innumerable factors of the embedding in which the Sender-Receiver duality functions. The same is the case with the difference between the Hearer and the Receiver—their difference is by no means only an acoustic issue! The knowing subject became just an element of a properly unfolding act of conversion. The result is a most unimaginable silence about the role and presence of the subject in digital expertise. Do not forget that the subject was one of the foundational and often un-reflected powerful positions in the classical Occidental philosophy. In the context of the digital cognition and culture is this silence meaningful because it silenced the newly conceived meanings of conversion. Where no subject is functioning or detached, is conversion active and made appropriate, as all digital theories and fragments of digital techniques approve.

The above pages signalized a transition from the classical knowledge concept into the dynamics of conversion. Forthcoming pages must for that reason indicate some of the major components of these thoughts which might master the reality of tomorrow. One of the central issues is in any case the different understanding and effectivity of what was in classical theories called 'the subject'. In that framework—a cultural framework that completely characterizes what is generally called modernity—became the role of the subject importantly reduced. We mention various important mainstream thought patterns which play a role in this transition, such as the awareness of *the flow character* of evolutions in thinking and cognition. Attention is furthermore paid to the various modern components of *narrativity and the human subject*, including the transition to the concept of discourse. The latter explorations give access to the problem of the naturalness as a character of cognition and its phenomenal plurality.

The correctness and efficiency of *functioning* in a network of meanings and data, which itself is functioning in more encompassing networks, seems the ultimate criterium of today's awareness and techniques. Differences between speaking and writing, nuancing and accurateness are, if not neglected, converted into proper features of the system, resp. the qualities of data. Knowing is not the same as speaking, hearing, or writing in earlier centuries. It has the tendency to rupture functioning knowledge and to favor the system, network and/or data patterns.

But this conclusion is not definitive, it does not define but only suggests how *cognition* became submitted to *conversion*. This will be exemplified in cases of conversion which are discussed today. We mention the position of *conversion* in the frame of the traditional philosophical transcendence, the multileveled language types and their expressivity as well as the digital coordinates named DAC (Digital–Analog Conversion) and ADC (Analog–Digital Conversion).

References

Bakhtin MM (1981) Speech genres & other late essays. University of Texas Press, Austin

Bakhtin MM (1984) Rabelais and his world. Indiana University Press, Bloomington

Benjamin W (1982) Das Passagen-Werk. In: Gesammelte Schriften, vol 1 & 2. Suhrkamp Verlag, Frankfurt a. M.

Broekman JM (2016) Meaning, narrativity, and the real. Springer Switzerland

Broekman JM (2019) Rethinking law and language, the flagship 'Speech'. Edward Elgar, Cheltenham

Broekman JM, Fleerackers F (2020) Legal thoughts convert, Springer briefs in law. Springer Nature Switzerland
Buber M (1923) Ich und Du. Insel Verlag, Leipzig
de Spinoza B (1996) In: Elwes RHM (ed) Ethics. Penguin Books
Eco U (1979) A theory of semiotics. Indiana University Press, Bloomington
Fourier C (1808) Théorie des quatres mouvements et des destinées generales, Lyon
Grier PT (2020) Language and law: artificial and natural. J Comp Law XV:1 (Wildy, Simons & Hill Publishing, London)
Hegel GWF (1812) Wissenschaft der Logik. Erster Band. Die objektive Logik. Erstes Buch. Das Sein
Hegel GWF (1949) Phänomenologie des Geistes [Phenomenology of the spirit] (trans: Miller AV). Meiner Verlag, Leipzig, Foreword by J.N. Findlay
Hegel GWF (1986) Werke, Gesamtausgabe (1832-45) Eds. Eva Moldenhauer und Karl Markus Michel Suhrkamp
Heidegger M (1929) Kant und das Problem der Metaphysik. V. Klostermann, Frankfurt a. M.
Jespersen O (1922) Language, its nature, development and origin. Allen & Unwin, London
Levinas E (1987) Reality and its shadow. In: Levinas E (ed) Collected philosophical papers, Dordrecht
Lindner B (ed) (2011) Benjamin Handbuch. J.B. Metzler Verlag, Stuttgart
Mannoury G (1949) Signifika. Een Inleiding. Servire's Encyclopedie. Den Haag
Ponzio A (2012) Alterity. In: Favareau D, Colbey P, Kull K (eds) A more developed sign. Tartu University Press
Scholem G (1957) Die Jüdische Mystik in ihren Hauptströmungen. Metzner Verlag, Frankfurt a.M.
Sebeok TA (1978) Sight, sound, and sense. Indiana University Press, Bloomington
Sebeok TA (2001) Global semiotics. Indiana University Press, Bloomington
Theunissen M (1966) Der Andere, Studien zur Sozialontologie der Gegenwart. De Gruyter & Co., Berlin

Chapter 2
Fluidity and Flow

Two terms, loaded with complex meanings and an intense social relevance, were introduced around the midst of the twentieth century. They were not totally unknown before and functioned already in specialized regions of sciences and philosophy, but their meaning and function became surprisingly broadened and empowered in the century before our days. That occurs when consciousness is studied philosophically and related to various forms of acquiring knowledge, such as thought, visual, audible, or even aesthetics. One term related to all of this is the socio-philosophical term '*discourse*' and the other the everyday term '*flow*', related to 'fluidity' and comparable analog-language metaphors. Of course, one should give attention to the fact that both expressions are familiar with several other terms in modern language, and that this familiarity appears sometimes closer and tighter than we ever would think of. But both directs us, eventually, to hitherto unknown directions.[1]

Until now, we thought that our modernity is a superior starting point for thinking about such a closeness, because we supposed that we could bring new types and qualities of relation to the fore. The same is true for the tightness of components, which *discourse* as well as *fluidity* demonstrate in each case of a great speech or an official oration. Were discourses and their argumentative power not overwhelming to underline modern values, norms, and insights? The question contains a most powerful confirmation of itself. All issues seem anchored in experiences, which characterize the human being in its own specificity: its cultural, political, or religious differences included. So, what 'objective' view or fact is there to expect? We should indeed strive for an open-minded participation and exclude any hubris in accepting our own experience as a source for the genesis of our knowledge. But would that untie the questions of tightness and closeness and bring the idea that complicated human experiences can become dissolved and understood rationally? That

[1]Notice how *the flow*, already present in Ancient Greek thoughts (Herakleitos), came in the last centuries to high currents by means of studying *dynamics* which in a digital culture lead via *mirroring* towards a new understanding of *communication*.

J. M. Broekman, *Knowledge in Change*, Law and Visual Jurisprudence 8,

viewpoint holds even in our contemporary world, which is molded by sciences of all kinds. It makes our attempts to understand cognition and thought formation the more interesting. Various expressions sustain us and several disciplines (scientific as well as philosophical) lead to the reinforcement of philosophical insights or our search for profiles beyond traditional philosophical path. Is this the path to walk?

2.1 Cognition and Flow

Whilst considering various expressions related to fluidity, one seldom encounters the term 'the flow' in this context. 'Fluidity' might be regarded as one of the flow's major characteristics. Zygmunt Baumann explored the expression already in 2000 when he spoke about '*Liquid Modernity*' and later, when he underlines in 2003 the fluidity of concepts and meanings in modern life, about '*Liquid Love*'. He used the term '*Liquid Society*' in his 2004 essay and completed together with Carlo Bordoni a more encompassing theory supporting that idea of liquidity as a feature of life in their 2014 '*State of Crisis*'.[2] They argue that the crisis facing Western societies should be understood as rooted in a continuous and profound series of transformations. The latter stretch far back in time and are producing long-lasting effects.

However, 'fluidity' seems not enough to become a basic expression and thought pattern that sustains a theory of social life structures and vital experiences. An important critical element is that fluidity and flow are too vague for being a marker of qualities characterizing our economically, politically, and socially complicated days. That was particularly the case in social processes, which never occurred before. Indeed, the 'flow' seems vague—and 'vagueness' never inspires the formulation of a sustainable social theory!

But—on the other side—the flow is not solely anchored in the regions of social sciences and affined fields of structured togetherness. The vagueness is not vague, but on the contrary perhaps more vigorous than any conceptual understanding could provide. Vagueness of the flow remains vague despite all various properties of the flow one discovers, and thus might vagueness cause interesting viewpoints in the light of cognition, in traditional philosophy named 'epistemology'. Modernity is for instance classified in the flow as belonging to the category of 'not-yet-understood' phenomena. Attempts to understand modernity are leading to pre-scientific expressions, which are in themselves already beyond the grip of any positive science. And if vagueness is recognized as the flow's inner power, then that cognition gives a very first impression of how to appreciate the implied cult of the flow's subject. The subject is indeed constantly present, and determines the many meanings embraced in fluidity and flow.

Umberto Eco discussed those dimensions in a 2015 essay and a year later in his book entitled '*Chronicles of a Liquid Society*'. The crisis that colors the traditional

[2]Baumann and Bordoni (2014).

cult of the subject today is in the 'unbridled individualism' of contemporary subjects, he suggests, and thus he concludes: 'people are no longer fellow citizens, but rivals to beware of.' The latter broke the walls of their cult and their identity by their acceptance of 'the collapse of any general call for a sharing of values that allowed them to feel part of something that understood their needs.' [3] Fluidity in social patterns does not replace what collapsed and does not provide new social powers and lifestyles. Are we able to perceive the flow and yet live up to our features of the contemporary culture? In other words, do we find in modern thought formation any patterns that combine the perception of the flow with insights into modern thought formation, which embraces the genesis and application of contemporary cognition?

This leads again to the flow's substance. Is Bauman's notion of 'crisis', Ferrari's 'weak textualism' or Eco's 'fluidity' helpful for our understanding? It should be underlined, that the collapse of sustaining common values is in fact not the final and complete result of a flow characterized by terms like 'crises or 'fluidity'. Flow is, after all: change, movement, flux, drift, gush, or stream of values. The issue to be studied is thus the specificity of the flow's dynamics rather then its syntax! 'Change' is a key word for this approach. Fluidity and change belong together, but it seems extremely difficult to determine the inner structure of their togetherness. New versions and different appreciations unfold if one changes position or opinion, attitude, or lifestyle—there is a change, a conversion, a differentiation, perhaps even a hitherto unknown pattern of activity that replaces them. But who'll find the right terms? Who determines what? Does a flow transcend any determiner? Do we correctly understand the many aspects of our handling the flow in which our lives unfold? The questions are many and their critical attitude is convincing. Where or when did we lose our grip on knowing the flow in which we live?

Or: did we ever know the flow?

One aspect of a possible answer to this essential question might be the idea that linguistic terms and their specific contexts provide the insight and knowledge we need to understand the basic features of the flow. Expressions, disciplines, and insights as well as profiles would elucidate them. But the flow demonstrates the contrary, namely that life and cosmos are more than linguistic categories ever express! Everyday languages, forms of social speech, varieties of artificial or newly conceived types of expression, resp. linguistic activity, are not only in philosophy or sciences qualified as limited means of acquiring knowledge! The flow might also emphasize such insights and experiences. One of the background reasons for the latter might be, that linguistic categories are studied and used without appropriate estimation of the implicit dynamics at hand. The cult of the subject is often based on designs of static patterns—and these can ruin a proper knowledge of the subject's qualities and its culture. It is enlightening that each flow embraces thinking as well as the dynamics of *re-thinking as a constitutive epistemological component*!

[3] Eco (2016), pp. 2f.

That notion leads beyond the patterns of linguistic expressiveness as a key to knowledge and insight. Which component of cognition is not present in our usual attempts to acquire knowledge and understanding of the flow? One of the many possible answers might surprise: analyses or insights in the flow are seldom acknowledging *time as marking the flow*. Even pointing at linguistic expressions as an equivalence of thinking time and flow does not solve that problem. We normally consider grammar and clock as our most reliable instruments to know reality—the more since our smart phone combines both and thus overshadows any possible doubt about time. But thoughts about experiences of flow do not make time disappear! On the contrary: we say that time flows and we thus do express in that manner how time mediates all components of our existence. The theoretical physicist Lee Smolin, who strived for a reevaluation of the role of time in the universe, mentioned how the clock seems the most authoritative of all machines. He stated in the introduction of his 2013 study entitled '*Time Reborn*': 'Time will turn out to be the only aspect of our everyday experience that is fundamental. The fact that it is always some moment in our perception, and that we experience that moment as one of a flow of moments, is not an illusion. It is the best clue we have to fundamental reality.' [4]

That 'best clue', related to the moment being a flow of moments, leads to a questioning of the inner structures of human knowledge. The almost antique philosophical term 'epistemology' seems a key issue of human experience and at the same time of cosmic reality—an issue we share in flow character. The latter was once defined as knowledge, but in our days of very diverse scientific disciplines and approaches together with equally diverse types of linguistic expressivity, one hesitates to embrace that definition.

What remains is the idea that when nothing changes (or: if there is no change) time has no meaning. *It is precisely this semiotic relationship between change and time that keeps our interest in the flow alive*. If we ever acquire any knowledge about our self as a component of the 'cult of the subject', it is thanks to awareness of the flow: awareness is a moment of one of the (cosmically anchored) flow of moments. An unconventional conclusion seems to become visible at the horizon of thoughts about time, as for instance presented by Smolin. He concluded that there is no possibility to consider time in thoughts, languages, or sciences without reference to human consciousness. The argument might astonish the reader, because it sounds like an old-fashioned appeal to re-examine the traditional concept of the subject. 'In the real world is always some particular moment, a dynamical system, occurring in time, evolving in time, able to absorb bits of information from the past and process them, able also to create anticipation for the future,' Gleick underlined in his well-known essay on Smolin's publication. [5] It means, in the real world is always a moment called consciousness—despite our problems to profile that exclusive moment. Consciousness *is* time and *unfolds in* time. But that insight does not suffice.

[4]Smolin (2013), p. xxxi.

[5]Gleick (2013), pp. 46 f.

There is still a powerful surviving of what we characterized as 'the cult of the subject'. Does a final reference to the place and function of a consciousness not revive that cult through references to its special momentary character? We read Smolin again: 'One further aspect of consciousness is the fact that it takes place in time. Indeed, when I assert that it is always some time in the world, I am extrapolating from the fact that my experiences of the world always take place in time. But what do I mean with 'my experience'?' [6] Fluidity does not solve the problem, and the need to recognize the character of a flow does also not do that. The factor 'time' may clarify some structures and inner relations of reality, but 'flow' and 'consciousness' remain a riddle in that context. Does it contribute to a new understanding because it is a riddle? Perhaps only, if we accept the vagueness of the expression 'flow' and remain aware of its general presence, in all times and on all occasions of a culture—Occidental culture not being an exception.

This view became supported by a fascinating example from the actual world in which various types of expression—primarily the analog and the digital type, but also AI terms and elements of Quantum Thoughts—function. That example is anchored in the general understanding and influence of Plato's dialogues. Reading and comprehending his texts as well as understanding his views on reality—of which the two are often considered to be dominating instruments—are determined by a mixture of linguistics theories and social values. But only in the last two centuries unfolded an insight that those dialogues are literary figures, [7] fitted to carefully formulated and precisely arranged questions.

2.2 Plato's Dialogues

A confirmation of the flow's importance in issues of human mind and culture as implied in terms like 'consciousness' and 'subjectivity' thus play a role of importance through the ages of the Occident. The inner relations between Plato's dialogues and Aristotle's metaphysics and ethics are studied in that context. Gadamer's study brought the conclusion that 'today it is an established fact that in the entire traditional Aristotelian works we never get back to a point where Aristotle was not a critic of Plato's doctrine of the ideas.' He adds a further thought and completes about Aristotle in a salient manner: 'we never arrive at a point where he really ceased to be a Platonist.' [8] The remarkable fact about this insight is that Gadamer does not concern a commonness of utterances and texts between Plato and Aristotle, but that he focuses in the first place on background structures and schemes of thought formation among the two. His views pertain to what we link with language and consciousness: to knowledge formation. Gadamer's insights thus relate to the flow in

[6] Smolin (2013), p. 270 (Italics are mine, JMB).

[7] Initiated by Schlegel (1772–1829) and Schleiermacher (1768–1834).

[8] Gadamer (1978), p. 8.

which we (as well as Plato and Aristotle in their days) unfold our thoughts and thought patterns founding knowledge.

A major question arises when the genesis of the epistemological patterns of Aristotle and Plato are exposed in this light. Our confidence in discerning developmental phases in Aristotle vanished—does the same not hold for Plato? The conclusion that also 'our historic-genetic way of viewing Plato's writings' disappears, has importance for understanding our proper position in knowledge and thought. Our fascination awakened by Gadamer's views reaches beyond his theme and philosophical framework. The initial wording seems limited and perhaps no more than a specialist's criticism when he suggests a specific causal chain: 'Aristotle's presumed evolution from a politics of the ideas ... through a still hesitating distancing from himself from Plato ... to the 'mature' and self-confident position ... is an arbitrary and contradictory construction'. But the actuality of almost half a century later fascinates. 'The development schema ... slowly begins to come apart': the fate of this schema is an important component of today's thought formation.

Gadamer's pioneering studies in hermeneutics during the midst of the last century were rooted in a thorough knowledge and emotional engagement with Ancient Greek thought formation rather then in a specialized study of specific texts. This constituted a unique emotional, philosophical, and scientific participation in the flow that accompanied Greek sages. Only the latter made recognizable for us what he calls the 'development schema', expressed in his sketch of the relationships between Plato and Aristotle. Gadamer mentions the schema, which should have been the frame of Plato's work and wisdom: 'the postulation of the ideas apart by themselves, then participation of the appearances in the ideas, the dialectic of idea and appearance, and then, at the end, the equating of idea and number.' Plato aside: one recognizes at a first view the limitations of the schema as an only means for his and our knowledge. Gadamer looks us in the face when he noticed the major issue at stake: 'Plato is obviously fully aware of the paradox in a participation or taking a part (Teilhabe) that does not take a part but participates in the whole—as the day participates in the light of the sun.' [9]

Was Plato aware of the flow?

He understood the difficulties to validate and understand the problematic relationship between the 'whole' and its 'parts' that always colors the dialectic of unity and multiplicity. But his development schema fades away in tensions pertaining to the whole. These also characterize our understanding of knowledge formation and (in a wider sense) of our self. Plato's schema might be no more than a weak sign. In other words: it is perhaps a hardly audible signal of the flow in which human—that is also: Plato's—consciousness and its Self unfold. But the growing irrelevance of the schema enveloping the formation of thoughts and thinking does not milder the importance of the components scattering around in our mind when we are asked to, or even forcibly brought to understand our understanding! That tension between irrelevance and importance characterizes today's approaches to today's different

[9] Gadamer (1978), p. 11.

context of human consciousness. Today, some almost global features pertaining to concept and experience of consciousness are to attend. They confirm the strong but hardly knowable ties between consciousness and flow.

Those features are anchored in a diversity of insights and facts. Edelman & Tononi refer already to that situation in their 2000 publication entitled '*A Universe of Consciousness*'. They suggested that 'although all scientific theories assume consciousness and conscious sensation and perception are necessary for their application, the means to carry out scientific investigations of consciousness itself have only recently become available.' But a special property remains of importance: 'Conscious experience arises as a result of the workings of each individual brain ... people's reports about their own consciousness cannot reveal the workings of the brain underlying them ... one must take special approaches to bring consciousness in the house of science.' [10] As a result, any text is in all regards a respectable attempt to enter the enigmatic regions of consciousness on the one hand and on the other to translate from the singularity of a consciousness into the consciousness experiences shared by human individuals at all times and in all cultural contexts.

One should underline how the core issue of consciousness relates by Edelman to the term 'dynamics'. The latter does not only emphasize that any consciousness is involved in continuous changes but also in plurality. Hence the philosophical fascination of one of the central conclusions of Edelman's research: 'Consciousness ... being a process, not a thing, is both continuous and continually changing. Conscious states typically flow seamlessly and maintain a high degree of coherence over time.' This inspiring observation becomes underlined by the suggestion that consciousness 'can maintain its unity over time even if its composition may be constantly changing, which again is the signature of a process as opposed to a thing'. [11] It seems interesting that all those remarks are a modern answer to the question 'what is a consciousness?' But Edelman's study shows how even this consideration cannot free itself from issues, which are in his study reduced to concluding remarks about (a) language and the growth of a self, and (b) about thinking. There seems no answer to the question how those two vital processes connect with consciousness as a process—an issue that gained importance in the two decades after Edelman's text.

This brings us back to concluding remarks of Smolin, who finalized his considerations about the phenomenon of time by underlining the complex and puzzling experience of human experience. Consciousness and the riddle of thought formation accompanied by cognitive processes are incomparable with our attempts to understand reality as an ensemble or pattern of physical interactions among particles. This insight fascinates since philosophical and scientific modernity focus on particles understood as a cosmic substance—a focus, which is supposed to originate in the operational power of a human mind and its consciousness. But a view on the process character, i.e., on the flow more than on the particles, seems to highlight the exceptional properties of human thought formation, constitution, and consciousness,

[10] Edelman and Tononi (2000).

[11] Edelman and Tononi (2000), pp. 150 f. (Italics JMB).

which play a role in human experience. How does consciousness relate to experience? 'What's missing when we describe a color as a wavelength of light or as certain neurons lighting up in the brain is the essence of the experience of perceiving?', Smolin asks. That essence has a name in philosophy: *qualia*. 'Why do we experience the qualia of red when our eyes absorb photons of a certain wavelength?' he considers and calls it 'the hard question of consciousness'.

These remarks bring us back by what seems the riddle of the epistemological conditions of *consciousness in activity*—in other words: our knowledge formation in which language and time are constitutive powers. The relation between consciousness and flow remains a challenge in the context of this axial question.

The neurologist Antonio Damasio concluded in his 1999 book *The Feeling of What Happens* '. . .that, in the end, consciousness begins as a feeling, a special kind of feeling, to be sure, but a feeling nonetheless, . . . consciousness feels like a feeling, and it feels like a feeling, it may well be a feeling. . . . The idea of consciousness as a feeling of knowing is consistent with the important fact, I adduced regarding the brain structures most closely related to consciousness: such structures, . . . process body signals of one sort or another, from those in the internal milieu to those in the musculoskeletal frame. All those structures operate with the non-verbal vocabulary of feelings'. That observation would have pleased Ch. S. Peirce, who remarked already in his *Second Harvard Lecture* on April 2, 1903, that 'there should be a regularity between feeling and certain notions of matter'. Most interesting is, that these notions of matter also seem to be notions of neurological quality—this insight broadens the field of consciousness and its results. This does not impede a further explanation of Peirce, articulating that '. . . a quality of feeling is not intelligible, either. Nothing can be less so. One can feel it, but to comprehend it or express it in a general formula is out of the question. So, it appears that unintelligibility does not suffice to destroy or refute a Category'. And with his widely respected sense for precision: 'The quality of feeling is the true psychical representative of the first category of the immediate as it is in its immediacy, of the present in its direct positive presentness. Qualities of feeling show myriad-fold variety, far beyond what the psychologists will admit.' [12]

A second suggestion from Damasio sustains our preceding considerations. He states: 'presenting the roots of consciousness as feelings allows one to glean an explanation for the sense of the self, . . . that is the owner of the movie-in-the-brain emerges within the movie'. [13] But how the movie is generated, especially from its quality sources on and upwards, remains an unsolved and often neurologically debated question. Essential is, however, that *a self does not seem to be able to determine the basic features of itself* by means of epistemological considerations. Does it have to enter the world of selves without a possibility of self-knowledge—or is self-knowledge a product of the world rather then of any individual self?

The latter questions emphasize the importance of the flow.

[12] Peirce (1998), pp. 150 ff.

[13] Damasio (1999), pp. 312 f.; Broekman (2010), p. 47.

We *first* underline that the 'flow' embraces various states of a human consciousness. But consciousness as a totality and perceived as a whole, which is: as an independent entity, does not seem to flow or to be a flow!

Secondly, a flow of consciousness is not a flow as a specific and definable particle or any psychological instance that symbolizes certain perspectives or occurrences in consciousness. It is even problematic to decide whether consciousness activity is a moment of the larger unity of moments named 'time'.

Thirdly, an act of turning attention to the flow does not constitute the flow but characterizes an activity of human consciousness. But the latter is not able to transform its proper experiences into knowable issues.

Fourthly, the term 'feeling' was already a risky denomination. A consciousness might withstand the possibility of acquiring any knowledge about its own features and functions. That is central for epistemology. In other words: if the flow must become reflexive, it just keeps it's flowing without reflection as its genesis or source of energy.

Gadamer illustrated in the case of Plato's dialogues how epistemology collides with its proper limits in an active consciousness. That activity will not have the flow as a knowable issue—neither as an object nor as a subject. Our concept and experience of consciousness touches the heart of the language phenomenon. It states harshly: there is no linguistic means to express a human consciousness completely and directly; its knowledge creation and thought patterning included. No word, digit, or quark nor any combination of the three will be able to present a lingual context in which a consciousness expresses itself purely and directly. Forms of indirect expressivity thus compensate the absence of specific linguistic means—as all natural languages on the globe prove. It means that all utterances of a consciousness are necessarily linking to cultural values, psychological experiences, social situations, and related components of human culture. The latter function as transmitter, transistor, translator and other 'trans- 'phenomena. Bluntly formulated: nobody knows or can precisely express what his or her consciousness or thought formation resp. knowledge pattern is. One should consider that this observation weights heavily on what in earlier centuries was cherished as 'the cult of the subject' ('die Kultur des Subjektes' [Kant, Hegel, Nietzsche]). This weight is primarily shaped by the riddle of human experience. Any experience expressed in a natural language will refer to a subject-object relationship, including the complicated event of self-experience. But if the subject-object scheme—distancing a knowing subject from a knowable object—cannot be realized and become functional, silence comes down. This limitation is determinative for articulating all expressions saying 'I' (first person singular) in whatever natural lingual means. No grammar, no syntax escapes from this fundamental determination.

This remark touches multi-dimensional problems. One of the major issues is, that if language is not explored as a medium of communication it unfolds into an all-embracing form of life as a flow. Beyond strict communication, for instance in aesthetics or in literature and art, unfold phenomena that cannot be traced back at all: not through sciences or philosophy, not through historical analyses or archeology. Each word beyond communication demonstrates a vague presence crafted by elements of culture, social relations, fragments of traditional knowledge or related traces. It is as if it possesses mechanisms to protect any extra-lingual grasping of its essentials. This notion—which could be characterized as a deeply hidden self-defense of all forms of expression—could eventually lead to the conclusion that our human 'being-in-language' is an existential feature. Its consequence would be, that questions posed, reflected, and answered beyond proper linguistic identity are classified as impossible. Archeologists encountered that opinion, and philosophers often experience the same issue. Psychoanalysis, structural or trans-cultural studies in anthropology share the question. They encounter incoherencies, inconstancies, irregularities, exceptionalities in patterns and practices, which ultimately bring to the fore that we will never dispose of a final and all-embracing 'objective' definition. All thoughts about what language is find ultimately their form and place in language! This observation colors the relationship between consciousness and flow.

2.3 Voegelin's Flow

The German/US philosopher Eric Voegelin (1901–1985) published 1966 his study: '*Anamnesis: Zur Theorie der Geschichte und Politik*', a work that was revised and translated into English and published in the USA in 1978. [14] It does not surprise that an attempt to acquire insight into history creates an existential interest for human consciousness, its foundations and boundaries. This interest generates a feeling for one of the constitutive features of history, namely its fluidity. No wonder, that this author should be characterized as one of the few philosophers in the twentieth century which gave attention to 'the flow' as a counterpart named 'human consciousness'. [15] The latter idea is underlined for its general importance. Voegelin states: 'The concrete consciousness of concrete man is the only consciousness given in our experience. Such constructions as a collective consciousness – either the consciousness of a society or the consciousness of mankind in history – are hypostases that have no standing in theory'. He emphasized that 'we are in the realm of freedom of the concrete consciousness.' That realm is not vague or missing profile. 'Reality, it is true, can move into the position of an object-of-thought intended by a subject-of-cognition, but before this can happen there must be a reality in which human beings with a consciousness occur, he underlines.' And that reality is not unstructured by its nature—it is the product of human beings and their consciousness anyway. So, man's conscious existence is a reality event that results from man's consciousness which is 'quite conscious of being constituted by the reality of which it is conscious ... intentionality is a substructure within the comprehensive consciousness of a reality that becomes luminous for its truth in the consciousness of man'. This insight brings the conclusion that 'The truth of consciousness, its

[14] Voegelin (1966).

[15] Voegelin (1966), Chs. 1 & 2 (pp. 3–36) and Ch. 11 (pp. 200–206).

verification and advance, could not be identified with either the truth of statements or the truth of experience; it was a process that let its truth become luminous in the procedural tension between experience and symbolization'. [16] Note the important words indicating the 'procedural tension'. The latter were exposed in the above pages in the words of Edelman, Damasio and Smolin as well as Gadamer profiling the thought patterns of Plato and Aristotle. Were the tensions between experience and symbolization not identical to tensions between events, knowledge, and feelings on the one side and linguistically formatted articulation on the other? Focus on those tensions implies the 'flow'.

Although it is recognized as a manifestation of human consciousness, the flow has not received a place in the classical philosophy or the more specified epistemology. The truth of consciousness and the possibility to acquire a complete knowledge of it shows features of the flow.

We conclude: *Knowledge of a consciousness is*

(a) a process that lets its truth
(b) become luminous in
(c) the tensions between experience and symbolization.

One of the foundational remarks of Voegelin should be noticed. He underlines, that 'neither the experiences nor the symbols could become autonomous objects of investigation for an outside observer. The truth of consciousness revealed itself through participation in the process of reality.' Damasio would agree and state that 'feeling' accompanying consciousness is a social event; Edelman would confirm the neurological importance of participation and relate brain developments with social events, Smolin would accept the idea that participation in the process of reality is a major means to experience and understand the qualities of time. However, all emphasis remains on *tensions* and not on *analytical analysis*!

However, this seems not enough to understand the flow and its relation to human consciousness. The flow is first effective in sensuous perceptions like time, tone, or color. But a possible completeness of knowledge, especially knowing consciousness, is not achieved via such perceptions. Can one get beyond the 'fleetingness' of sensuous awareness and name that fleeting 'the flow'? Two remarks should be made. *First*, one must consider that consciousness has a physiological limit—which for instance becomes clear when sensuous issues such as color perception, time awareness, audition challenges come to the fore without solving the question how we know about the conscious factors in the case. *Second*ly is the constitution of consciousness not the same as its awareness. If we see a color or hear a tone, the flowing may be registered—but its cause is in consciousness, and therewith not unraveled! What remains in every consideration is the following:

(a) The 'flow' does just impress by its character of being a limit on every occasion of experience or observation, and

[16] Voegelin (1966), p. 11.

(b) Our tradition to understand human consciousness as the origin of the flow implies that this consciousness itself does not flow—it remains a stable, reliably structured type of causality in analysis and reasoning. What is there to say about these two?

They do not contribute to an understanding of human consciousness—of which the flow would be the most important mediator—but they try to force our knowledge of a consciousness into a centuries old pattern: the subject–object schema. The expression 'flow' does, however, imply the contrary and state that no consciousness ever fits to categories reducible to subjectivity or objectivity. So, does Voegelin's unique considerations of the flow result in the conclusion that a human being is gifted with a consciousness that is unable to fit to any category or movement of knowledge? In other words, is an unknown and unknowable power called 'consciousness' of essence for a human being? And is a 'flow' an unknowable sign of its presence?

2.4 Immanuel Kant's Desire

No wonder that the grammatically expressed 'first person singular', the 'I', was a move towards language in general and the uniqueness of consciousness. Voegelin was careful and critical in view of that step and formulated: '…it seems to me that there is no 'I' that would be the agent of the constitution of a flow of consciousness'. And he completes his thoughts on the subject by saying: 'The 'I' seems to me to be no given at all but rather a highly complex symbol for certain perspectives in consciousness'. So, what should guide us is a sort of naïve realism, expressing that 'Man's conscious existence is an event within reality, and man's consciousness is quite conscious of being constituted by reality of which it is conscious.' [17] Is this all there is to say, not only about consciousness but also about the flow? There are two terms in these considerations, which should lead us to further thoughts in this context. The first is that any 'I' relates to the phenomenon of language, and the second is that this special linguistic category of the 'I' is named the 'first person'. Both might fascinate—we emphasize the first observation and deal with the second in a following chapter.

With any mentioning of the 'I' is language introduced—not any preferred social relationship or any related 'ego'-position in life. But the step from this category of the first-person singular into the wider field of understanding knowledge and its consciousness is not simple and direct, the famous and foundational thoughts of the German philosopher Kant already showed in a radical way. [18] His thoughts are therefore a key to our possible understanding of the flow and its consciousness, and ultimately to cognition. So, we spend for a moment attention to his philosophical

[17] Voegelin (1966), pp. 19, 11.

[18] Immanuel Kant (1724–1804).

ideas in this context. These are a focus on an everyday-language component, which is a trusted element of human consciousness expressed in almost all so-called natural languages around the globe as the 'I', the first person singular. Kant had this important term in mind when he suggested that knowledge in general is related to a firm identity of human reason with itself. Not only in his days, but also in ours is this identity is not a psychological but a purely structural need. The specificity of our second decade of the third millennium is however, that a new plurality of expressivity is becoming dominant: the plural of the *analog* and the *digital* type. Kant's desire includes an understanding of all knowledgeable features of consciousness but could not reach to that immensely important plurality. His desire embraces a harmony of 'reason being the key to a philosophical approach' to knowledge. When we say 'I', it should have a place in this harmony: that desire embraces many views, standpoints, social components, and presuppositions of which Kant was aware. His desire was much broader than the wish that everyday relations should not embrace conflicts.

Kant's famous 1781 '*Kritik der Reinen Vernunft*' (Edition A; the second version published in 1787, traditionally named Edition B) mentions one of the key terms that characterize a human person and its consciousness: that person is described as a numerical identity. [19] That description is in his text called the 'Third Paralogism of Personality'. In this term is Kant's desire enclosed: despite all plurality one encounters in studying the human person, an identity should prevail once it qualifies itself via the 'I'.

One conclusion about his desire to gather knowledge of a human being becomes already understandable in this light. Kant shows that the 'I'-position is not exclusively a domain for psychological, social, or anthropological studies, but for a substantial epistemological approach in the very first place! That position was in Kant's days normal and represented an attitude, which characterized Occidental philosophy until the end of the nineteenth and the unfolding of the twentieth century. Subjectivity-structures were given priority above analyses of knowledge processes only since the days Edmund Husserl formulated his phenomenological insights. Kant's emphasis on the subject as a key to human knowledge was unique—even when it ultimately had his days to serve the interests in processes of analysis and knowledge formation. Note, that all those aspects are folded in the Kantian term 'Kritik' [Critique]. This remark has a very important implication. The identity, which contributes to the understanding and knowledge of the person, is in no way a static moment! It refers, on the contrary, to the dynamics of all components of the ego that fascinated Kant. This identity is dynamic—that insight dominates all components of the ego's perception, as Kant illustrates in his thoughts on the various forms of transcendental apperception. Any human perception is thus understandable via the various components of the ego as well as those of the self-consciousness.

The 'flow' has never been so near to the core issue of any theory of knowledge. That proximity leads to a deeper understanding of the Kantian concept of 'numerical

[19] Kant (1781) [The numbers refer to the original pages].

identity', and Kant's term 'identity'. The motivation of our reference to this concept and its Kantian interpretation is in this proximity to dynamics—fluidity and flow—as the key to our understanding a human consciousness. Indeed, the numerical identity has never been a static data in the Kantian approach. Dynamics enable our understanding of a certain order in the innermost regions of consciousness. That order is needed because a consciousness is composed of various components so that each appearance and each functional moment of a consciousness creates a specific order to manifest itself and become active in a human life. This creative ordering is the essence of a being; identity is the result of a constant creation process that brings a specific order. Identity—because of the many components to be ordered continuously—and difference—of these multiple components—are the two powers that constitute consciousness. And the two can never fulfill their task without a temporary order named 'identity'. Identity is in this context an act; it is the act of togetherness of all consciousness components, a togetherness, which is characterized by a regaining of all components, the parts of what in ultimo will be the human 'I', a 'Subject', a 'Self' or a 'Person'.

However, Kant was analytical in viewing its process character as well as the need for a fixation in linguistic categories, the 'I', the 'Person', the 'human being'. But he also underlined what for instance Husserl, James or other twentieth century contemporaries often neglected: the stream needs the continuous completion of order! If there is no order, there is no expressivity, and then there is no language, no communication or identity. Kant had his difficulties to interpret and clarify the differences and multitude of the components to be ordered at any moment of an appeal to consciousness. He therefore brought a crucial metaphor to the fore: the comparison of consciousness and reason in activity as participants in a Court of Justice. The Court should bring the calm of a legally determined situation. Every critical philosophy, he suggests, should unfold on the basics of respectfully observing disagreements among the components of consciousness ('Veruneinigung der Vernunft'): only trough that approach will human reason be able to create clarity. There is no clearer description of Kant's desire: it is the striving for a harmonic reason, which can radically come to its senses.

All these considerations do not form an ethical command, but they represent an insight in the complex differentiations, which characterize the components of reason and thus of human consciousness—a consciousness continuously in conflict with itself (B767). Kant even provided names for such contrasting components when he for instance described a 'searching reason' ['forschende Vernunft]' contrasting an 'examining reason' ['prüfende Vernunft].' Both strive to realize their own ideals, he suggests, and each appeal to reason is therefore embedded in tensions caused by their contrast (B492). This most remarkable position has a very important consequence. The dynamics of consciousness illustrate that the ego is in essence nothing but performance, experience, or execution.

This flow does, however, not only concern the inner structures of a human consciousness. It is also functional in view of its external structures, the reality with which a consciousness relates—in other words: with the real world. The being-in-the-world based on consciousness comprises intentional relationships with all outer objects: with 'the world'—Kant underlines. The state of being conscious of a self is in his view identical with being conscious of worldly objects. Our inner experience is only possible when external experiences can be made: 'our inner experience, which Descartes did not doubt, is only possible under the condition of our external experiencing' he concluded. [20] That sentence contains the key for any human consciousness to articulate experiences through linguistic means. In other words: the theme of language returns in the heart of a complex epistemological structure.

One should re-think that structure, because it might be the most important in connection with our knowledge concerning consciousness. As a matter of fact, it has not directly to do with a possible theory of knowing the world as an objective fact. The Kantian observation refers to human expressivity—and that is not evident and not easy to understand: the idea of language and a human mastering of this subtle and complex instrument asks for a strong sense of differentiation. This sentence right from the heart of his major work suggests that inner experience is conditioned by external, and vice versa. We repeat his sentence here: 'our inner experience, which Descartes did not doubt, is only possible under the condition of our external experiencing.'

This articulation of experience, both internal- and external, is lingual by nature. That is for Kant a central issue. The 'I', the 'human consciousness', differs from the objects of reality in the sense that the subject is never origin or creator of its own experiences—but the 'I' is the fundamental exception in this context. The 'I' posits itself as an object of its inner experience and that inner dimension relates to the reality of the outer world. Kant differentiates between 'affection' and 'self-affection', and the 'I' is unique in that it affects (and thus creates) itself. It 'posits' [German: 'setzt'] itself as object of its inner experience. The 'I' is itself and at the same time creates itself as an object—that is the structure of the constitution of the 'I'. It happens in the flow, the stream of consciousness, because the subject can be affected by its authentic Self: 'the consciousness is not incidentally and now and then affecting and affected—but as a finite Self is it this tension between affecting and being-affected.' [21] All human self-knowledge is therefore in its deepest sense a Taking and a Giving. All self-knowledge is therefore marked by tensions between inner dialogues and external forms of speech. Human language is ultimately no more that a flow of modifications between those two forms—there is no subject and no 'I' possible without the continuity of self-modification. [22] Indeed, in Kant's eyes is the human subject nothing but the dynamics of performance, experience or execution articulated as an 'I' and/or a 'Self'.

Voegelin, Baumann, Ferrari or Eco would not connect Kant's philosophical ideas with their considerations of the fluidity concept. Today's studies often exclude Kantian insights because these are generally qualified as no longer relevant. But

[20] Kant (1781), Edition B (1789) 275.

[21] Kant (1781), Edition B 68.

[22] Kant (1889), p. 124.

they developed a very special insight in the deep structures of human subjectivity and their outreach to reality. Kant distanced himself from any purely rationalistic metaphysics and understood the human ratio in its position as a reflecting judgment power as described in the 1781 '*Critique of pure Reason*' with the words: 'Our consciousness is, even by means of its imagining and experiencing, never the cause of the object . . . nor is the object the creator of the reason's images of reality. Purely rational concepts can therefore not be abstracted from and are never the basis for any sensorial reception of experiences; they must have their origin in the nature of the soul – but not before the object causes them to take that position or the senses create them,' he already wrote to Marcus Herz on February 22, 1772. So, there is no doubt that human knowledge is related to and even fundamentally limited by sensory experiences. This leads for Kant, as well as later for Hegel and in the twentieth century for Husserl, to positions characterized as 'transcendental'. The latter remark is important in the context of understanding the flow. Husserl formulated that the Kantian analyses of subjectivity did indeed provide a unique insight in the dynamics of epistemological processes. That insight might provide a special attention for the internal movements that produce knowledge. But, as Husserl formulated in his 1936 '*Krisis der europäischen Wissenschaften*', [23] this remains an insight into 'transcendental' spheres—and those are difficult to place in an epistemological context.

2.5 Stream and Flow

Any rethinking of the flow as a philosophically relevant concept occurs in the shadows of Immanuel Kant's desire to clarify the structures of reason and consciousness. He stated that a consciousness is not incidentally and only now-and-then affecting and affected, but that *each consciousness as a finite Self* is this tension of affecting and being-affected. It is beyond doubt a matter of dynamics, in other words: of flow. This illustrates in an exemplary manner that the ego is for Kant in essence a process characterized by performance, experience, and execution—a conclusion implied in Kant's German term: 'Vollzug'. He refers more than once to this conclusion and remarks that it is the fruit of his 'Subjektivitätsanalyse'—an analysis of subjectivity—which is by no means to understand as a kind of psychology but rather as a problem of expression. In the language of analyzing a consciousness, Kant underlined, one can only envisage the path to go in understanding the constitution of reality. That path is not impassable but is just a specific form of self-understanding. *But in what type of expression might this self-understanding unfold?* This question is not formulated in the days of Kant or later, but only in the beginning decades of the third millennium.

Envisaging that path includes a confrontation with the flow, which was the heart of our desire to know a knowable and knowing consciousness. But there is more

[23] Husserl (1954), pp. 82 ff.

than this: the envisaging of the flow is in our days also a confrontation with the particularities of a specific type of expressivity—which is either *analog* or *digital.* All authors in this chapter took the *analog* type as their evident and only form of expressivity. But when considering the flow, one has today to consider this limitation. In other words: the forms of understanding human history were until the last decades of the twentieth century exclusively concentrated on one lingual type. Today, in the beginning decades of the third millennium, has this situation changed. An important self-expression is in the term *conversion*—a term which is also linked with our self-understanding via the concept 'flow'.

No, there was in the Kantian analyses no confrontation with *THE* flow—maybe with *A* flow! Kant's thoughts lead us to the human being as a subject, including all its components, as well as naming them and qualifying their mutual relations. They delivered the image of a flow in analog expressivity! But this did not mean that it embraces the flow as the name for our epistemic apparatus and its function of knowing and understanding knowledge.

Kant refers to the fact that he distinguished two characteristics in the frame of what we named 'A Flow': (a) a language of the Self, which functions within the structures of subjectivity, and (b) a language of the external world of that Self. Both relate closely and unconditionally to each other, in theory and practice. Like there is no word without a language and no language without a word, is there no flow without The Flow. The flow's multiplicity is not diminished by a flow's uniqueness. But all these considerations are valid within the pattern of analog expressivity.

How is the flow understood in the third millennium's digital expressivity?

A few suggestions for such an understanding are at issue:

(1) The word 'stream' or 'streaming', which is today often used to indicate 'the flow', belongs to a large *variety of analog expressions*, which are seldom strictly divided among each other. Streaming is in analog expressivity used as 'flow over'; streaming expresses liquidity and fluency, both literal (e.g., as a water-engineer) and metaphorical (e.g., as a psychiatrist). Flow and stream can both be equalized with 'flux', 'torrent' or even 'jet'. The word 'streaming' makes us in any case understand that the flow is no longer the unique and only linguistic expression for this form of life's dynamics.

(2) Today, the word 'stream' or the verb 'streaming' takes place in the sphere of *conversion of analog terms into digital.* In that process comes a strongly *reified* version of the *flow* in digital context to the fore. It is in nearly all digital contexts represented by the term *stream* or *streaming.*

(3) Streaming is indeed *reified in forms of media* that must directly and unconditionally be accessed via computer networks. With this electronic and digital restriction is the word at distance from the many comparable analog expressions. Its reification makes it into *a product*! It thus becomes an issue with one strict reference and one special form which enters the field of *economy* and its *digital zones.* Via this conversion will the term play a role in social life, politics, and many other regions—even in the depth of psychology.

(4) *Streaming* relates with the direct *distribution or sale* of video images, films etc. via computer networks. It brings its general digital features to the fore via instances or networks like Facebook, Twitter, Instagram, YouTube, Pinterest, and others. *Streaming* is therefore to be understood as a highly institutionalized process which embraces specific digital meanings that access recent block-busters or special top series.
(5) Streaming products can only in exceptional case be conserved, downloaded, or kept on a hard disc. In most cases, it is *a one-time only* occurrence. These elements show a parallel with the conversion of the analog Speaker–Hearer into a Sender–Receiver model. The Speaker as well as the Hearer are constitutive in the *analog* world of lingual communication. But since the beginning of the twenty-first century are they replaced by conversion processes which introduce *digital* meanings. The Speaker resp. Hearer lost in this conversion its subject-character, its character of personality and its function and features of constituting social life. They were, in the words of Martin Buber, no longer recognized as an 'Ich' and a 'Du' and conversed in a world of 'Es' relations. That happened also with the 'one-time-only' features of *stream* and *streaming*. Its dominant character is mirrored in human hands grasping the smartphone. Their gesture and ownership characterize the world of the 'Es', Buber would have remarked.

Voegelin considered: 'Reality, it is true, can move into the position of an object-of-thought intended by a subject-of-cognition, but before this can happen there must be a reality in which human beings with a consciousness occur.' [24] A serious implication of rethinking the flow is, that one will be confronted with the fact that the flow has a powerful inner drive, which can be understood as a continuing process of reformation, changing, and converting. The meaning concept is never a fixated and stable given in the flow—in other words: there is no meaning which is not flowing with the flow, within the flow, at distance from- as well as in the heart of the flow. Rethinking the flow delivers a firm standpoint: the flow is an always-changing embedment of meaning and sense. The fascinating language of the Self articulates this feature as an astonishing foreground phenomenon.

References

Baumann Z, Bordoni C (2014) State of crisis. Polity Press, Cambridge

Broekman JM (2010) Firstness and phenomenology. In: Wagner A, Broekman JM (eds) Prospects of legal semiotics. Springer

Damasio A (1999) The feelings of what happens. Body and emotion in the making of consciousness. Harcourt Brace & Cie., New York

Eco U (2016) Pape Satàn Aleppe. Milano [Engl. Transl. Dixon R (2017) Chronicles of a liquid society. Vintage, Harvill Secker, London]

Edelman GM, Tononi G (2000) A universe of consciousness. Basic Books [Perseus], New York

[24] See Voegelin (1966), p. 11.

Gadamer H-G (1978) Die Idee des Guten zwischen Plato und Aristoteles. J. C. B. Mohr, Heidelberg [Engl. Ed.: Christopher Smith P (ed, transl) (1986) The idea of the good in Platonic-Aristotelian philosophy. Yale University Press, New Haven]
Gleick J (2013) Time regained! In: The New York Review of Books, 6 June 2013
Husserl E (1954) Die Krisis der europäischen Wissenschaften und die transzendentale Phänomenologie: Eine Einleitung in die phänomenologische Philosophie (1936). Husserliana, Bd VI, M. Nijhoff, Den Haag 1954
Kant I (1781) Kritik der reinen Vernunft [Critique of pure reason] (Ed. A), A 360
Kant I (1889) Nachlaß. In: Reicke R (ed) Lose Blätter aus Kants Nachlaß [Separate pages from Kant's posthumous Work], vol I, p 124
Peirce CS (1998) In: The Peirce Project (ed) The essential Peirce, selected philosophical writings, vol 2 (1893–1913). Indiana University Press, Bloomington
Smolin L (2013) Time reborn. From the crisis in physics to the future of the universe. Houghton M. Harcourt, Boston
Voegelin E (1966) Anamnesis: Zur Theorie der Geschichte und Politik. Piper Verlag, München [Engl. Ed. Transl. & Ed. by Niemeyer G (1978) Anamnesis. Notre Dame Press, Notre Dame]

Chapter 3
Post-dialectics

Several notions, terms and descriptions in the preceding chapters seem old-fashioned, and many were foundational in the fields of conceptual tensions which reign the actual world. They appear to be locked in the process of *conversion* (mainly from analog to digital expressivity and reverse) which appears to be of global importance. The latter do ultimately determine our cognition in the actuality of flowing conversions. It means, that in forthcoming analyses and reconsiderations old-fashioned terms might function in new contexts and semiotic lights. Most of them—such as 'dialectics', 'harmony', 'transcendence' and even 'harmony'—play a role at the borderlines between analog and digital expressivity. They should be reconfirmed and reconstituted in that attitude. It means, that philosophy and thought formation in the third millennium has constantly to decide what words, terms, expressions and thought patterns must play what semiotic role in actual problems. There seems no strict uniformity and linearity in philosophical reasoning anymore.

'To mean' became a venture, and 'to be' a hazardous undertaking.

The inner dynamics of thought formation was already an actual theme during the discussions of the Ancient Greek, and it is still the case in modern times—not only in the types of traditional analog language but also in the context of recent language types like digital and quantum types of expression and reasoning, which sometimes parallel the analog language. It fascinates how the notion of 'particle' (Latin: 'corpusculus') appeared in all these contexts as foundational in various moments of philosophy and physics. Both disciplines are almost entirely determined by the very special dynamics of particle localization, mainly regarding the thought patterns of these disciplines as well as the organization of their materialist or rationalist research in three-dimensionality. But one must venture a step further in this perspective: particle localization includes the designed by a term which indicates no longer a primordial issue although its importance is greater than the history of philosophy suggests: the term 'dialectics'.

This insight reinforces, remarkably enough, an omnipresent focus on particles understood as a *planetary,* perhaps even *cosmic* substance. Within those frameworks highlight narratives the flow of insight and knowledge—hence the specific

J. M. Broekman, *Knowledge in Change*, Law and Visual Jurisprudence 8,

expressions indicating the effusiveness that characterizes knowledge. The term 'particle' seems therefore to be chosen by the Occidental mind as a basic component of all expressivities which unveil the dynamics of thoughts and their flowing formation.[1]

3.1 Conversion and Dialectics

The flows of meaning that characterized the art of conversation and its implicit thought formation received in the days of Kant, Hegel, and Marx the name that comprises all those elements: dialectics. Walter Benjamin confirmed in the first lines of his *Passages*—later translated as *Arcades Project*—how "dialectical thinking is the organ of historical awakening. Every epoch, in fact, not only dreams the one to follow but, in dreaming, precipitates its awakening. It bears its end within itself and unfolds it by cunning."[2] That method of seeking the truth unfolded by means of a peculiar reasoning which should be understood as a historical process surviving many centuries. Today, the term is often used to ironically circumscribe a sophistical reasoning or to forward a pejorative expression. *Dialectics* is indeed a term, which (in its most general sense) indicates the inner dynamics of moving ideas, notions, expressions, words, and abstractions, implying their constant link to wholeness and movement.

'No word, digit, or quark, nor any combination of the three will be able to present a context in which a consciousness expresses itself purely and directly', we stated in the preceding chapter. The birth of such an expression occurs repeatedly. Not because history must focus on such events, but because the progress of time and life does not condone their interruption. History is not the life motive of the present, but of a life's progress in general, wherever in the cosmos! History concerns the soul of life—man and culture included: the duration, the progress, the flux or flow which is never identical with time. The 'time-piece' we made and universally accepted may have completely obscured our understanding of that duration and flow and made its presence indisputable. Perhaps is that observation the main reason for our lacking (or at least difficulty) to understand the flow.

In the flow are vested positions of knowledge impossible—a standpoint is dissolved because any standing will be freed from the static and thus safeguard its dynamics in the flow. *Positions* are external to flows but *steps* feature flows: that is one of the most clearly visible changes in the traditional knowledge-acquiring schemas. It implies a specific distance to the particle-focused thought patterns that dominated the twentieth century. Traditional 'subject–object' positions deliver insight and knowledge as 'steps' in our thought patterns today. But what does this conversion from 'position' to 'step' say about the fundamental dualisms we cherish

[1]Broekman (2016), Part II, p. 151 f.

[2]Benjamin (1935).

in traditional epistemology? What does it tell us about our own priority to positions in contrast to steps e.g., moments of insight and wisdom?

We prefer the tree and do not perceive the wood.

But there is no part without a whole.

When observing the wood, we understand how sap is the fluidity of the tree trunk, how birds are nested in the tree because the tree is for them the wood in which they live. The ecological complexity of tree and wood should teach us how to approach our own reality, and thus how the whole determines part and particle in which we take a walk. Insight in that determination is not a final stadium but just a beginning: even our positions in thought processes and the acquiring of knowledge are steps, which cannot be made without a firm notion of the whole.

Dynamisms also unveil thought formations that are embedded beyond psychological boundaries, especially in social contacts and their lingual utterances. Note, that not only the properties of the objects we talk about in daily life, but also the unfolding of social contact between the participants, creates a conversation already essential for Plato and his friends. In other words: the dynamics of question and answer was their central issue and indeed a major condition for grasping the flow of understanding and knowledge. Reflecting on a given thing or situation (often imagined as a particle) implies formulating interrogative propositions: such sceneries determine the dynamics of speech qualities in questions and answers. The conversation of the soul, the Ancient Greek stated, is a conversation of the soul with itself to grasp the fluidity and dynamics of matters it is investigating, as the *Theaetetus* underlined. Today's expression that thought is an inner dialogue of the 'soul', resp. 'the inner human being', is still anchored in such reflections. Its survival through the ages is important and emphasizes the central position of dynamism in reasoning and its thought processes.

The term 'dialectic' indicates for Kant and Hegel as well as for Marx and Engels a movement that creates and supports thoughts patterns and thinking in general. An interesting example is in the difference between a 'dialectics of the mind' like Hegel's and a 'dialectics of materialism' like Marx's. Dialectics describe in general the flow of thought formation by exploring an order of 'thesis', 'antithesis' and 'synthesis', the latter being able to function as another 'thesis' provoking other components ad infinitum. A difference between Hegel and Marx interests in this perspective: Hegel emphasizes the 'thesis' as a starting point of attention that enflames the dynamics of thought formation and Marx emphasizes the antitheses for this same purpose. Hegel's developments touch the unfolding of the human mind's thinking process, whereas Marx' views are a social criticism represented by a term that embraces antithetic positions. The latter imply a criticism pertaining to the thesis, which brings new synthetics in social life: social justice being one of the ultimate positions to be forwarded in concrete, and not in a socially vague transcendence like in the case of Hegel.

One should underline, that the outlined contrast existed only between two types of understanding the flow of thought formation as an issue of the nineteenth century thinking. Engels underlined how sudden revolutionary changes are a fundamental feature of the universe understood as a whole. The question why there are changes and developments, and never a standstill, fascinated him. Changes, continuity, breaches, gaps, struggles of opposites were themes which did for him not reach beyond question and answer: they are an observation that is basic to dialectics. If tensions would be lacking in the universe, things would remain identical to themselves, since there would be no challenge to change, Engels concluded. This necessary distancing from any fixated identity was in his eyes the deepest truth of dialectics. Gradual physical changes are omnipresent and cause an enduring transformation of quality.

The implicit dynamics of such transformations are the ultimate powers of the Creation, he confirmed in his innermost proximity to Hegel. The latter had already called attention to the gradual steps towards an explosive revolutionary break in thought patterns and culture. In the *Preface* to his *The Phenomenology of Mind*, Hegel foresaw a gradual disintegration, which did not alter the general look and aspect of the whole, but became interrupted by the sunrise which, as if it occurs in a single flash, brings to view the form and structure of the new world. The character of a sunrise and its effects prove the importance and overwhelming power of movement, flow, and progress in Hegel's thoughts. He underlined the importance of total movement with his famous remark: 'The true is the whole. However, the whole is only the essence completing itself through its own development.' Development is the most important, and its form—dialectics—is also for Hegel to be reminded. Hence his illustrative consideration in the already quoted *Preface*: 'I have posited that science exists because of the self-movement of the concept . . . In the meantime, I can bear in mind that, for example, the excellence of Plato's philosophy has sometimes been said to lie in his scientifically valueless myths, and there have also been times . . . in which the Aristotelian philosophy was esteemed for the sake of its speculative depth and when Plato's Parmenides, perhaps the greatest work of art of the ancient dialectic, has been taken to be the true disclosure and the positive expression of the divine life.'[3] The (ancient) dialectic was evidently the name for the flow, the development, which is the stream-without-name and was the main subject of Hegel's philosophical concern, as Marx, Engels and later philosophers noticed. That name was omnipresent, also for Marx and Engels who wanted to have the dynamics of thought formation as an unquestionable form of the unfolding of social positions, forms of life and ideals of sociability. Would that name survive the ages to come? The same consideration regards the stability of the particle and its spread in well-defined spaces.

Physics want to view the particle as an identifiable object, as a unit of transition or of rotation specifically: is the particle indeed a result of conversion? That question is only efficient and acceptable in the third millennium. A particle is in earlier years considered effective in space-time to have forms of extension to study its properties and develop conceptual ideas about it, like size or duration. Such approaches created questions about the appearance of 'split' particles or 'pairs' or 'groups' of particles, which all lead to measurements based on various types of technology. Note, how the

[3]Hegel (1949), p. 25 f.

fact that the quantum state of each particle taking part in a pair or group of particles can for instance *not* be described without considering the state of other particles—even when extreme distances separate them. A description or measurement seems therefore important because these techniques can cause an irreversible collapse on the particle while changing the quantum state of particles, as the '1935 EPR paradox' (Einstein, Podolsky, Rosen) already suggested. The 'entanglement' issue—focusing on the 'particle' concept, its constitution, properties, and meanings, and above all its dynamics—is yet of central interest in today's quantum theory/technology as well as the research concerning differences between quantum theories and classical physics. But keep in mind: any entanglement as described in the above lines, deviates from the term 'dialectics' as a general indication for the continuous change, movement, unfolding and stream that characterizes human knowledge and its epistemology. One should not neglect that deviation!

Classical philosophy sustained a strong and stable interest in the positioning of particles, their flows, and dynamics. It is remarkable how positions functioned as a meaningful indication regarding the inner dynamics of what philosophy characterized as being and sense. The importance of dynamics is to underline. No wonder, that the term 'dialectic': *the proceeding of reasoning by means of question and answer*, was often identified with *logic*. An analysis of Immanuel Kant's writings made clear that this process of question and answer as a general view on reasoning and thinking showed that the principles of sciences embraced contradictory aspects. He thus focused not on them but on the realm of subjectivity during an important period of his life and philosophical research. Hegel suggested that the entire world history itself followed a dialectical path, so that in the course of time(s) all sorts of contradictions would be transcended. But neither time nor thoughts disappear in that transcendence: the importance of dynamics and duration always becomes underlined by the fact that the transcendence of contradictions gives rise to new contradictions in following periods of history, which also require resolution. The latter inspired for instance Marx and Engels, so that for them the term 'dialectic' concerned the art to master (and often justify) the course of events, i.e., of the world, or of reality itself. Indeed: one emphasizes the course of reality when considering the latter.

This emphasis was in the mind of Hegel when he wrote his 1807 *Phänomenologie des Geistes*, a masterwork often translated as *The Phenomenology of Mind* and sometimes as *The Phenomenology of Spirit*. He was driven by the notion that minds of human beings are progressing towards an insight that the world is not alien or hostile to humans but a part of themselves. That is the case, because the Mind (Spirit) is all that is real in Hegel's view, and each human mind is a part of that Mind (Spirit). Understanding that fact is a process, which is solely brought to a standstill when the understanding is completed. Marx was profoundly inspired by this idea, because once understanding a society as such a basic form of life, it includes that society itself could solve conflicts and thus lead to a final solution of the riddles of human life. In that situation, dialectics would achieve its goal to format human thoughts in such a way that common interests of all humans focus on the dynamics of changes as its basis. Mastering the immanent dynamics of life would help to reach this goal, and *dialectics* should be the term to characterize this human power. That approach includes a notion, which transcends even philosophical disciplinary attempts to understand reality and its history: beginnings (in Peirce's terminology: 'Firstness') and finalities function clearly as Signs of the General. And there is no generality without or beyond dynamics.

The transcendence of the concept 'dialectics' as a determination of 'dynamics' characterizes the twenty-first century on a global scale. Any transcendence of 'dialectics' suggests that a new terminology expressing different ideas, attitudes and awareness might rise at the horizon. Hegel already focused on broader perspectives, which a human being's *Mind* could realize. They characterize an actual unfolding and create a wholeness that encompasses analytics and dialectics that absorb partition. The two form a major nerve of rethinking our thought formations, and color many dimensions of today's social experiences. Growing awareness about the cosmic powers, which influence terrestrial situations seem to have put the Cartesian ego widely in perspective. Newly arising notions of wholeness and dynamics do already heavily influence life-prospects in the third decade of the actual century. They cannot fixate all components of change scientifically or philosophically or color them definitively.

A general remark might be the steppingstone for further considerations. Dialectics is not only a term to indicate an order of thesis, antithesis, and synthesis. The three phases are not to be considered as independent and fixated: the three are anchored in the flow of standpoints, which is marked by the three, or two, of perhaps only one of them. But a consequence should empathically be underlined: there is no thesis without anti- or synthesis, there is never a thesis on its own, without context, without effusion. It is the flow in its proper sense, which requires our attention, our conceptualization, for short: our deeper understanding as a completing force that is characterized in its entirety as 'dialectics'.

We refer in this context to the term *conversion* as a basic component of human knowledge. Wholeness and conversion are closely affined but by no means identical. The first dominates the foundations of Occidental culture; the second stems from a wider understanding and application of expression types linked to specific disciplines. *Wholeness* and *conversion* are important viewpoints in the debates on knowledge and perception, which characterize the last decades. *Conversion* is often defined as a state of change in character, form, or function; it closely parallels changes of attitude, emotion, or personal viewpoint, often from antagonism to acceptance. But the major issue is the fact that *conversion is always understood in connection with the opposites of fixation and standstill.* Conversion is thus in the frame of our interest in understanding the dynamics of cognition. The term has often been understood as 'ethical turn', in proximity to metanoia and therefore as a switchover from logos to ethos. Our introduction and application of the term will, however, take distance from religious thoughts, from revolutionary rhetoric or works and viewpoints of literary character.

Speaking in general, we underline that thinking conversion seems a matter of radical participation rather than guiding or steering. It is a matter of individual minds being together and requires no outstanding or fixated 'self' that acts as the originator of thoughts and thought products. There is for that achievement no road ahead of the thinker and there is no list of profiled problems to solve, there are even no precise goals to achieve. There is, to use a metaphoric expression, a cloud that makes us experience the multidimensionality of thoughts and thinking—not a fixated Speaker-Hearer model. In that regard is conversion in essence the energy and the necessity to rethink our thoughts and knowledge processes in general. It means, not only the 're- ', (the object of thought) but also 'think- ', (the process itself) is differing from individualisms and other conventional patterns.

We thus formulate an act of *conversion* as '*entering a/the stream of thought formations*'. Hegel intuitively understood this process, when he concluded that *wholeness* and *generality* dominate us in all aspects of our thought formation and its effects.[4] Knowledge is in this perspective a means of entering wholeness through determining a 'something' as its very temporary 'object'. Only sensual security concerning that object justifies for him the question, which is central in knowledge processes: 'what is this?' And with the question comes the answer—both are impossible without language! The latter is therefore essential in any process of knowledge acquirement and human speech its global means of articulation. Determinations of the 'something' take place in speech; changes of view and appreciation are never beyond speech and signs are created as linguistically relevant even when they are conceived beyond language patterns. And so is dialectics a concept that determines the 'something' in its relevance for linguistic determinations, even if the latter depend upon the phase in which the dynamics of dialectics unfold—the phase of thesis, anti- or synthesis or stadia beyond them. Dialectics is Movement, Flow, Being, Mind/Geist before, during and after fixation (mostly by means of concepts)—it seems a never-ending process and its components seem seldom captured.

3.2 Negative Dialectics

Jean-Luc Nancy, in his 1997 study on Hegel, entitled his work in accordance with his attempt to embrace dialectics, as the '*Restlessness* of the Negative'. But in how far do 'negative dialectics'—title of the major 1966 publication of Theodor W. Adorno—represent a step in the unfolding of a twenty-first century philosophy?[5] If we outline an answer, we understand the negative in a positive sense. What is the central issue here?

In a short but deeply rooted analysis, Walter Benjamin wrote a century ago, in 1918, a text *On the Program of a Future Philosophy*[6] which impressed Adorno and his colleagues in the Frankfurt School. Any forthcoming philosophy, the text suggested, must concentrate on the relation between experience of reality on the one side, and epistemology (theory of knowledge) on the other. Benjamin critically

---

[4]Hegel (1949), 1807, p. 82.

[5]Buck-Morss (1977).

[6]Benjamin (1963), p. 33 ff. And: Benjamin (1977), p. 117 ff.

analyzed the ways this was developed by Kant, his precursors and followers included. In the deepest regions of epistemology became 'experience' resp. 'reality' an element of speculative, rudimentary metaphysics, he suggests. Two ideas, which are elements that challenge the philosophy of the twenty-first century as well, are important in that regard:

(a) the idea that knowledge and experience are always relate to a human empirical consciousness, and
(b) the idea that knowledge is always and in any regard the product of a relation between subject(s) and object(s).

A forthcoming philosophy is therefore challenged to critically consider the character that clings to the subject of the knowing consciousness ('die Subjekt-Natur'). The basic structure of the latter embraces the pattern of a consciousness that experiences itself as a subject! That was essential for Kant, and it is still a challenge for the modern empirical subject in daily life. Benjamin characterizes 'that subject's self-understanding reinforced by objects around him' as a metaphysical rudiment in his ideas on a theory of knowledge. His words express a vision, which focuses primarily on the value- and functional levels of a knowing consciousness. However, today is a renewed view at stake, especially on the criterion that determines the value-differentiations which are produced by *all types* of consciousness. Note, that all experience in his philosophical view—Adorno's friends and the Frankfurt School included—is grounded in the common notion and understanding of a *transcendental* consciousness.

Those ideas inspired—but are they still relevant? They are, in any case, inspiring to appreciate a critical approach and even the negation of traditionally loaded subject-object foundations inherent to our thought patterns. The *Preface* of Adorno's text suggests indeed relevance: '... as the latest aesthetic discussions feature the 'anti-drama' and the 'anti-hero, this Negative Dialectics in which all esthetic topics are shunned might be called an 'anti-system. ... It attempts by means of logical consistency to substitute for the unity principle, and for the paramountcy of the supra-ordinated concept, the idea of what would be outside the sway of such unity. To use the strength of the subject to break through the fallacy of constitutive subjectivity – this is what the author felt to be his task.' 'Concretion' is the keyword at issue. 'Concise, concrete philosophizing'—words of Benjamin's commentary on Adorno's 1937 lines pertaining to a meta-criticism of epistemology—is the goal 'that requires the strength of the subject to break through the fallacy of constitutive subjectivity.'[7] Herewith is the distinction between a 'pure philosophy' on the one hand and a 'philosophical thought pattern based on formal sciences' on the other hand a powerful motive at the horizon. A closer look at the effects of this distinction might clarify some aspects of the negative dialectics.

[7] Adorno (1973), p. xx.

(1) One should be aware that in the days around 1963/1966—the period in which Adorno wrote his major philosophical work—was the term negative understood as critical. The critical dimensions of philosophical regions and domains, expressions, and articulations concern today not a specific attitude but a field and flow of research in which the role of the critic is enveloped. Developments of the concept 'dialectics' therefore caused Benjamin, Adorno, and others to focus in the first place on the basic meanings of the subject and managed by it. And with the recalling of the subject occurs an act which seems an inner motive of the Creation: *the naming*. With the combination of the two: subject and naming, embraces Adorno's problem of the negative dialectics a recent theme in actual philosophy, called language.

(2) A reference to language does not simplify or solve the problem of *meaning* as such or the term *negative* itself in the expression *negative dialectics*. The latter focuses primarily on a new and different understanding of dialectics. No longer fixed to identity, its appearance is recognized to be inherent in thought itself, in its pure form and its flow. To think is to identify; any conceptual order is therefore screening what thinking seeks to comprehend, so that truth and thought entwine. The 'revelation of the limits of knowledge', pursued in the wholes of purely theoretical thinking, is the true feature of the negativity of this new form of dialectics. Philosophy is obliged to ruthlessly criticize itself; the term 'negative' expresses this attitude. And: what about the subject? The answer is clear, challenging, and yet confusing: *tell the subject to perform this negativity, and let the knowing subject become aware of the fact that this performance implies a hitherto unknown resp. unpracticed project of de-subjecting!* It means all in all: enrichen the subject with the insight that philosophy's conceptual knowledge is not the absolute of philosophy! Adorno adds: 'this insight, for all its inescapability, is again due to the nature of the concept. It is not a dogmatic thesis, much less a naïvely realistic one. Initially, such concepts as that of 'being' . . . To change this direction of conceptuality, to give it a turn toward nonidentity, is the hinge of negative dialectics. . . . Insight into the constitutive character of the non-conceptual in the concept would end the compulsive identification, which the concept brings unless halted by such reflection. Reflection upon its own meaning is the way out of the concept's seeming being-in-itself as a unit of meaning'.[8]

(3) A challenge pertaining to the true nature of the subject is the idea of *identity*, which also plays a role in the framework of a negative dialectics. Remember Adorno's words: 'to think is to identify'. It is a slogan that should support the major idea, that 'no longer fixed to identity, its appearance is recognized to be inherent in thought itself, in its pure form and its flow.' But we need to think to understand, and the outcome of that thought formation astonishes. Our thoughts about identity do not only consider a sameness or equality in a specific (for instance linguistic or logical) framework, but also in the heart of philosophy

[8] Adorno (1973), p. 12.

> itself. Identity has indeed been a complex and central theme since Leibniz, and it also plays its role in the understanding of 'negative dialectics'. Wittgenstein has given much attention to the issue in his famous *Tractatus Logico Philosophicus* as well in the pages published in 1945 as *Philosophical Investigations*.[9] They were not without effect on Adorno's view. When Wittgenstein writes: 'Roughly speaking: to say if two things that they are identical is nonsense, and to say of one thing that it is identical with itself is to say nothing.'(5.5303), it resounds in Bertrand Russell's introducing words from 1922: 'Mr Wittgenstein ... banishes identity', which 'removes one method of speaking of the totality of things, and it will be found that any other method that may be suggested is equally fallacious: so, at least, Wittgenstein contends and, I think rightly. This amounts to saying that 'object' is a pseudo-concept. To say 'x is an object' is to say nothing'.[10]

Both philosophers already express what Adorno had in mind: what is said about 'identity' is meant to be valid for all philosophy as such! There is no philosophy about philosophy that is not a philosophy. We thus read: 'Identity is the primal form of ideology.' Why, and how? 'The force of consciousness extends to the delusion of consciousness. It is rationally knowable where an unleashed, self-escaping rationality goes wrong, where it becomes true mythology. The ratio recoils into irrationality as soon as it fails to grasp that the disappearance of its substrate—however diluted—is its own work, the product of its own abstraction. When thinking follows its law of motion unconsciously, it turns against its own sense, against what has been thought, against what calls a halt to the flight of subjective intentions. The dictates of its autarky condemn our thinking to emptiness; in the end, subjectively, the emptiness becomes stupidity and primitivism. Regression of consciousness is a product of its lack of self-reflection. We can see through the identity principle, but we cannot think without identifying. Any definition is identification.'[11]

Identity thus seems beyond the thinkable.

So, does identity change our thought patterns? But to grasp 'identity as an ideology' represents only a moment of a far more encompassing process: the laws of motion that characterize our thinking express its existence and motion. They seem an auxiliary plea where words are failing, and philosophy appears primitive. However, Adorno suggests in one of his most central thoughts to distinguish between identifying- and identitarian thinking. This distinction seems a crux of any dialectics, and most certainly of a *negative dialectics*. Identifying thoughts seek to say what something is, he explains, whereas identitarian thoughts say what something exemplifies or represents, and what, accordingly, it is not itself. The distinction becomes important when it suggests: 'The more relentlessly our identitarian thinking besets its object, the farther will it take us from the identity of the object. Under its critique, identity does not vanish but undergoes a qualitative change'. The burden of ideology

[9]Wittgenstein (1958a, b).

[10]B. Russell: *Introduction*, in: Wittgenstein (1958a), p. 17.

[11]Adorno (1973), p. 34.

diminishes whenever the change from one type of thought formation to the other takes place.

An outcry that unexpectedly formulates thought patterns of a future philosophy thus appears amidst of analytical phrases: 'To define identity as the correspondence of the thing-in-itself to its concept is hubris.' But further explanations direct the reader only back to traditional philosophy: 'identification is reflected in the linguistic use of the word outside of logic, in which we speak, not of identifying an object, but of identifying with people and things. Dialectics alone might settle the Greek argument whether 'like' is known by 'like' or by 'unlike'. If the thesis that likeness alone has that capacity makes us aware of the indelible mimetic element in all cognition and all human practice, this awareness grows untrue when the affinity—indelible, yet infinitely far removed at the same time—is posited as positive. In epistemology the inevitable result is the false conclusion that the object is the subject. Traditional philosophy believes that it knows the unlike by likening it to itself, while in so doing it really knows itself only. The idea of a changed philosophy would be to become aware of likeness by defining it as that which is unlike itself.'[12]

All in all, does the power of thinking, the exploration of thought patterns, the activity of human consciousness in general, reach into its own gloss! The essential of this insight was already formulated: 'Dialectics – literally: language as the organon of thought – would mean to attempt a critical rescue of the rhetorical element, a mutual approximation of thing and expression, to the point where the difference fades. Dialectics appropriates for the power of thought what historically seemed to be a flaw in thinking: its link with language, which nothing can wholly break. . . . It is in the rhetorical quality that culture, society, and tradition animate the thought.'[13]

Do those insights suffice to understand the essence of negative dialectics and in ultimo of philosophy itself? Nothing is said furthermore about the law of motion, or about motion or flow—an expression already often mentioned in the above lines. Is motion the missing expression amidst all those words and the wealth of their considerations? It is, miraculously. *In all considerations of a negative dialectics is no word about its specific dynamics.* Wittgenstein was correct to conclude in his Investigations 5.5301: 'That identity is not a relation between objects is obvious.' At stake are the nature of the thinking subject expressed in his or her thoughts, and the possibility of thinking the totality of things, thoughts included. Are they fallacious? They might be if the modes of thought formation are not an issue, in other words: if the dynamics of dialectics is not considered in its uniqueness. If identity is not a relation, as Wittgenstein suggested, then is identity a moment of the flow of thought formation. The characteristic of the first is not a feature of the second—both belong to a flow, the dynamics, an evolution, a mode. The latter are neglected and do not appear as an important issue in its own right.

Our traditional view on dialectics seems determined by its 'flow'-character rather then by any other type of characterization—but are we aware of it? Steps in the flow

[12] Adorno (1973), p. 149.

[13] Adorno (1973), p. 57.

remain essential when those dynamics are respected—but when, why and how? Let us not forget we characterized beginnings and finality as signs of the general. There is indeed no beginning without any imagination of its possibly forthcoming totality and no first step without notions of the path to go. This pertains to the hidden dynamics of what we register as an entirety or what we imagine as the meaning of our thought formations as such. That inspiring idea must guide us also when we consider the stadia or steps featuring any dialectics. No step is named, analyzed, or performed without this background. No thesis, anti- or synthesis will be recognized beyond an idea concerning the features of its proper totality.

No step in that totality will be taken beyond such an idea.

That is the riddle of the dynamics inherent in the flow of knowledge characterized as dialectics.

A step is 'a somewhere'—nobody denies. But a next step is somewhere else, and that is often denied or at least difficult to accept. When we go, we go somewhere, but where do we go while we move? Do we always move, and is the flow of words and thoughts in which everyone participates, including directions or other identity providers? Are we able to understand rationally and clearly that we, as living humans, belong to the flow of life? Did we ever take the famous adage 'everything flows' serious in its relation to the qualities of our subjectivity? 'And yet, she moves'—Copernicus' heliocentric words are not a joke!

A remarkable difference of expression fascinates when dialectics as a flow are considered in relation with human behavior. Participating actively in a narration differs from participating in a flow, or a streaming named dialectics. The first is usually considered as a position (often also as a role) and we characterize the second as a step. Both have their fascinating relationship with the problem of identity: positions are identifying- whereas steps are identitarian thinking, Adorno would have said. Steps, in contrast to a position, declare an identity or position in the process in which they are involved. A step should therefore be understood as 'an indication of the multiplicity of the one', whereas a position is 'a narration of singularity', which is powerful thanks to its uniqueness claimed as a form of 'being'.

This observation supports the idea that making steps characterizes the realm of dialectics. A step from thesis to antithesis is often very consequential, difficult to perform and requiring an open mind. That is the case when two different subjects are making those steps as well as when the step occurs within the mind and attitude of one and the same person, resp. subject. What is more: the order of steps is neither a natural phenomenon nor an occurrence beyond intelligence and responsibility of the performing subject. Any step (even those made solely corporeal or psychic), is made in the framework of knowledge and/or the knowable. So, a step in the flow of dialectics is a most fascinating phenomenon. A step can be made to create a thesis, an antithesis, or a synthesis—to restrict oneself to classical names of the three phases. But one can also take a step to create an antithesis with the consciously planned purpose to go from there and generate a thesis! That step will beyond doubt influence the forthcoming synthesis and at the same time throw a different light on the thesis in its position of first step—the latter, the first step can thanks to its other name (anti-) change its character and function. A first step became thus a complicated constitutive process that would receive its name and function in dialectics as a functional entirety. In modern prose would such an epistemological move be named 'critical'. A slogan for the actual street thus originates: 'Take the critical step, make that step utmost important and search for a possible origin in a thesis, so that your critical step can be named 'anti- ', and go on, while your 'anti-' as well as its foresighted 'syn-' are symbolized by for instance 'a yellow vest'!' Indeed: modern streets became a semiotic climate of importance by means of embracing the dynamics of dialectics.[14]

The Occidental cultures narrated how language was of axial importance through a very special activity, which God assigned to the first man: the process of name giving: 'God formed out of the ground every beast of the field and every bird of the sky and brought them to the man to see what he would call each one; and whatever the man would call to a living soul is its name'. Is it not remarkable, that the name giving in the framework of the Creation is described in this narrative as a Human affair and not as a Divine activity? But the naming in the way it is marked here in these text fragments could never be qualified as a Divine activity because there was a fundamental imperfection involved!

Most attention has been given to what was famously characterized as the absence of a 'helper' of the naming authority, i.e., the first man. The Bible's *New King James Version* tells us: 'But for Adam there was not found a helper comparable to him.' This absence does not in the first place articulate a lack of any 'Other' for the first Man on the planet. No, it expresses that *Man's linguistic capacity was incomplete*. His name giving did not unleash any dynamics of question and answer. That process of the name-giving becomes even clearer profiled if one focuses on the order of events, which go with the acts of naming. The remarks stated that language unfolding in the activity of name giving was the major component of the Creation. But the imperfection reins from it's beginning: the absence of another 'helper', a 'woman'. The male part of the human brought the female part into being via naming: a naming into an already named world. Eve was named by the male part, which was himself not been named by God. But only the two, after the completion of the man's name giving process, were able to explore deeper knowledge incited by the serpent, the 'more cunning than any beast of the field'. Man's finalizing his original activity, which is the assigning of names, occurs *before* the naming of Eve. The nomination Eve is thus equal to the naming of all other living creatures. So, the name Eve (given by the first man) highlights *the flow of assigning names* as the essence of the creation of humans and not the activity of the serpent and the 'first sin'.

The order of the events narrated in the traditional text comprise a most important issue. It is the insight that the completion of the name giving by the first man must be understood as having priority over the occurrence of the 'Fall of man' and the 'first sin'. The latter brought a widening and completion of knowledge in the context of the naming process—the Fall of man should, in other words, not interrupt the Naming! This included the naming of Eve, who only after the Fall was named by the first man. In other words: the broadening of knowledge by the Fall could only

[14] Broekman (2017), pp. 1–37.

take place after the completion of the naming process. This order of events underlines that the Naming would comprise the dimensions of knowledge after the Fall. Only in that order of events could the role of language be understood: the name giving was the basis for the linguistic dynamics of question and answer—the creation of the 'helper' to the naming first man was in effect a creation of the dynamics of language. Language as a means of communication, and above all of conversation, exists in this phase of historical events thanks to its dynamic properties. It is a first time in which occurrences like 'question, answer and communication' are linked to these dynamics. The contrast between this phase of linguistic evolvements of language and the preceding name giving occurrences is most striking.

At least one aspect of this insight leads to modernity.

The task of *naming* changed into the layered task of *answering* and *questioning*, that is: to a dynamic of language, which was impossible in the language before the Fall. The central theme amid language's new dynamics is the self. The discovery of the human pair that 'they were both naked', which the Torah put next to the episode of the Fall brings awareness of a human Self and, what is more, insight about the complexity of that Self. The birth of the two children Cain and Abel also changed their Selves: Eve told Adam a most inner experience of herself, when saying: 'When He (God) created me and my husband, He created us by Himself, but in the birth of this child, we are partners with Him'. Dialogues unfold, speech occurs, questions and answers become formulated.

The Self has entered the ages as one of their major issues, clad by language. The world is only 'world' thanks to the name giving that created a world. The latter was missing when the first man unfolded his meaning creation, which was ultimately confirmed by the creation of the helper he himself named Eve in the performance of his final name-giving act. Her existence is a breach; her meaning erodes and does not rename the reality she is confronted with, nor the tasks she must fulfill: to accompany, and to create new lives. Eve's Otherness is based on what is already named, and thus finds its origin in acceptance and not in any Adam's name giving. Since her creation will her 'acceptance of otherness' be the naming that creates life on earth. A double sense of the modern desire to understand human subjectivity is announced herewith: the Creation's reality is the transcendent and only reality of God, and at the same time man's capacity to make the world. The two form one subject. Its riddle and challenge are at the end of the Creation process, God had done—but the making/naming of man moved on and has no end. The subject must stumble over the names and words through which he forges reality. Did Freud understand this, when he formulated that 'the ego is not master in his own house'?

3.3 Dialectics and Firstness

Is Eve's life a symbol in the heart of Creation that surpasses the reality based on- and outlined through Adam's name giving? The grand narratives confirm a most remarkable fact: Eve enters her life in the already Created World, which is fully named, but she herself is named before the name-giver Adam was given his proper name! As if 'the first man' as the Creation narrative calls him, did not belong to the unfolding world.

The narrative that introduces Eve displays a fascinating feature: the dialectic character of evolvement always circles around *firstness*: Eve is the 'first named' by Adam, which acted as the 'first name-giving actor'. Her name was given after the Fall: that is the formidable event of *broadening human knowledge*. Adam's name is mentioned only after the completion of the naming process.[15] One must conclude: the narrative of a human genesis and the creation of the globe are marked by *tensions around firstness*. No wonder that also modern philosophers were fascinated by this problem. Their interest brought them to leave the traditionally cherished positions and (often without knowing and analyzing) to face steps that feature the flow as an epistemological narrative that displays its own special features. Each philosophical approach structuring likewise might be inspired by the intuition to interpret dialectics not only as a scientific method but also as a form of participation in the flow. Tensions between positions about reality and consciousness formulated in narratives and steps in the flow of dialectics are sensible.

Ch. S. Peirce articulated such tensions whilst warning: 'do not confound thought with thinking!' The steps of dialectics (the latter not being a 'method' but temporarily named: 'fluidity') determine. Positions imply the totality of the story, the narration in which steps imply dynamics without fixing the story's beginning and finality. New impressions come into existence: positions in the narration are almost intuitively viewed as specifically structured steps. A dominating feature is that those steps, once recognized as composites of positions, represents a different structuring of though formation. They are performed not to rest and stabilize but, on the contrary, to change into new and/or different views and viewpoints.

That structuring, we emphasize, circles around what is experienced as firstness. Every step is made to evoke a new beginning; each step can choose another direction; all steps can require different types of language to express an overall intention. Indeed: steps are always made in the context of an intention, which is also understood as the whole that embraces the parts. But the parts, even their composing particles, are not submitted to the whole—they are, in contrast, expressing an immense freedom of creativity. Post-dialectics is in this light not a term to indicate 'leave dialectics', or 'condemn them as a bad progenitor' but rather a term indicating the challenge to reach beyond themselves, indeed: beyond dialectics and see the flow, the unfolding, which dialectics truly indicates. Post-dialectical components

[15] See Genesis 3.

guide us from positions and methods to insight and unfolding of knowledge, thought patterns and consciousness.

And there is another mark in the context of firstness to be mentioned. We underline, that *there is no Firstness without its context.* That awakens the notion that (a) Firstness is a step on a path, not a fixated or fixable position (Peirce speaks of a 'possibility'), and that (b) the path must be a path loaded with meanings, because Firstness is, and always must be experienced as meaningful. The two are basic for what is seldom discussed: (c) Firstness is a special form of Presence. The actual, a breach in the fluidity of the historical, the step that sustains the dynamics of life, underlines the close ties between Firstness and Presence. Peirce was insightful when he wrote: '... nothing is more occult than the absolute present. ... It would be something which is what it is without reference to anything else within it or without it, regardless of all force and of all reason.' The light we so badly need is there when we understand the ties between the present and its firstness. Peirce registers that 'such isolated flashes come to the front'. The most inspiring flash of conscious knowledge might be, that there is no notion of Firstness without Time. In that regard we remember Smolin's introductory suggestion: 'Time will turn out to be the only aspect of our everyday experience that is fundamental.' And Firstness is a key issue of that daily experience. Philosophy requires our rethinking the relations between Firstness and Time, and Smolin enriches that requirement for us when he writes: 'The fact that it is always some moment in our perception, and that we experience that moment as one of a flow of moments, is not an illusion. It is the best clue we have to fundamental reality.[16]'

Indeed—there is no consideration of Firstness without taking Time as a constitutive element and not an incidental context.

This is the more appealing to us because all human individuals should be understood and even be characterized as 'being radically bound by 'beginnings' in life'. The focus on Eve and Adam in a named world, on their multiple beginnings (before- and after naming, before- and after the Sin, before- and after aware of being naked) are in themselves a beginning for an unfolding of human lives. The narration makes clear how each being that lived or lives on earth, on the globe and the cosmos is a component of history. We must remember moments of that history to build knowledge and explore possibilities of our consciousness. Even the modern eco-centric view on life and humans seems surpassed by this insight. Any First belongs to Firstness as well as Beginning or Start and the Before or After, which characterize them. Those belongings and their patterns, varying with their culture, make—not unlike the Flow itself—the strong impression of an all-embracing natural evidence. This question is, in other words, a most fascinating issue: must the Flow ultimately become understood as the most natural experience among all components of human consciousness? If one affirms the question, then the experience as well as the naturalness is to be philosophically questioned.

---

[16]Smolin (2013), p. xxxi.; Charles. S Peirce: *The Collected Papers of Charles Sanders Peirce*, Ch. Hartshorne & P. Weiss, [Eds] Cambridge MA, Harvard UP, Vol 2, p. 85.

Our feelings of natural evidence in Firstness and Beginning do indeed imply a pertinent question: does that evidence exist in life's unfolding? In other words: is the idea named 'natural evidence' undisputed? That question touches the fundamental structures of human existence. It says: does every human being, embedded in one of the cultures around the globe, enter social life by means of leaving the realm of natural evidence? The Torah/Bible narrative about Creation suggests that move: after 'the Sin' was the realm of natural evidence named 'Paradise'. It appears that this issue is embedded in a foundational narrative to be found around the globe in numerous variations.

Do we indeed have to perform a step out of the realm of natural evidence to become perceptive individuals? This was certainly suggested by Peirce's whistle of the train or the sheriff's hand on his shoulder. They should be understood as signs of a breach with our pre-existing natural evidence, of which we are not aware.

Awareness of evidence and breach of it seem to co-exist; they engender at the same time in a process of intensifying consciousness. It interests how psychiatrists—in contrast to philosophers—did not encounter any 'natural evidence' as a general human property! On the contrary, they encountered multiple and very different forms of existence, deviations from even the most common human properties, psychological and behavioral standards. Not the epistemology of one specific breach and its ontology seems at stake. Natural evidence seems rather one form of an immense variety of interpretations and experiences pertaining to such a breach. Psychiatric patients tell us how they do not experience a breach with any pre-existing natural evidence because that evidence never existed for them. They witness a bewildering separation between evidence and breach. A breach did never take place for them because there was nothing to depart from, nothing to be driven out, no Paradise of natural evidence! The basic problem of their symptoms is that they did not possess any natural evidence related to their Selves!

This challenges philosophical problems. It has often been discussed that psychiatric patients enrich or expand the scale of 'normal' phenomena of human life while representing 'abnormal' life situations and experiences. That was particularly highlighted in existentialism, philosophical anthropology, and existential psychiatry during decades before and some years after the Second World War. Those movements most prominently understood how 'abnormality', 'the abnormal' or 'the schizophrenic' could be the theme of a regional ontology in the sense of Husserl. But they also underlined that an abnormal or a schizophrenic person, a psychically ill human being, could never be approached in that same ontological context. An existential theory about human beings based on a general ontology is contradictory and therefore not feasible. Therefore, Heidegger stated that the philosophical expression 'ontology' should have a different meaning as soon as a human being and its existence are at stake. His interpretations in the famous 1926 publication 'Sein und Zeit' [Being and Time} are in that regard understandable as interpretations of Husserl's Lebenswelt [Lifeworld] in a specific ontological *Einstellung* [attitude]. In other words, the expression 'to be' has a meaning, which depends on whether it is applied to objects or to humans. If there are multiple regions of ontology, how then should we articulate the word 'to be' and how do we discuss the question whether any pre-existing natural evidence should be awakened by a breach that 'exists' for all humans alike?

Husserl articulated how a human existence is founded upon a plurality of ontological structures, so that existential-anthropological interpretations are themselves embedded in a plural ontology. A phenomenological ontology on its own may never be sufficient to grasp the dimensions of human existence and deliver any insight into its subjectivity. Human reality, he highlights 1929 in his *Formale und Transzendentale Logik*, is a universe of multiple transcendences. So-called abnormal modes of existence belong to constitutive processes, which include all dimensions of any human nature. A plural and in essence transcendental ontology embraces limitless variations of being, which are altogether foundational for the understanding and realization of human life. In other words, the question pertaining to 'the 'being' of reality' relates to a plural ontology in which multiple modes of understanding 'to be' are implied. That is basic for a 'structural anthropology', which includes observations about the virtual and cyberspace as explained in the preceding paragraph. All are accompanied by what Husserl called an 'attitude change' and this change remains foundational for semiotics. As we will see in the next chapter, remain Firstness and attitude change closely connected in the context of a plural ontology.

Peirce's interest in pre-existing natural evidence was, however, not primarily ontological. His question was not whether naturalness exists in an ontological sense of the word, but how naturalness is philosophically, linguistically and semiotically understandable. Because that point of view is important, he proposed a breach with natural evidence as a major factor in the epistemological conditions of a human being. That caused his interest in what he called the indexical properties of such a state of being. If its foundation is an ontological issue, it is the ontology that founds human communication tout court—and that is exactly what Husserl characterized as a regional ontology, expressing how a plural ontology is needed for understanding each specific property at hand.

A problem with the idea of a loss of natural evidence is expressed in W. Blankenburg's 1971 study: *Der Verlust der natürlichen Selbstverständlichkeit.* (The Loss of Natural Evidence).[17] The psychiatric situation highlights the question: How can one lose what one does not possess? The answer appears to be, that only if the world of words possessed by others is the sole hold and criterion for the self. This is Anne Raus's problem, as her case study in the Blankenburg publication clarifies. The case represents important categories of thought formation. It should in the first place be underlined, that the expression 'natural evidence' was coined by Anne long before the psychiatrist met her. It was apparently her life-theme, perhaps the sole fruit of her entire life-tree, and she kept using the expression in all her conversations. Essential fragments of a phenomenology of her case are in the notes of her psychiatrist, such as: '. . .she spoke of 'thoughts imposed on me' and: 'everything was powerless against them'. But, as he further states, it was not apparent that she

[17] Blankenburg (1971), pp. 60–121.

experienced an imposition or any hypnotic compulsions. Most striking, and never observed before, were facial behaviors, nearly grimaces, and a strong excitement, which articulated beyond doubt the dangerous nature of life in general. As far as could be clarified, these were behaviors or reactions—even fragments of complete scenes—belonging to others, which she felt compelled to imitate. The latter form of social contact, especially through language, was for Anne Raus: imitation, and not creation. A further analysis of the implicit dialectics of that inherent power appeared not to be in the hands of the psychiatrist. Blankenburg's study challenges in this regard to perceive the patient's possibilities in the broader perspectives of linguistic utterances beyond the grammatical and syntactical standards of language in general. The conflict between linguistically correct speech and lingual imitation should be takes seriously: it determines qualities of the flow we seldom encounter.

Characteristics of Anne's conversation were that much *unsaid* remained standing in the room. Her gestures and facial expressions helped her, especially when she clearly touched the boundaries of the unutterable. ... 'What am I missing? Something very small, it's comical, something important without which one cannot live. At home, with my mother, I was not there as a human being. I had not grown. I was simply there, just there, but not with them. I need a bond, which guides me so that not everything is artificial ... now I have always to see that I do not lose everything ... I simply feel that I still need a hold ... that might be natural evidence, which I miss'... 'To find boundaries and experience limits is becoming an adult...I take things always like others do and could never take an opposite position—I could never trust my own judgment' she told her psychiatrist, who reports about many years with an important variety of therapies and continuous residence in the clinic, until in an unattended moment she committed suicide. There are indeed several issues to underline in our attempts to understand Firstness.

(1) The importance of a pre-existing natural evidence for understanding primordial experiences and perceptions is clear. Natural evidence in the sense of a plural ontology helps differentiate the often-rigid debate of a 'to be' or 'not to be'. To suppose that there is any natural evidence beyond cultural and anthropological differences is untenable. Peirce's interest was not ontological but pertained to semiotics as a general theory of signs.
(2) In most cases is a pre-existing and thus natural evidence understood as self-evident. The use of the concept 'nature' in this expression serves the understanding of a human epistemology and is thus an important anthropomorphism. It plays a major role at the level of human experience rather than at the level of positive facts. This also functions as a basic observation to enhance experience and knowledge but does not solve ontological questions.
(3) Any confrontation with a primordial function of natural evidence underpins the social dimensions and social needs in human life. Life is definitively a life with others. The quality of a sign leads always to others, as in the footprint that Robinson Crusoe found in the sand was an index for another creature existing on the island. However, life with others is only possible as a self. That insight

dominated in the case of Anne. It surprises how natural evidence as well as natural self-evidence is an epistemologically relevant condition.

(4) Anne's loss was not a loss in the sense of normal life, and it could not be such a loss, because she had not developed a self. Natural evidence (as well as natural self-evidence) has *a self as precondition*. Her loss was solely a loss in so far as others (who contrasted with Anne successful in developing a self) articulated her situation as a loss. It was the language and its meaning of others she had missed and would never possess. Her psychological handicap could only be articulated and experienced in the language of others, as much as her psychiatric anamnesis could never be in her own words, because she did not have words at her disposal. Together with this lack, she was psychically ill because she did not have what others told her is a possession, a self.

Anne complained about her loss of natural evidence whilst articulating this loss as a form of missing. She showed in her situation of psychiatric patient how natural evidence is an issue of semiotic nature, which requires a well-developed self. So, one must conclude, that *Firstness confirms how the language of 'a self related to others' is the foundation for natural evidence,* in other words: something bewildering which is not there 'by nature'.

References

Adorno TW (1973) Negative dialectics (trans: Ashton EB). Routledge, London & New York

Benjamin W (1935) The Arcades Project (trans: Eiland H, McLaughlin K). German volume edited by Rolf Tiedemann, Harvard University Press Cambridge, Massachusetts, London, UK

Benjamin W (1963) Über das Programm der kommenden Philosphie, (Ed. Gershom Scholem) 1918. In: Horkheimer M (ed) Zeugnisse. Theodor W. Adorno zum sechzigsten Geburtstag. Europäische Verlagsanstalt, Frankfurt a. M.

Benjamin W (1977) Gesammelte Schriften. Band II,1 Suhrkamp Verlag, Frankfurt/M.

Blankenburg W (1971) Der Verlust der natürlichen Selbstverständlichkeit. (The loss of natural evidence). F. Enke Verlag, Stuttgart. Second Edition: Parados Verlag, Berlin 2012

Broekman JM (2016) Meaning, narrativity and the real. Springer International, Switzerland

Broekman JM (2017) Street' as theory. In: Marusek S, Brigham J (eds) Street-level sovereignty. The intersection of space and law. Lexington Book, New York, London

Buck-Morss S (1977) The origin of negative dialectics. Theodor W. Adorno, Walter Benjamin, and the Frankfurt Institute. The Harvester Press, Ltd, Hassocks/Sussex, UK

Hegel GWF (1949) In: Hofmeister J (ed) Phänomenologie des Geistes. F. Meiner, Leipzig

Peirce CS. In: Hartshorne Ch, Weiss P (eds) The collected papers of Charles Sanders Peirce. Cambridge MA, Harvard UP, vol 2

Russell B. Introduction. In: Wittgenstein: *Tractatus*, Op. Cit., p 17

Smolin L (2013) Time reborn. Houghton M. Hartcourt, Boston, New York

Wittgenstein L (1958a) Tractatus Logico-Philosophicus (with an Introduction by Bertrand Russell). Routledge & Kegan Paul, London

Wittgenstein L (1958b) Philosophical investigations. Basil Blackwell, Oxford

Chapter 4
Flow and Firstness

4.1 Divine Desire

'God loves odd numbers', Abu Hamid al-Ghazali (1058–1111) mentioned[1]—and Kings, Queens, Governors, and Presidents take the floor, are given priorities, come first and consider Firstness as their natural milieu. And for the God of the Torah, Bible, and Koran narration—the One Who Creates and is not created—is Firstness beyond every possible definition of the concept. All that must be understood at a deeper level than order and number suggest. This is the case, because, as Ch. S. Peirce formulated in his *Third Harvard Lecture* on April 9, 1903, the category 'the First' 'is not susceptible of any degenerate or weakened modification.'[2] The sanctifying itself is a sign of the precept to fully encompass the Creator's Firstness. The encompassing concerns literally everything—in the quoted words are man and animal equal, and equally underlining a universal requirement.

Is Firstness the Creation's Divine Evidence? The question is important. Interest in any pre-existing evidence is not primarily ontological. In other words: the question is not whether evidence exists in an ontological sense of the word, but how it is philosophically, linguistically and semiotically understandable. A breach with natural evidence thus seems a major factor in all epistemological conditions of a human being. That viewpoint caused Peirce's interest in what he called the indexical properties of such a state of being. If their ontology founds human communication tout court (what Husserl characterized as a regional ontology) then a plural ontology is needed for understanding each specific property at hand, he argued. There are various descriptions of an index as understood by Peirce, but none of them exist apart from a sign. A sign is for Peirce anything that determines something else (its interpretant) to refer to an object to which itself refers (its object) in the same way—the interpretant becoming in turn a sign, and so on, ad infinitum. Two features

[1] Burrell and Daher (1995), p. 117 f.

[2] Peirce (1998), p. 160.

J. M. Broekman, *Knowledge in Change*, Law and Visual Jurisprudence 8,

(which relate directly to the idea of a pre-existing naturalness) are essential in this description. If something will become understood as a sign, one must understand (a) the concept of difference and its reality, which we use to qualify as the 'something/someone *else*', and (b) one must grasp the *process* character of reference, resp. interpretation.

An index is in Peirce's view a sign, which would lose its specific character that makes it a sign if its object were removed—but not if there were no interpreting activity anymore! This fits to the idea of a pre-existing natural evidence, which would be independent from an interpretant as well as from any encompassing leads to evidence that could be called Firstness. 'Such, for instance, is a piece of mold with a bullet-hole in it as a sign of a shot; for without the shot there would have been no hole; but there is a hole there, whether anybody has the sense to attribute it to a shot or not.' wrote Peirce.[3] And in another context, he stated: 'That footprint that Robinson Crusoe found in the sand, and which has been stamped in the granite of fame, was an Index to him that some creature was on his island'. Any process character is based on difference and is essential for each referential activity. With it, an existential totality is evoked, a world of action and resistance in need of being articulated as a 'some-thing'. However, that world presents itself as a 'no-thing' if any form of positivism does not give life to its so-called naturalness. A breach with the idea of pre-existing naturalness and self-evidence is thus like such a positivism. Without it there is only a world as a permanent menace caused by the shadows of the 'no-thing'. One could thus say that the world of a pre-existing naturalness is most forcefully understood in the Peircean index-character: it is a world awaiting its indexation, its signs awaiting their assignation. No wonder that absence of any experience of such an assigning can be qualified as the realm of Divinity. Life in a world without expectation of being assigned is not a human life!

4.2 The Road to Firstness

The road to Firstness, Charles S. Peirce's cherished expression we all embrace, seems a road that first leads backwards before it can move forwards and establish its essence. The latter must wait until a certain accomplishment took place: a step, or several steps. Only in the perspective of parts (resp. moments or steps on that road) are we able to judge and create a consciousness about this dominating feature. That is philosophically to be understood as *a step*, a step backwards and/or forwards, an *interpretation* and never a *fixated position*. Formulated in other words: Firstness is the qualification of a step in the flow, and thus always depends upon another step. And time is connected to each correlate: what was is now, and thus qualified as a beginning, a cause, a quality, a motive, a claim, a situation at this moment—that is in

[3]Peirce (1998), p. 145 f.

all cases: as a specific occurrence in the flow that determines the flow at this very moment and thereafter.

We understand Firstness in the context of consciousness' creation of knowledge and experience; it lights up far beyond the dialectical schemes from Hegel to Husserl and seems a magical constitutive point. We mentioned already in the preceding chapter that each being (living or having lived on earth, on the globe and in the cosmos) is a component of history. The latter has the character of flow in any culture—flow rather than a fixated composite of texts. Moments of that history build our knowledge and explore possibilities of our consciousness. Even the modern eco-centric view on life and humans inhabiting the planet seems to be surpassed by this insight. To repeat that view: any First belongs to Firstness as Beginning or Start just like any Before or After, so that all characterize Firstness. No wonder that Peirce does not stop to underline in the various phases of his work, that the Firstness of any idea appears as present and immediate. It never takes the risk to be experienced a second to any representation.

Therefore, we claim that the title of this paragraph, the term: 'road to...' is *inadequate*! Firstness is not a stable and determinable position, which can be treated as a well-defined or definable goal for scientists and philosophers alike. Its dimensions described with words like 'Beginning' or 'Before' are wrongly conceived when its inner dynamics are not fully exposed. They should be understood as a flash of a Beginning—and Walter Benjamin's favored expression 'Blitzartig' (a lightening flash) should be remembered here.[4] But how do we expose those dynamics?

The ineptitude of the expression road to Firstness forms a true challenge.

We must meet the issue not as a singular and very special issue amidst of a multitude of philosophical questions. A precise correlate to Peirce's ideas could be final for ideas on the working of consciousness and the results of thought formation. But that is not the case, and for that reason are several topics to register, of which we mention only a very few.

(1) Firstness and the Peircean 'Triadomania'.

Peirce, the philosopher using the term more frequently than any of his colleagues, was aware of a more-than-terminological complexity at hand. Despite his frequent uses facing the many consequences of the term, he considered Firstness as a vague concept with determinations that are difficult to precisely determine. The desire for determination was never fulfilled because of the many correlations with related issues once a definitive understanding was attempted. One of the many tensional implications can be put into words only indirectly: Firstness is per definition independent of anything although it necessarily depends on the category of continua we named 'the flow'. However, the belonging to continua is realized through articulating non-distinctiveness.

[4] Broekman (2010), p. 45 f.

The issue is important, because all sorts of triads appear in Peirce's thought patterns; hence Stjernfelt's quote of the term *triadomania* and his reference to an almost globally read letter, which Peirce send in 1904 to Lady Welby.[5] One could formulate the thesis that the frequency of triads is underlining the importance of the Firstness in Peirce's thoughts. An enrolment is therefore more important than the literature on Peirce registered until now. Any mention of Firstness indicates fact and value of the flow—and does not describe how to understand or define Firstness as a particular indication. The latter (the defining) is an act of acquiring knowledge about a specific item—the first (the inherency to the flow) is an epistemological act engendering insight in man, culture, and terrestrial life.

(2) Firstness and the 'Unlimited Semiosis'.

Firstness is a matter of the human mind, resp. consciousness, whereas Secondness and Thirdness unfold empirically and are ultimately cosmic processes (mostly registered by the human mind as 'fact' or 'data'). Mind and cosmos are perhaps equivalent in their task to inspire human experience—but they remain distinguishable powers in flow. That remark is not only reflecting continuity as a major constitutive element of sign and semiosis, but also (and perhaps in the first place) the flow character of semiosis and thought formation.

Where signs are at stake, positions are defined or otherwise described. Where Firstness is at stake, steps are indicated—their dynamics and various characters included. Peirce's intuition to consider his semiosis as 'unlimited' seems meant to emphasize *the dynamics of semiotics*. There is no semiotics or sign-function in a fixated and completely stable world. The road to Firstness is part of a flow, a flash, an innumerable number of steps. But the same expression embraces other insights. The 'unlimited' character of semiosis—the latter meaning no more than 'caring of signs'—relates to the Second- and Thirdness evoked by the Firstness. A footnote in Stjernfelt's 2007 text opens the path to a further understanding of this issue.[6] We should indeed strive for an open-minded participation and exclude any hubris in accepting our own experience as a source for the genesis of our knowledge. But we cannot decide whether complicated human experiences can become dissolved and understood rationally.

(3) Firstness and Subjectivity.

Does Peirce's triad-philosophy represent a philosophy without—or beyond any need of—subject/subjectivity? His thoughts on Firstness seem to resemble the activity of a consciousness that positions itself as a subject. Firstness is never an actual

[5] Stjernfelt (2007), pp. 16, 17, 427; 13.

[6] Stjernfelt (2007), p. 17: 'In Peirce's evolutionism, he even ventures the hypothesis that Thirdness is growing as a tendency towards the appearance of still more correlations between even more Secondness events. The relation between the three categories as presented here may be given two different interpretations. One is structural, picturing the a-temporal relation between the three. Another is temporal, supposing that Firstness is also first in a temporal sense, so that the growth of Secondness and Thirdness are cosmological processes empirically taking place'.

phenomenon in the actual world and cannot be understood as any type of correspondence theory. Firstness is a sign produced as a sign—that is the essence of Peirce's insight in semiotics. But he did not primarily focus upon 'subject–object' relations as a basis for knowledge, a thought pattern embraced by many German philosophers from Kant on and even centuries later inspiring thinkers close to semiotics or significs in the beginning of the twentieth century like Martin Buber.

But here is again a viewpoint at stake, which focuses on the criterion determining the value-differentiations, which are produced by all types of consciousness. Instead of researching the activities and properties of an acting subject might Peirce be understood as searching for syntheses of action and patterns of thought: 'Peirce's greatness lies in his genius for synthesizing, for breaking down old habits of thought and recasting composite ideational materials into new form, new Firsts' Kevelson wrote. 'At the end of his life Peirce has begun to grasp the process whereby synthesis, as happens in everyday life, in commonsense thinking, may be deliberately used as an instrument for making, inventing, new ideas. Peirce sees this instrument as a new mode of reasoning, that is, a new way of understanding how reasoning works. This new, expanded account of the process of thought making is, in its hare bones, logic. This logic Peirce calls Semiotics (earlier, Semeiotic).' A few years earlier, she already mentioned: 'It is a mistake to honor Peirce for his individual achievements, in any aspect of philosophy, of the mathematical and other sciences, if doings so distracts us from his one fixed idea: to bring together all these various points of view into a more intensive general place, or, in other words, to take the several mediums, disciplines and discourses of an earlier stage in the evolution of us and edit them into synch.' Those fragments culminate in a remark, which clarifies that Peirce's ideas are characterized by a 'special option of 'consent' as a partial, provisional relationship, based on the 'agreement' between relates in some but not all aspects, underlying Peirce's affirmation of relationship between relates, rather than internally within an individual.[7]'

A conclusion fascinates.

Meaning is in Peirce's view not the result of any type of constitutive power of a subject, but the result of relations between elements.

So, patterning is the issue, not subjective concerns! Modern philosophers with knowledge of digital features would strongly agree. Already Peirce wanted us to be aware of the complexity of this philosophical viewpoint and its planetary relevance. Thinkers knowing the digital might agree what he wrote already in 1885 to William James: 'If the universe is thus progressing from a state of all but pure chance to a state of all complete determination by law, we must suppose that there is an original, elemental, tendency of things to acquire determinate properties, to take habits.' No subjects as origins of thought patterns, but physical laws, laws of nature embracing (yes, even identifying with) the subjects we think of, determine properties—that would be the consequence. And he adds in a triadic mood: 'This is the Third or mediating element between chance, which brings forth First and original events, and

[7]Kevelson (1999), p. 192 f.; Kevelson (1996), p. 6.

law which produces sequences of Seconds.' Looking back, he adds: 'I make so much use of three-fold divisions in my speculations, that it seems best to commence by making a slight preliminary study of the conceptions upon which all such divisions must rest. I mean no more than the ideas of First, Second and Third—ideas so broad that they may be looked upon rather as moods or tones of thought, than as definite notions, but which have great significance for all that.'[8]

Insight in (a) the triadic reasoning, (b) the importance of Firstness and (c) patterns rather than subjective statements, belong together. There is no reason to reproach Peirce for not constructing an Occidental philosophy with the central position of subject and subjectivity. Patterns prevail in his thoughts. Language confirms his approach. He shares linguistic understandings with De Saussure while understanding that texts are patterns of relationships among linguistic components, which create meaning through sign relations. Moreover, he opens an understanding of discourses that was impossible and absent in 1885, the year of his just quoted consideration. Discourses are because of his view signifying ensembles, which should be understood as equivalent to speech acts.[9] And so are narratives, for instance concerning the Cosmos Creation!

These remarks do not simplify the philosophical understanding of thinking and thought creation in general. There is no call to redeem subjects for patterns and change the basic structure of our reasoning accordingly. There is no absolute and safe distinction, let alone an opposite, between subject and structure. The same is true for relations between exclusive subject-centered thought formations and patterns of structural ways of thinking. Thinking does not evolve solely in subject spheres or by contrast solely in structural formations: *the flow in which thoughts arise is a golden mixture* of both. But how do we procure insight and practices of such a mixture: are these to be created at all by a human mind and its cultural context? A first consideration would regard the conditions for that flow, which we are able to distinguish. They are for instance encapsulated in communication, contact, lingual expression, levels of knowledge and insight, forms and intuitions of constitutive structures, dialogues, and other types of language.

One should keep in mind that Firstness is not exclusively a Peircean concept and neither an exclusive approach to reality in the field of philosophical investigation. The road to Firstness is partially made by each philosophical attempt to understand the human cognitive approach to reality. Not any philosophy is uniquely and completely dedicated to and characterized by that concept, but all are—as we will experience in the forthcoming pages –inspired by it! The actual interest for a comparison of Peirce's realism and Husserl's phenomenology is an example of that inspiration.[10] It has a common denominator in specific substances of the flow, of which the process of conversion is the perhaps most important.

---

[8]Peirce (1992), p. 242 f.

[9]Jan M. Broekman: *Structuralism. Moscow, Prague, Paris.* Synthese Library, Vol. 67. Dordrecht, Reidel/Springer Science + Business Media, Dordrecht etc. Ch. 4, p. 70 f.

[10]For instance: Shafei and Pietarinen (2019).

4.3 Peirce, Husserl and Firstness

Mutual insights in the philosophies of Peirce and Husserl became an issue of almost global interest. Why? 'Do not confound thought with thinking,' Peirce once warned. He may have been rethinking Descartes' famous slogan: 'Je pense donc je suis', but he adds: 'Thought is the Object that you think. Thinking, as contradistinguished from feeling and from the effort of attention, is the operation of the mind by which you strive to make out the Truth. You expect to extract it from the object before your mind, the Thought. That thought, then, is (or you hope it may be) a Sign of the Truth. Thought then is a Sign.' and he should have added: being the truth of thinking evolves through the sign, and the latter is ultimately the creation of thoughts.

He did not forget to mention the *semiotic implications* of his insight: '... and Firstness is all around every sign and sign-activity'. Sign and Firstness belong together because no sign will ever be independent from the dynamics of our thought formations, which he called 'the moving images of thought'. Those images are thoughts in themselves, which implies that the recursive character of thinking dominates every inch of our epistemological movements in life. Firstness is the concept in which the relations among the works of Peirce and Husserl are anchored—a concept that touches the inner dynamics of thought formation and cognition in general. These are the basic features of the flow, which Peirce indicated by means of his epistemological interest in 'moving images'. The central observation characterizing this expression is therefore.

Peirce–Husserl relations are primarily in 'Firstness as an all-embracing expression for the meaning and sense of their philosophical work'.

When knowledge is concerned and consciousness questioned, some type of subject seems necessary in our eyes. That involvement is a major issue to discuss when changes and conversions in the flow are rethought. Subjectivity seems to be an ultimate and cosmic requirement of thought formation although flow processes are only considerations at the limits of subjectivity. Is such a limit their correct and adequate position, or do they need the consideration of a renewed bearing? The question was at issue when Kant split the Ego/Subject as if it exists in parts, and when Peirce rethought the many consequences of this view exploring Firstness and a knowing subject's various forms of attitude. Cognition is always a moment in our perception, in our management of life, in our orientation on the road we must go in even cosmic contexts. Knowledge is never an illusion at distance from reality, and it presupposes in our eyes of Occidental culture always a knowledgeable and knowing subject.

The flow challenges us with the often-overwhelming idea that knowledge without a knowing subject would be possible. Do we know how? How do we know? Its cognition would incorporate subjectivity in the stream of cosmic dimensions, which can be miniaturized in every human situation. Is that the crux of an epistemology based on a plurality of language types? It transcends our idea that cosmos and reality are knowledgeable by describing and developing knowledge of all physical interactions among particles in a most subtle way. The flow brings us to answer the question how to obtain knowledge about what the world and its reality really is, can be modeled and represented under the condition that we surpass that knowledge and see the flow's links with consciousness. Both Peirce and Husserl would be fascinated to recognize a pattern of their own interest being formulated thusly. Insights shared by Peirce and Husserl interest philosophers and scholars in the first decades of the twenty-first century.

A recent and broadly based publication presents various supplementary studies on specific fields, such as Logic, Mathematics, Signs, Intentionality, and the Arising of the 'I'.[11] They refer explicitly to the 2007 Stjernfelt text, which places the Peircean Diagram at the center of interests that fascinated both philosophers.[12] That position, which is now located in the diagram, was indeed an important topic for Peirce as well as for Husserl. Shafei and Pietarinen claim priority for the diagram.[13] The triadomania is a theme to consider seriously when studying relations between Peirce and Husserl. That is also the case with the other studies, in particular the mentioned articles on Signs, Intentionality, or the Arising of the 'I'. The latter support an inclusion of images, Husserl underlines—and that makes us again think of Peirce! The image of the object in the knowledge-acquiring mind will during the process of knowledge formation support the latter through forms of similarity. Husserl's insight in the role of the image in knowledge formation will later in his life be completed by his ideas on an eidetic reduction as one of the crucial phases of non-naïve ego attitudes.

We read those considerations today with a renewed interest since important dimensions of communication in non-analog language types focus on the relations of images in the process of acquiring knowledge.

However, not the 'eidetic reduction' or any comparable term of Husserl will bring us to add a specific theme to the fore to be enlisted in the above-mentioned Peirce–Husserl observations.

No, there exists not a safeguarded list of themes to accomplish!

All ideas of Firstness and its multiple characteristics (in Peircean as well as Husserlian sense) lead us *to understand the flow as essential component pertaining to the riddle of cognition related to conversion*. This should sharpen our awareness. The suggestion should not be read as a critique concerning Peirce's triamodania or

---

[11] Shafei and Pietarinen (2019). See Ch. I: A.-V. Pietarinen, M. Shafei and F. Stjernfelt: 'Mutual Insights on Peirce and Husserl', pp. 3–13; and the references at pp. 13–15.

[12] Stjernfelt (2007).

[13] Pietarinen, Shafei and Stjernfelt: 'Mutual Insights on Peirce and Husserl', *Op. Cit.*, p. 5. 'Once a diagram of a general conception is attained it is possible to reason about that object by manipulating and experimenting with the diagram according to certain rules of the system. Husserl, half a generation younger than Peirce, was influenced by the emerging critiques of the use of diagrams that we see emanating from the works of Pasch and Hilbert in Germany, and for such reasons was inclined to meet claims made in favor of the epistemological centrality of diagrams with a great deal of skepticism. Husserl would rather consider diagrams instrumental, as auxiliary tools of philosophical theorizing and mathematical proof. … Husserl famously claimed that knowledge could evolve only from direct acquaintance, not only regarding empirical objects, but also with general, categorical structures, such as numbers, grammar, logic, or general concepts.

his phaneroscopy. On the contrary: ideas seem to be confirmed, which are inherent to the term 'transformation'. This term holds a prominent position in various semiotic contributions of researchers and philosophers during the second half of the last century and firmly underlines their dynamic character.[14]

The closeness of Peirce and Husserl is in their notion of Firstness. Three aspects clarify that view: a closer look at the dynamics of Firstness in Peircean thoughts and experiences as well as the context of Husserl's phenomenology with it phases of reduction. And both lead to the third question how to qualify Firstness as an expression of a philosophical understanding of consciousness and the constitution of human knowledge. In Peirce's thoughts is Firstness the power that generates continuity. But: how? It hardly matters what continuity is *meant*; and what is *perceived* as continuous matters just as little. *Firstness is the grab handle of all aspects of the flow*. One reads Peirce's frequently quoted explanation in a 1904 letter to Lady Welby: 'I should define Firstness, Secondness, and Thirdness thus: Firstness is the mode of being of that which is such as it is, positively and without reference to anything else. Secondness is the mode of being of that which is such as it is, with respect to a second but regardless of any third. Thirdness is the mode of being of that which is such as it is, in bringing a second and third into relation to each other.'[15]

One should rethink the relation between the three stadia mentioned in Peirce's definition and ask whether Thirdness is not a form of Firstness. Do Secondness and Thirdness not, each in their terminology and context, reach out to be or be qualified as Firstness? Would Peirce not have appreciated the simple line we quoted: 'God loves odd numbers'—a line already written by Hamid al-Ghazali around the year 1100? Is continuity created before any reality could enter it, as odd numbers confirm? Are we prepared and able to focus on that continuity (by Peirce expressed in numbers and especially in triads and by Husserl in phases towards transcendence) before we enter the world of realities that could become outnumbered? Is this interrogation of the thinking mind not the great challenge of Peirce's definition resp. triad? Let us have an even closer look at Firstness:

(a) Firstness, the major odd number, is in Peirce's mind the final articulation of incomparability with anything else, the inexplicable as such, in other words: the pure sign. The numerical character is confirmed by the insight that 'Firstness is the Mode of Being of that which is such as it is positively and regardless of anything else. It is thus an abstract possibility. It can therefore only be known to us immediately.'[16] And Secondness is in this light: 'an essential part of Thirdness though not of Firstness, and Firstness is an essential element of both Secondness and Thirdness. Hence there is such a thing as the Firstness of Secondness and such a thing as the Firstness of Thirdness; and there is such a

[14] 'Peirce meets Husserl on Skype' in: Broekman (2016), p. 71 ff.

[15] Peirce (1904).

[16] *The Logic Notebook* | 1905-06-01 | MS [R] 339:242r. 'Firstness'. Term in M. Bergman & S. Paavola (Eds.), *The Commens Dictionary: Peirce's Terms in His Own Words. New Edition*. Retrieved from http://www.commens.org/dictionary/term/firstness.

thing as the Secondness of Thirdness. But there is no Secondness of pure Firstness and no Thirdness of pure Firstness or Secondness.'[17] The road to Hamid al-Ghazali's insight seemed clearly outlined in Peirce's eyes! Constitutive for any initial understanding of firstness and its pragmatic-semiotic project are at least two components: Beginning, and Relations.

(b) Firstness is neither unfettered beginning nor pure immediacy. Reference to firstness is never a recapitulation of any Genesis. Firstness is *not* the same as a Beginning. It is the process of taking a step in the flow, not a matter of knowledge and rationality but rather a matter of orientation, awareness, and dynamic activity. Firstness is indefinable, a concept that emerges only when accompanied by retrospection.

(c) Firstness is unique in as far as it is in an absolute sense a matter of relations—structural, logical, conceptual, semiotic, linguistic as well as social. If things do not act upon one another, there is no meaning. Signs must be in relation to other signs, sign systems and eventually language, to be a bearer of meaning.

So, *meaning is in Peirce's view not the result of the constitutive power of an individual subject but rather of relationships between elements, which became understood as components of reality*. The position of an active subject in Peirce's philosophy seems an issue of special consideration, and—like Firstness—unthinkable if separated from continuity. *This confirms many observations of digital character!* It interests therefore to underline how Firstness seems for that reason an all-embracing expression for Peirce's philosophical work. Is that also the case in Husserl's work, and what is the importance of this eventual parallel? And how elucidating is it to unpack their respective understanding of Firstness?

4.4 Attitude

In the sphere of knowledge, knowledge creation or even knowledgeability has the concept of *attitude* a central position and a crucial meaning. It colors the field of activities of a subject, which seems continuously involved in acquiring knowledge. It unfolds in whatever geographical and cultural condition around the globe. No wonder, that philosophical projects as well as structures of the subject related to the dimensions of cognition are changing fundamentally, even beyond cultural barriers and transcendental dimensions touched by the philosophizing subject. The latter changed, as was mentioned, together with the strong and new global determinations of a *digital* patterning of knowledge and knowledge acquirement—a conceptualization and formation which determines the first decades of the third millennium. This development of the digital as a global feature of knowledge and culture forms the basis for the combination of *cognition* and *conversion* as mentioned in the title of this

[17] Charles. S Peirce: *The Collected Papers of Charles Sanders Peirce*, Ch. Hartshorne & P. Weiss, [Eds] Cambridge MA, Harvard UP, Vol 1, p. 530.

study. In view of that particular and unique coherence is the concept of attitude important and even crucial—neither the concept nor its changes should remain unquestioned since they are challenged by new forms of thinking and its dynamics.

We will in the light of these developments give an intensified attention to the *plurality of positions of the subject* respectively *the ego* as a focus of various positions which create many fields of human knowledge. Husserl has demonstrated its importance during the entire development of his phenomenology. But his analyses did only take place in the context of analog thought formation and a philosophy which positioned the subject centrally. That challenges our insights the more since today is a period which is characterized by a plurality of forms and types of expressivities which were unknown when the phenomenological foundations became articulated. Let us therefore begin with an undisputable insight.

Firstness always occurs first.

There is no way to let Firstness wait until we focus on other categories, acts, or interesting views. That influences our experiences as well as our insights into *attitudes*. When Firstness really unfolds, there is nothing more important than this unfolding itself, including its attention, caring, and sharing. Peirce and Husserl would underline that this characteristic property of Firstness should be respected. But their forms of respect and reverence are different. Reaching out to the untouchable, to what seems beyond relations and thus is independent from any other Self, requires an understanding that is distanced from what should be *understood* (Peirce) and *argumentized* (Husserl). The latter underlines the continuous *repetition* of *Firstness* since *each new attitude of the ego always unfolds in relation to all other positions*. Husserl distinguished a variety of ego-positions resulting from the predominant process of position change.[18]

Do not forget, that the term 'attitude' is complex. It means 'adjustment' as well as 'employment', 'setting' as well as 'awakening' or 'affection'.[19] These differentiations are important because Husserl's phenomenology is characterized by *the phenomenon of change*. Husserl would have remarked that *a human being freely changes his attitude—as he does his mind*. And what is more: he can freely master those changes so that the pure or transcendental ego results of a free activity called attitude-change! The *eidos ego* is thus a pure possibility of the *factual ego*; the two embrace a different attitude. But 'attitude' is in that case a matter of exclusive evaluation, an ascription of value which all attitudes capture in freedom, and therefore ultimately a Firstness.[20] Of course, that freedom is socially embedded. The channeling through social norms, values and expectations is forceful enough, but those forces direct the application of structures in phenomenology. The split, the

[18] Original German expressions are 'Ego-Einstellung', and 'Einstellungsänderung'.

[19] Ferrarello (2019), p. 194 f.

[20] In Husserl's mother tongue: 'ein ausschließliches Geltenlassen'.

Ich-spaltung, the partition of ego-parts, seems omnipresent and throughout constitutive in the eyes of a phenomenologist.[21]

One should underline *the freedom to change* attitude, which is in any regard active and takes position. Firstness in Husserl's sense shows that ego-passivity (a non-dynamical positioning) must nevertheless be understood as a form of attitude change—Peirce would have embraced this qualification referring to his differentiations deeply within the level of Secondness, as Ferrarello explained.[22] Husserl's 1920 commentary refers to a bewildering conclusion, which could be viewed as a new notion of his Firstness. He formulated: 'There is a most remarkable Split to be mentioned, which evolves through the decision in the ego-subject to perform a phenomenological attitude'. The ego-subject '(... the same, which possesses the experiencing, theoretical, esthetical, practical attitude, which composes his daily life) now steps out of this natural life and rises to the higher level of reflection and looks at this life not only with the eye of an onlooker but of the researching thinker.' Two pages later he summarizes: 'I am whom I am, live a secret but always thematically disclosing life, an absolute life, a life as a flow of consciousness concerning... But in this position, I have only in the phenomenological reflection and reduction an absoluteness (namely a consciousness, which is itself a consciousness concerning a something) as its theme'.[23]

Those considerations, especially the understanding of the term 'attitude change', are therefore the basis of explaining Husserl's interpretation of Firstness. There are indeed numerous attitude changes in the lifetime of a human ego. Firstness is immensely and intensely repeated in this context—every change creates a new change, often experienced as a beginning. A human life with the nameplate 'ego' is composed by those changes, which are baffling and powerful. Only one of them is in Husserl's phenomenology identified with Firstness: an *attitude-change* from *a naïve-natural towards a non-naïve-natural* experience. That *change of attitude* provides an entire philosophy, Husserl remarked. That change is a germ of insight and knowledge caused by distancing from the evident. It is not a cheap play with words, to express that *a change of attitude is continuously different!* This change is on each occasion a new breach, and often a new beginning in another context. But the multiplicity of changes is basic to the continuous flow of cognition and consciousness.

In his younger years Husserl read Friedrich von Schiller's essay: '*Über naïve und sentimentalische Dichtung*'.[24] The text imposed the idea that different types of

[21] 'Einstellungsänderung', which took a central position in Husserl's phenomenology, does not only relate to 'Einstellung'-*attitude* but also to 'Anschauung'—a term often determined as *experience*. Ego-positions differ from experience. Our explanations under the heading 'attitude' as translation of 'Einstellung' are therefore to be completed by 'experience', 'view', 'vision', 'notion', 'awareness', or 'opinion'—but focus in the first place on 'position[ing]'.

[22] Ferrarello (2019), p. 195.

[23] Husserl (1959), p. 422 ff.

[24] See F. von Schiller: 'Über naïve und sentimentalische Dichtung'. Its essays were separately published in *DIE HOREN* 1795 & 1796. They formed a completed essay published in 1800 in the

literature will be created strictly under the influence of genuinely different attitudes (Einstellungen). That remark touches all creative writing and can be an instrument to understand worldviews as well as philosophical and scientific approaches. Hence the various expressions at home in everyday language, which Husserl mentioned in his philosophy via his focus on 'Attitudes'. It could mean that all philosophical views must always be understood based on various attitudes as their major component. The Nobel Prize Winner Orhan Pamuk confirmed this view in 2010. Spontaneity in writing a novel or composing a poem as if a completely natural act is opposed to any 'reflective' sensibility, he mentioned. 'Being a novelist', Pamuk concludes not unlike Szondi,[25] 'is *the art of being both naïve and reflective at the same time*. These two attitudes determine not only literature but also the complete expressivity of mankind, which is a treasure of philosophy.

Husserl states clearly: the Copernican turn is a sign for attitude change.[26] Firstness is thus determined by the 'ego-position' that belongs to a 'naïve attitude' or (as mentioned already) a position of 'self-determination'. Therefore, the quoted Copernican turn became a new philosophical method with the phenomenological reduction as its axial activity. And it thus elucidates the question why Firstness is crucial in Husserl's phenomenology. A methodological self-reflection upon naïve thought formation and the possible turns towards other, non-naïve and non-natural ways is needed. They lead Husserl on the road from Firstness to a transcendental philosophy. Attitude change is for him a new type of philosophical theory, so he writes: 'We humans are subjects who experience the world, know, evaluate, and treat it; and at the same time, we are an object of that world and thus objects of our experiencing, evaluating, and acting. ... As theorists we understand and grasp the universe; as humans we belong to it.'[27] This double participation in managing changes of ego-position includes *ethical dimensions of human understanding as well as structural views of acquiring cognition*. No wonder, that Husserl remarked already in 1924: 'Phenomenological reduction is nothing other than *change of position*.'[28] Is *a change from analog to digital positioning not the major attitude changed we are challenged to experience*?

In its close ties with attitude change is Firstness primarily engaged in the abrogation of any naïve ontology, any un-thinking thought about reality. It is an all-embracing change from thinking in naïve-natural ego-positions towards thought formation in non-naïve positions. The reader of Husserl texts should therefore be careful to understand the word 'natural' because it indicates a naïve- as well as a non-naïve possibility! The latter opens to a whole world of further positions, which

same German Journal established by F. Schiller. The Journal was named after three Greek Goddesses: Eunomia, Dike, and Irene—now issuing its 253rd volume. See Broekman (2016), p. 54 f.

[25] Pamuk (2010), p. 13; Szondi (1978), p. 59 f.; See: Broekman (2016), p. 54.

[26] See the central German term 'Einstellungsänderung'.

[27] Husserl (1959), p. 239.

[28] Husserl (1959), p. 422 f.

Husserl describes as steps in non-naïve positions. He names three of them explicitly. They excel in an order once the transition from naïve-natural attitude (also named pre-reflexive) to non-naïve natural attitudes (also named reflexive or phenomenological) is performed. *First, there is in realm of non-naïve positions the attitude again named 'natural', second is the attitude named 'phenomenological' or 'eidetic', and third the 'transcendental' ego-position.* Those positions delineate the field of his new philosophy called phenomenology.[29]

A diversity of ego-positions makes him articulate the various reductive phases that characterize the ego in its 'non-naïve-natural' character. This illustrates an assignment of the ego-parts leading towards phenomenologically based cognition.[30] One of the most important sources in the beginnings of the twentieth century, the second volume of his *Logische Untersuchungen,* focuses on an elucidation of cognition based on such ego-positions.[31] Such articulations embrace far more than just mutual insights of Peirce and Husserl: they form a broad and decisive insight in Occidental philosophy. One encounters different terms and variant thought patterns in philosophical prose when only a few years into the twenty-first century.

Attitude change is a split: the split between a 'naïve-natural' and a 'non-naïve-natural' position in viewing and understanding reality. Both types of Firstness are positioned to create clarity in the field, order in the stream of positions, insight in the flow and its undefined developments—and insight in what normally is not distinguished or distinguishable.[32]

4.5 Cognition and Transcendence

Why mention the concept of transcendence? Is any understanding of transcendence possible in digit patterns? Why and when could we become referring to 'a higher state of mind'? A related question is: why focusing on a highly-senseful state of the knowing subject? The later reaches the profiles of our general approximation: is the transcendental subject, i.e., a subject at its highest sense of sensibility, able to any cognitive activity? And if that is the case, what type of cognition is reached? Does transcendence mean something like 'supersensual'? That could very well be the case, but it then includes a form of subjectivity which is totally determined by analog expressivity. Can that be forwarded and accepted in our days? The answer is in the negative: there cannot be any thought formation in the twenty-first century which

[29] Broekman (1963), p. 71.

[30] Broekman (2016), p. 60 ff.

[31] Husserl (1921), p. 128 f.

[32] 'Einstellung' translated into English with 'attitude', and 'Anschauung' translated into English with 'experience' resp. 'intuition' is of interest to clarify that the 'Anschauung' retains in all cases an essential relation with the 'Ausdruck' [expression], which concerns the implicit ego-position and its meaning. The two keep a close relationship: they hold a palpable togetherness and thus create a changeable but nevertheless stable unit.

does not recognize the expressivity of analog *and* digital features. This is an extremely important view of the foundations of cognition.

The flow of ego-positions always includes a transcendental position and its inherent continuity. That is the case with those that appear as a Firstness: they are marked by the breach with the naturalness of all naïve-natural positions. The name 'transcendental' indicates only a specific condition and a position fully loaded with special meanings. But even that term appears to be one of the innumerable constitutive elements of a human consciousness! Husserl named and studied three of them and profiled their characters through indicating their field of application: the '*natural*', the '*phenomenological*' and the '*transcendental*' position. The first is importantly broader than the last. Keep in mind, that all those positions are visible and understood for the very short moment of their appearance within a much wider context named the '*non-naïve-natural attitude*'. Indeed, from Firstness to the Transcendental is for an epistemological mind an important path in the field of positions!

Occidental philosophy shows a tendency to unleash ties between subjectivity and cognition. The ego-positions, of which only a few are clearly distinguishable and could be given a name, are steps in the true sense of the word. They are moments of a wider, more complex, and all-embracing process one calls *cognition*. Neighbored and equally important components are for instance the various linguistic ones or even those who are today understood as *a planetary processes*. They are never understood as specific forces on their own. Their intertwinements with space and time are important powers to create cognition. Never is such cognition the private property of a constitutive subject or the single relation between a subject and an object.

'Transcendent' as well as 'transcendence' are during the last centuries treated in philosophy and cognition as a *name*. This long-living approach seems to change in the first decades of the twenty-first century. The approach was, as if the two words were a name for a final human situation, for a step away from normality, for a situation at distance to troubles, pain, or fear. The 'beyond' was loaded with feelings of change, or at least of reaching a point of no return. Hence the feeling that self-transcendence—a grip on life accepted since Kant—was psychologically acceptable and a feature of broader personality determination. Those forces made the concept of 'transcendence' indeed a crucial life situation. Husserl underlined, that in the languages of the naïve-natural worldview exists no name for the transcendental in its particularity. On the other hand, is the transcendental a term at home in the field of human cognition which remains accessible in its anthropological specificity. The transcendental is not inaccessible for human understanding like the Kantian 'Ding an Sich'. It is understandable and can be understood, is open and can be unfolded via a human capacity named self-experience. Center as well as periphery of the transcendental is the *human subjectivity*, which can reach into the depth of the self. But with the acceptance of a name comes the epistemological consideration of the name as a process of name giving, or naming! That appears as a form of acquiring cognition—an appearance affiliated to Kant's epistemology. Has the latter, which must be reconsidered in the context of relations between cognition and conversion (the manifold connotations of understanding 'transcendence' as a possible position of human knowledge) an acceptable *form* of a process to acquire cognition?

Is *naming* such a process?

Let us not forget, how Kant brought the term 'transcendence' or 'transcendent' in connection with the general process of knowledge formation. This was accepted for the centuries to come since 1781 and is still debated. Two presuppositions are at work: (a) the qualities and conditions of the name giving process, and (b) the inherent function of a type of cognition creating subject. The first is most general and endured the centuries: the question of identity between the act of naming, the name itself and the object named. That is indeed a complicated issue. Some make it easy and say that the name is the same as the thing or issue or object named—including with that thesis an enormous power of cognition of the name giver. They note that the name differs principally from the thing named. Others underline that name and naming are identical but different from the thing named. They consider that the name can (but must not) be identical with the thing named.

The three annotated positions concerning name, name giving, and the object of the name, embrace differences, but can in fact not be experienced without an open mind for the close ties or even implicating positions of the subject-in-name. One should note that the differences embrace constitutive positions of the subject in the name and name giving, but the specific properties of assigning names embrace participations and implications of a subject beyond such a power position. Only the latter fulfill a role in language and linguistic expressiveness! The lingual expressivity of a name and the semiotic process of naming are never without internal or external reference to any form or function named 'subjectivity'. That reference must always be performed in linguistic means. In the concept of 'transcendence' are those means to be discovered as specific forms of a 'subject' and/or a 'self'.

This is a key issue in all cases of the transcendental, transcendence or transcending as a philosophical activity. They can be experienced as happiness, chance, talent, or serendipity—for short, everything that is recognized as belonging to subjectivity but remains beyond control of a subject. 'Transcendental' thus describes anything within the spiritual, non-physical world. The expression brings us back to the Kantian thoughts which we often characterized as 'the split ego'. Any moment of experiencing the transcendent is in its essence a moment in which a 'subject' and a 'self' play a constitutive role. The relation between those two is perhaps the most important here; a relation between the abstract and the concrete self becomes articulated in the transcendent, the non-physical world. The goal is to enrich and to have the concrete self fully function, even in the abstract functioning of a subject structure.

An important issue in our contemporary philosophical prose is about subjectivity as a main center point of constitution. A general outline of cognition in our twenty-first century's second decade sustains the notion of *categorization* as a primary factor in *cognition*. The notion suggests that each actual object involved in a specific regularity, which is concretely observable, can fulfill the constitutive role of what is traditionally seen as the role of subject and subjectivity. The idea goes back to Husserl's 1920 distinction between sensual and categorical 'Anschauung' and relates to the major outlines of the actual *digital* components of modern culture. What in English language is considered as 'attitude' is to be broadened in the latter by expressions like 'experience', 'view', 'vision', 'notion', 'awareness' or 'opinion'.[33] The question remains, which is in this context the meaning and sense of the term 'kategoriale Form' (disputably translated as 'categorical intuition') as a completion of our understanding a statement in its entirety? That question seems to belong to the philosophy of the twenty-first century and its digitality features. The suggestion comprises namely that a statement or a lingual sentence is complete when uttered by a constitutive subject and formatted by an observable regularity.

Cognition is in this light no longer only a matter of a subject and its actions, but often in the first place a matter of a specific situation and its characteristic powers, which regulate and thus re-cognize reality.

With this constitution of a specific context is a digital approach configurated. The essence of that question leads us back to the idea of a 'split ego'. *Experiencing the transcendent* helps us to understand that *the split character of the ego is a moment of self-understanding*! The latter embraces both dimensions of the ego, the subject dimension as well as the categorical. It teaches us, that there is not one dimension without the other. Its ultimate meaning is that the split is itself an always-present feature of the ego and as such an important epistemological insight. *Speaking or rethinking one part* (for instance the subject dimension) *constitutes the other*. Any transcendence would be impossible if that were not the case. Contemporary philosophers who want to exclude one of the dimensions will ultimately fail in the structuring of any self-understanding; with that failure they miss to view the key dynamics of knowledge formation. Their lack of recognizing a transcendental experience in their epistemological view on life and reality is a serious sign of misjudging a proper philosophical attitude. That insight might be one of the most important conclusions from the ego position called transcendental since the days of Immanuel Kant and his contemporaries.

When the *Handbook* of *Categorization in Cognitive Science* was published in 2005 and republished in 2017, the *categorical dimension* seemed, despite its evident complexity, defined, documented, and prepared to function in the philosophical approaches of cognition as contrasted to the subject-dimension.[34] Neither the expression 'subject' nor the word 'transcendence' was mentioned in the more than thousand pages of the handbook. The *positioning of the self beyond the self* was its philosophical secret. That positioning became achieved via the exploration of categorical dimensions, which apparently neglect the power of the constitutive ego-positions as Husserl outlined. The handbook does not provide a direct answer. The fixation of categorical dimensions related to special fields of knowledge seems problematic within the field of research itself. Husserl understood the term

[33] The reader of Stjernfelt's 2007 *Diagrammatology,* should therefore be aware of the difficulty when 'Anschauung' was translated as 'intuition'; is intuition indeed a form of awareness or worldview?

[34] Cohen and Lefebvre (2017).

'categorical' as 'without any doubt or possibility of being changed'. He speaks of 'the categorical, the absolute difference between form and matter of representation'.[35] The 'absolute' is decisive in cases of characterizing the categorical. Stevan Harnad's contribution to the Handbook articulates those relations between cognition and categorization. He summarizes his ideas in a few lines, which express what Husserl envisaged as an assigned ego-position. He formulates as a starting point: 'We organisms are sensorimotor systems'. Function and exclusivity are clearly based on that definition of a human organism so that he concludes: 'Things in the world contact our sensory surfaces, and we interact with them based on what that sensorimotor contact affords. . . . All of our categories consist of ways we behave differently toward different kinds of things—things we do or do not eat, mate with, or flee from; or the things that we describe, through our language, as prime numbers, affordances, absolute discriminables, or truths. That is all that cognition is for, and about.'[36] His thesis: 'to Cognize is to Categorize' seems based on an interpretation of the ego as an organism with its possibilities of contacting reality via senso-motor capabilities. Those are, insofar as categorization is concerned, more basic than abstract objects like goodness, truth, or beauty. They are namely all grounded in a sensory experience, which is quite similar and predictable for most members of our species. What difference is thus constitutive for human togetherness and cognition? The Handbook changed the linguistically relevant *ego* into a *point* of perceptive reference—in other words, the background thesis is, that *a change from verb to stimulus leads to categorization as the general source and activity of human cognition.*

But what is the essence of this change, this differentiation of accents, this newly designed point of reference? Is it a new vision, a renewed choice between well-known points of view, or just a transition from language to a different form of activity and awareness based on sensory capacities? Husserl understood language as the evident means of expression and dependence—how is it in the above explained light of the categorizing explained in the *Handbook*? One answer could guide us in these considerations: there is evidently a stronger interest in the recognition of dynamics involved in human activities—cognition included! As if there is a renewed fascination concerning the sensual dimensions as contrast to the categorical. Husserl contrasted the sensual with the categorical view [sinnliche und kategoriale Anschauung]. The entire human experience, the sensual as well as the categorical, seems dominated by the cognitive dimensions with their senso-motoric dynamics as a virtual point of reference. *Became cognition newly conceived based on its recently understood dynamics?* What will the experience of transcendence tell the subject involved in unfolding itself contribute to that point of reference and its dynamics? The lingual and epistemological dimensions of this reference lead to the observation of recently conceived dynamics and expressivities in our twenty-first century. They mirror the effects of combining cognition and conversion.

[35] Husserl (1921), p. 136.

[36] St. Harnad: 'To Cognize is to Categorize' in: Cohen and Lefebvre (2017), Ch 1, p. 20 f.

References

Bergman M, Paavola S (eds) The Commens Dictionary: Peirce's terms in his own words. New Edition. Retrieved from http://www.commens.org/dictionary/term/firstness

Broekman JM (1963) Phänomenologie und Egologie. Series Phaenomenologica Bd 12. M. Nijhoff, Den Haag, p 71

Broekman JM (2010) Firstness and phenomenology – Peirce and Husserl on attitude change. In: Wagner A, Broekman JM (eds) Prospects of legal semiotics. Springer, Dordrecht

Broekman JM (2016) Meaning, narrativity, and the real. Springer, Switzerland, p 71 ff

Broekman JM. Structuralism. Moscow, Prague, Paris. Synthese Library, vol 67. Dordrecht, Reidel/ Springer Science + Business Media, Dordrecht etc

Burrell DB, Daher N (1995) al-Ghazali: the ninety-nine beautiful names of god. The Islamic Texts Society, Cambridge, UK

Cohen H, Lefebvre C (eds) (2017) Handbook of categorization in cognitive science. Elsevier Science Ltd, 2005, 2nd edn, see also https://academiaanalitica.files.wordpress.com/2016/10/cohen-h-lefebvre-c-eds-handbook-of-categorization-in-cognitive-science.pdf

Ferrarello S (2019) On the arising of the I in Peirce and Husserl. In: Shafei M, Pietarinen A-V (eds) Peirce and Husserl, mutual insights on logic, mathematics and cognition. Springer Nature, Switzerland

Husserl E (1921) Logische Untersuchungen, Band II: Elemente einer Phänomenologischen Aufklärung der Erkenntnis. 2. Auflage, M. Niemeyer, Halle a.d. Saal

Husserl E (1959) Erste Philosophie (1923/24) Zweiter Teil: Theorie der Phänomenologischen Reduktion. R. Boehm (ed) Husserliana Bd VIII, M. Nijhoff, Den Haag

Kevelson R (1996) Peirce, science, signs. Peter Lang, New York etc.

Kevelson R (1999) Peirce and the Mark of the Gryphon, St. Martin's Press, New York

Pamuk O (2010) The Naïve and the sentimental novelist. London

Peirce CS (1904) Letters to Lady Welby; CP 8.328 'Firstness'. Term in Bergman M, Paavola S (eds) The Commens Dictionary: Peirce's terms in his own words. New edition. Retrieved from http://www.commens.org/dictionary/term/firstness

Peirce CS (1992) One, two, three: Kantian categories. In: Houser N, Koesel Chr (eds) The essential Peirce, vol I (1867-1893). Indiana UP, Bloomington, Indianapolis, USA

Peirce CS (1998) The categories defended. In: The essential Peirce, selected philosophical writings, Ed. the Peirce Project, vol 2 (1893-1913). Indiana U.P., Bloomington, USA, p 160

Peirce CS. In: Hartshorne Ch, Weiss P (eds) The collected papers of Charles Sanders Peirce, vol 1. Cambridge MA, Harvard UP

Shafei M, Pietarinen A-V (eds) (2019) Peirce and Husserl: mutual insights on logic, mathematics and cognition. Series: logic, epistemology, and the unity of science, vol 46. Springer Nature, Switzerland

Stjernfelt F (2007) Diagrammatology. Springer Synthese Library, vol 336. Springer Science +Busisness Media

Szondi P (1978) Das Naïve ist das Sentimentalische. Zur Begriffsdialektik in Schillers Abhandlung. In: Lektüren und Lektionen. Schriften II Suhrkamp Frankfurt/M

Chapter 5
Interludes

Changing Worlds Changing Words

An interlude is a musical concept which brings the participant feelings of freedom, contemplation and even a well-framed researching of conscience. That type of composition is traditionally used in opera performances and church music. The intermediary task of those compositions is important in view of a just performed past as well as an immediately following future. They should bring reconsideration, clarification, and a well-designed stress release for all participants, the musicians as well as the listening public. Individual words, languages, or speeches are seldom creating an interlude. To understand the concept in the context of culture and philosophy, one must switch and enter the realm of metaphorical language. That transition still needs a functioning linguistic grammar, syntax and the correct choice of words and phrases, but one could say that this parallels music in its social functioning.

But when a concentration on linguistic instead of musical expressivity is at stake, become flows in culture and political, economic, scientific, or philosophical movements the basics of the interludes' alphabet. One can in this light conclude, that since the first half of the twentieth century, several interludes in Occidental culture thoroughly influenced Western thought formation. Its second half could be described as a period in which newly conceived views, systems and ideologies were changing the patterns and instruments of thought far beyond traditional mainstreams. Even the contexts and interests about '*cognition*' changed fundamentally. They touched the theme of '*conversion*' like never before and challenged to revise and renew our interest in the 'naïve-natural world confronted with the non-naïve-natural' as mentioned in preceding pages. The urge for changes appears under the surface of several mainstreams of science and philosophy such as Semiotics, Structuralism, Phenomenology or Neo-Marxism, paralleled by new forms and insights of physics and natural sciences, not to mention climate- and planetary views. A package of terms (to elucidate what we traditionally name 'knowledge') is at stake—expressions and profiles included. Interludes are thus to be respected and require considerations, which at first glance don't fit to traditional frames.

J. M. Broekman, *Knowledge in Change*, Law and Visual Jurisprudence 8,

5.1 Word

Words are unique. But we don't know what they are, despite all our traditional and modern super-technical attempts to define, describe, understand, and make them effective! Words do belong to languages, but their belonging is not a matter of language itself and they do also not state what a language is. We nevertheless follow rules of grammar and syntax, which do represent certain languages without making clear to us what a language is. We can confirm that analog words, i.e., words belonging to (or being produced in) an analog language, function in a non-analog (today in most cases a digital) context, vice versa. Today, everyone has these analog words literally in hand via a Smartphone, iPhone, or any other digital instrument, but whether and how these fit to a type of language or possess other qualities remains unknown and unquestioned. How do we act when using analog words in all sorts of communication? The digital generally acts as also embracing the specificity of a word, but the essence of this idea remains unquestioned.

And there is yet another issue, which determines the character of expressivity by means of words. It is in the question how to mention the function or character of a word without any clarification of the phenomenon of language: the language to which a word essentially belongs. This widens the issue because such a reference between word and language seems uncleared, although nevertheless open for further determining relations like those between the language of a word and its cultural dimensions! We all are impressed by our daily experience of the fact that changing worlds occur all around us. But that does not bring any secure knowledge of the changes of words they seem to bring. And we all experience that fact while speaking words and having conversations with fellow human beings. In that regard represents the subtitle of this chapter, 'Changing Worlds Changing Words', a challenge to sources and contexts of our knowledge without clarifying the inherent language concept which seems a key to the understanding of this observation. This situation of *the word* has many implications and consequences. One of the most powerful in this context is the fact that *the word is not an act—even not a 'speech-act'—but an event*, an occurrence, a happening between individuals within a specific, mostly cultural, setting.

The event of an utterance of a word is not merely shaped by rules of language expressed in a grammar or a syntax and not exclusively by a determinable specimen or type of language, but rather by social power and status. An interesting example is recovered in what is named '*legal language*'. Within the context of practicing law can the speaker formulate words to the hearer whilst formulating the word 'I'. But that word is in legal discourse also understood as the totality of every individual 'I', which is an understanding that was investigated, documented, and even prescribed through the precious process of establishing law and legal discourse. This totality involves all pronouns that are incorporated in the basic legal term (and with it the legal language broader than any specific mother tongue) named 'legal subject'.

That example clarifies a more general issue. *The fundamental condition of all linguistic expressions is the presence of another individual.* In other words: an 'I' can only be expressed and even imagined when the position of an 'alter' is concrete in our thoughts or social reality. Only when the pronouns 'I', 'You' and all others can be provided, can the 'I' be spoken. The thesis in our example is, that indeed pronouns must exist in law so that law can exist. This is an unexpected variation on the theme explored already in the first chapter and named 'intersubjectivity'. That insight is also valid for language as such: *pronouns and other words must exist in life so that life can unfold.* It is true: the situation of *the word* has many implications and consequences. But the most basic insight is in this case, that a word is never solely an *act* but also always an *event.*[1] That remark is based on an observation which indicates the *double structure* concealed in the relationship between language and the intersubjective. When in earlier years the subject or the 'I' was given a priority role, it meant that one was living in a world which was *delineated* by the 'I' concept. That was foundational in the analog world. Today has the insight and its expression changed and do we have to formulate that we are aware of living in a world which is based on *networked* forms of the 'I' concept. The mentioned double structure is the doubleness of the analog and the digital approach to reality and its origination.

One meets here a seldom-articulated feature, which is a central issue of this interlude. It could be formulated. Linguistic features are anchored in a specific type of expressivity, and *thus in the first place a matter of inter-subjectivity.*

The qualities, the use patterns, functions, and meanings of certain words in daily- as well as philosophical and scientific language, included the changes which took place during the last decades, make a reorientation necessary The words with which they are re-thought must fit to changes taking place under our eyes. These include the fact that words function in a changing world. But those functions must take place in words that belong to the changing world(s) in which they are spoken. But the act of speaking is not a simple activity but characterized as an event! For this reason, we already underlined that all linguistic features are anchored in a specific type of expressivity, and thus in the first place a matter of inter-subjectivity. The two types we specified already many times are the *analog* and the *digital.* They are today the most important types reigning human understanding and communication.

In the light of one of the contributors to the *Amsterdam Significs Circle* (which was basic for the international development of *semiotics* in the third decade of the last century) one should keep in mind how philosophy must express the life movements of humans in the same sense as significs enables humans to take lingual expressions as a form of guidance in life. This is the case, as Gerrit Mannoury formulated in 1948, because 'no matter how vain, how fugitive a word may be, it does have a meaning. A meaning, not only for the speaker and the hearer, but also for those who will never hear it, but whose minds nevertheless will be influenced by it . . . it is not the speaker who utters the word; it is they who whispered it to his heart

---

[1]Broekman (2019), p. 216: 'Law's authority does not embrace any singularity, it denies engagement in the single. (. . .) The 'I', once articulated, is in law understood as the totality of every individual 'I'. Alter's presence is a necessary condition for the pronouns 'I', 'You' and all other to be in effect.'

and ear, who handed it down to him from generation to generation and who put their soul to thoughts into it'.[2]

This 'handing down' seems a basic process to be recognized every time one develops thoughts about the origin of language. Each word expressed by a speaker or received by a hearer creates a breach with any solo situation. There is no first person without another, in a second or third, or 'how-do-you-name-it' position. No wonder, that an accent on the *type* of thought and language plays a fundamental role.

5.2 Types

It surprises: the question of *type* of interaction, communication or interactivity is today urgently posed to me *as a speaker or hearer via my iPhone*! A choice of type comes to me not via a program or any deliverance institution, but via my touch on the instrument. The latter opens a world for me and makes me responsible, participating, liable and much more—even legally liable. Via the touch, I entered the patterns of the phone and became a subject with specific properties that choose a type of interaction. So, I will never ever be a subject alone. On the other hand, will the touch not always bring what I expected or wanted to see. We may have wanted to photograph a nice situation, a landscape, a butterfly, wonderful scenes, or your face amidst magnificent flowers. What they all did, was most prominently seen via the touch: the *portrait* called a '*selfie*'. Indeed: the analog portrait with its many variations and contexts in paintings or photography has been replaced by the digital selfie! Millions, perhaps milliards of selfies could be collected all around the globe, but nobody might be interested anymore: the selfie is momentarily and lost the feature of the long-living portrait.

You may face concerns that a selfie will not be exposed in a gallery like a portrait of the eighteen's century! Mind and self were honored in philosophical considerations when the subject was a riddle of the self. Both belonged to the human brain's activity and were rethought as a key to understanding not only language and expressivity but also to the foundations of human existence. That attitude seems lost: *subject* and *self* became a new cultural and social event—my iPhone made me to a multiple personage engraved in a diversity of social senses. Lady Victoria Welby was one of the very first thinkers who expressed feelings about the changing Self already in 1911 when she wrote: '. . . for the first time we emerge into the *answer-world* which has prompted our question and stimulated our discontent . . . It is true of course that the term 'self' was originally equivalent to 'same' and 'ego'. But now a self is what You *have* and are apt selfishly you pamper and work for'. And she added the closing remark '. . . what you *have* you cannot in the full

[2]Mannoury (1948), p. 15; see also: Broekman and Cata Backer (2015), p. 41 and: Petrilli (2009), p. 834 f.

sense *be*.' It fascinates how she articulates what she once considered as 'the first human query' in terms of the Self.[3]

All those thoughts were still in debt to an analytic approach which characterizes our ability of self-identification. It widens the difference between subject and self in a manner that relations between styles of expression are more visible. The reciprocal relations between the two creates fields of tensions among them. Speaking subjects appear to be de-centered by their own speech-activity. Lady Welby's observation reached far in the future centuries following her observations. The latter apply the distances and functions of the analog versus the digital styles we experience. The decentering of our speech-activity is basic for e.g., operating the i-phone, the smartphone, the desktop, Facebook programs and other digital means of communication.

Indeed, articulation is folded in the grammatical forms and prescripts that govern so-called natural languages. Pronouns occupy a central place in grammars. So-called 'pronounce games' unfolded during the ages which led to our actual world. Once openly and independently operated in lingual communication, three types come to the fore: the personal, the possessive and the demonstrative pronoun. None of them is represented by any triadic structure. They are dualistic, and dualisms govern the rules of grammar that structure our discourses and reinforce our awareness of digital structures. Most influential are in this context the first and second person singular: the 'I' and the 'You'. Their power seems endless, and one does not need to be egocentric to be convinced about their importance.

This exemplary and overall dominance of the 'I—You' relationship and the complete empowering by the first-person singular is basic for each language and linguistic relationship to understand. Languages are the most radiant sign that man does not intrinsically possess separate individuality. In other words: togetherness is embedded in- and created by language and not by any technical result of speaking. The mutual dependency of word and thought makes it visible that languages are means to discover the Unknown, which seems embedded in Culture and Self. All this underlines the importance of speakers (and their hearers) being bearers of habitual patterns of thought, which are firmly anchored in their language—their position in that language cannot be dissolved from other linguistic features, as the cluster confirms in all patterns of social activity. Modern multiplicity of languages plays an important role in this regard. One lives today amidst of words, thoughts and expressions, habits and worldviews that do not strictly belong to the mother tongue of the speaker but have become a far more general asset through radio, television, film, cell phone, computer, and other mass media. This puts the strength of the speaker/hearer position within a language pattern into perspective despite their regularly underlined empowerment as a first-person singular. That strength is a specific feature of those languages and philosophies, which unfolded in the natural/analog type of language.

[3]Welby (1903).

The mentioned word 'type' should not be used naively. On the contrary, it shows how a dominant 'Speaker-Hearer' model of language, which is continuously reinforced by the powerful position of the 'I', shapes the specific language types prevailing in most occidental theories. This position of the 'I' is mirrored in that of the 'Self', which appear to be structured and to function as a discourse. That makes language into a succession of rule-governed 'speech-acts', with a heavy accent on 'act', and the 'Self' as a problem of what was called 'the Flow'. It interests therefore to discover how already Hobbes' 'Magnus Homo' uncovered facts and consequences of the subject's central position in language. He focused on grammar, syntax, and at other linguistic levels and involved us in the social and political consequences of that position. But the actual level is the basic fact that characterizes our modernity: the plural of- and in language types. This plurality came to the fore when it became evident how the first-person singular was tied to the creation of a specific of world form. Thus, as structuralists around the midst of the twentieth century suggested, the subject should be de-centered.[4] Once this insight was formulated, the key question remained: 'what is a human being without the capability to position itself as 'subjectivity'?' Indeed: that capability changes with the world in which the word should be understood and spoken. It was the background idea concerning ego-positions, which were 'grips out of the wealth of positions' from the ego. Husserl's theory of phenomenological reductions was in this context ahead of structuralism when it proclaimed the subject's 'de-centering', which took in the beginning of the third millennium a further step in the digitalization that marks a global culture.

Not only the word, but also the world remains fluid, changing, leveled and plural.

The classical history of ideas did not perceive the serious tensions between the order inherent in the things themselves and the order induced by the cultural codes. Between the latter and any type of reflexive knowledge were no intermediations registered. That was the case since clear causes had to unfold strictly drawn consequences. The hallmarks of eighteenth century sciences were representation, equality, and equivalence. And those of the nineteenth century: origin, and continuity. The twentieth century envisaged a serious counterpart that had to find its final form in a change or an end of anthropomorphism to keep the globe changing and plural. No wonder, that Nietzsche had no more fundamental observation to describe than 'man rolling from the center towards an X'. Michel Foucault suggested in his 1969 *Archéologie du Savoir* how someone who wants to speak of man and interprets formalization as an attack on his soul and culture, merits either a philosophical smile, or a no-comment.[5] He could in his days not foresee how intensely the changes from analog language to digital expressiveness embraced those ideas.

The stimulus, which generates from that new positioning, profiles the cluster at stake. Jacques Derrida[6] outlined the need to recognize the multiplicity that

[4] Broekman (1974), p. 59 ff.

[5] Foucault (1969).

[6] Derrida (1967).

characterizes subject and language type, saying: 'the European tradition connects the human voice with the breath rather than the writing, with the spiritual rather than with the material.' That is a beginning to cherish an actively differentiating and multiplying insight pertaining to the first-person singular position. Who is hearing sounds, listens to a voice! Listening differs from hearing; it is a spiritual occurrence and includes understanding and interpretation, in contrast to the hearing, which is mainly a physiological fact. So, once the first-person, the Speaker is set aside as a fundamental reality, the Hearer seems only a truncated conception of the same type of language and person.

That issue called 'type of language' was perhaps unknown in the days of Peirce and Husserl, but especially Husserl's phenomenology unfolded already around the implications of such an insight. For that reason, we should reconsider the important effects of thinking about the subject as a first-person position in our days. The cluster demonstrates the importance of this stimulus. Most effects are namely about a problem that was new in the context of philosophy: the principal multiplicity of the powers of expression, which were hitherto only related to subject and subjectivity and mainly studied in their grammatical forms. One should thus consider that not solely the 'Speaker' and/or the 'I' position but that all words are touched by this multiplicity; they are always participating in processes of change. All our engagements with meaning and sense are complex and organic—no meaning of a word is ever fixed on one specific type of lingual utterance. But a word has never solely one specific meaning: this makes a word difficult to accept or maintain in the case of a unilateral type of language.

Is the latter ever in the safety of a unilateral feature?

The multiplicity of language types does not unfold in simple plurals of languages we know and use today. A multiplicity is in general not a summing up of definable and fixated elements. One encounters in the case of types of language a three very different ones: the analog, the digital and the quantum language. But these are not to simply sum up; there is no lingual situation in which basic elements of the three can function in any form of togetherness. Moreover, in the culture of today is the situation in which parts (or even elements) of one of the three just integrate with others also unclear. It seems that utterances of each type do function by means of circumscription eventually also in another type. Expressions in analog language offer articulations of digital nature in the own analog expressivity whereas in digital language analog concepts can and will be represented and functional. But how do they do? One encounters, furthermore, seldom a philosophical discussion about the question whether the word 'language' can be used at an equal level in these cases. The plurality remains complex but important in any case. Do not forget, that each of the three types knows a differentiation between that specific type functioning as a natural language and as an artificial as well as a technical language! All in all, it means that plurality is always the result of implication as well as enumeration of components.

That conclusion has the character of an interlude: a personal interlude in as far as our psychological attitude in the realm of text and speech is concerned—and a cultural interlude in as far as those two are embedded in a global culture characterized by approaching storms of digital as well as quantum character and energy.

5.3 Conversion

What once was cherished as *translation* (among analog languages in the days of dominating natural or analog language patterns) became at the end of the preceding century a *conversion* to meet the requirements of multileveled language types and their expressivity. Two aspects are definitively constitutive in the case of conversion: its application in an immense number of expressivities, and its consequences for the constitution of the human subject and its object (which is often treated as a process of de-subjectivation). The complexity and influencing forces of the cluster is a matter of dynamics, which reach beyond- and thus intertwine with the mentioned diversity of language types.

They are an independent and generally experienced factor, which is often difficult to locate or circumscribe, but under all circumstances (as the two preceding chapters show) a matter of reorientation for the subject and object position. Note, that conversion as indication of such changes concerns not 'language as such' but relates to the various types of language and their specificity. The term conversion, which is at home in the analog as well as the digital world and within reach of quantum expressivity, covers social and conscious dynamics in their changes of meaning and sense. The latter focus straightforwardly on language—not as a bloc of expressions, but rather as a major means of understanding languages in their often very diverse intertwinements. Also in today's actuality, has conversion been understood as 'ethical turn' because it has been understood in proximity to metanoia and therefore as a switchover from logos to ethos. But the contrasting argumentation is, that such a switch will ultimately take the form of religious prophecies, revolutionary rhetoric, or viewpoints of philosophical or literary character.[7]

And what is more: our understanding of the term changed, and that change *makes the concept called conversion function as 'an interlude'* in its proper sense. Conversions are today intertwined with analog as well as digital types of lingual expressivity. One encounters here various positions with an interlude character. One notices a predominant change of authority and its expression as well as ego-positions that contrast the Speaker–Hearer Model. The model shows important components of the *interluding* one should study when man and society are the topics at stake.

The Wikipedia site[8] offers an impressive choice in this regard. It focuses for example on *business* when it provides the path a consumer must take through the web in case of a desired action. The site is also informative on *computing*, its science

[7] Avanessian and Hennig (2019), p. 180.

[8] https://en.wikipedia.org/wiki/Conversion.

and technology included. It mentions *chemistry*: the ratio of selectivity to yield or the change of a molecule. The same also mentions *GPS*: in computer science a changing of the form of continuation-passing, of conversion between different units of measurement and data, on converting computer data from one format to another, as well as electric modification of a conventional vehicle to battery electric and energy conversion—all in all the process of changing one form of *energy* to another. Of interest is furthermore the *trans-coding* concerning analog-to-analog or digital-to-digital conversion of one video encoding to another, which parallels conversion coding and embraces the changing of one data type into another in computer science. *Economics, finance,* and *property law* are mentioned as well as the adoption of a new *religious* identity, and *psychiatry* relating to a disorder problem, a condition in which neurological symptoms arise without a definable organic cause, and conversion therapy, which is a pseudo-scientific treatment to turn a homo- or bisexual person into a heterosexual person.

A comparable feature is at the background of the Wikipedia list. The global outreach of conversion is even beyond limits of language types. This is already visible by the emphasis on the *Conversion of Units*, and the conversion between different units of measurement for the same quantity, typically through multiplicative conversion factors. That generally accepted form of conversion underlines an actual insight in the global importance of the term, which is at the same time beyond any specific limit. It leads to the view, that the positioning of language types always concerns *the intertwining of natural, artificial, and technical expressivity*. Each spoken or written or generally used word is in this view positioned in fields of dynamics in which intertwining of meanings and senses occur continuously. Everything in language and reality is on the move: the term conversion is often used as if it concerns a particular translation. In fact, is that translation everywhere in human life and existence—no word, no gesture or opinion is excluded. *Conversions are continuously converting, and these conversions also convert themselves.* To live means to perform the task of converting or being involved in conversion. The latter is not definable in words with a fixated and stabilized meaning, because words are continuously in motion, changing type and context of language, sense and meaning of intertwinement of type and specificity. One concludes that Life 'in conversion' is the ultimate definition of 'cognition unfolded' in a course of life itself.

After all, the commonness discovered in the relations between *cognition* and *conversion* seems the most important bridge between individuality and life. Is conversion not to discover and experience as the major characteristic of cognition—a terrestrial challenge and inspiration? Question and answer in this consideration convert themselves.

The question is not answerable through practicing definitions or any comparable lingual statement. The interludes we suggested were characterized as a process, a flow, a type of dynamics, an event and never a fixation or related fact. Answers occur and are not definitive facts and fixations. They occur in fields, which are to be observed beyond outnumbered or outlined sketches of an engineering mind. Those fields must be respectfully observed, and its processes should be studied as causing patterns in linguistic expressions and human thoughts. They thus reach beyond the boundaries of definition and the designs of opinion concerning what is destined as reality. They must be studied and experienced at the same moment and in that process of being process: they fulfill our need to activate human consciousness in an often-broader sense than any definition or rational calculation could do. A central domain is the region in which the passing from one type of language—almost globally characterized as analog—to another—understood today as digital—occurs. What in these interludes is called a *transition* is thus no more than an attempt to create an expression for the *digital* in the traditionally named 'analog' language. One speaks of a transition, a translation, or a re-naming, but cherishes philosophical consequences that are fundamentally analog because nobody knows to express its counterpart.

References

Avanessian M, Hennig A (2019) Metanoia. A speculative ontology of language, thinking, and the brain. Bloomsbury Academic, London UK

Broekman JM (1974) Structuralism. Moscow, Prague, Paris. Synthese Library, vol 67. D. Reidel, Dordrecht/Boston

Broekman JM (2019) Rethinking law and language. The flagship 'speech'. Edward Elgar, Cheltenham/Northampton

Broekman JM, Cata Backer L (eds) (2015) Signs in law - a source book. The semiotics of law in legal education III. Springer Verlag

Derrida J (1967) De La Grammatologie. Ed. Minuit, Paris; Of grammatology (Engl. Ed. G.-C. Spivak, Johns Hopkins UP, Baltimore & London, 1974)

Foucault M (1969) Archéologie du Savoir. Gallimard, Paris

Mannoury G (1948) Handboek der Analytische Signifika Deel II: Hoofdbegrippen en methoden der Signifika. F. Kroonder, Bussum

Petrilli S (2009) Signifying and understanding. De Gruyter Mouton, Berlin

Welby V (1903) Lady: what is meaning? Studies in the development of significance. Macmillan & Co, Ltd. London, Ch. XXVI. (Bibliolife, LLC)

Chapter 6
The Non-Naïve-Natural

The first decades of the twentieth century were marked by a philosophy that cherished fascinating contrasts. Facts were confronted with phenomena, the subject-object relation with differences in ego-positions and the flow of life seemed understood with series of positions and changes marked by reductions and no longer only an elongated discourse. A pattern of the flow of cognition together with its founding thought formations became visible when all those elements and steps were systematized. But such a pattern became not clearly presented or discussed.

6.1 Natural

One of the most influential and disputable elements is the understanding and operationalization of what was called 'the natural' in the light of a 'non-naïve natural' ego position. That was already explained and disputed when the structure and power of *no - thing* and *nothingness* were discussed and the concept of *intersubjectivity* questioned. The non-dialectical character of the two terms was related to patterns of interactivity maintained by floating identities linked with electronic devices. Yet, the two terms: the Natural and the Non-Natural, apart from their naïve- and non-naïve variation, require renewed attention as a preparation for obtaining insight in pluralities.

Understanding the natural is an activity which is extremely relevant for human cognition in general. But its knowledge remains nonetheless very complicated. That is especially the case because social patterns do today no longer refer to fixed identities or ego-positions which could be delineated. And what is even more important and formulated in the subtitle of this book: they became related to floating data linked to special electronic activities, which are not focusing on knowledge but rather on practical prescripts. It means, that such new *forms of inter-activity* must be understood to unfold insight in *newly developed emancipating forces* of the human mind. Those underpin *forms of identity which have electronic means that format*

J. M. Broekman, *Knowledge in Change*, Law and Visual Jurisprudence 8,

important social patterns—with communication as one of the first intermediary patterns at stake. Such developments changed the term, the meaning, and the psychological relevance of the term 'natural'. A foundational question in this surprising context is, whether what is at home in natural languages, will also find a place (or will be replaced) in digital forms of expressivity. Many notions and terms of analog language might not become translated, substituted, converted, or functioning in the world of digital expressivities. So, it is important and not simple to understand the term 'natural' as a new expression for the 'evidence' modern patterns of thought represent today in the combinations of analog, digital, AI and Quantum patterning.

Identities in social communication are in that context no longer independent from their technical embracement. This is a background for the conclusion that a *differentiation between the natural and the non-natural is fundamental in studying cognition*. The distinction between those two positions[1] thus remains functional in all studies and debates. A natural position is also named the 'simply objective'. Therefore, each person is supposed to occupy such a 'natural' position from time to time. Problematic is not to occupy and explore, but rather to leave and/or change that position. It means, that a 'natural' position in philosophy or any other scientific view will be subordinated to what could be called a sophisticated position.[2]

Non-naïve positions are often characterized as 'phenomenological'—their character of 'the flow' included. Husserl offered in his 1923/24 *First Philosophy* a differentiated set of distinctions characterizing possible ego-positions within a larger systematic framework. Emphasis is on the fact, that the field he characterized as the 'non-naïve-natural' position knows as a first phase also a 'natural' position (called 'non-naïve-natural') followed by a second and a third positioning (by him respectively named 'phenomenological' and 'transcendental'). Philosophical discussions since his *First Philosophy* unfolded mainly in those fields. Note, that this seems to inspire a better and more differentiated understanding as well as a renewed practicing of our native tongues in view of digital and perhaps even quantum expressivity—although these relations are a riddle at this very moment.

Of importance are such broader and plural fields of ego positioning offering us a broader insight in the various language-related and expressivity-dominated forms of cognition.

(a) We do acknowledge the fact that any 'natural' position to create and explore knowledge must be actively distinguished from a 'non-natural' position (vice versa).
(b) Within the reach of such an insight must all 'natural' positions distinguish a *naïve-natural* from a *non-naïve-natural* position.

[1]Husserl mentions 'Denkhaltung' as well as 'Einstellung' and both are often translated in English as 'attitude', which is a debatable interpretation and named 'position' in this case.

[2]See Husserl (1921), Ch. 1, p. 10; Husserl: Ideen zu einer reinen Phänomenologie und phänomenologischen Philosophie. Husserliana, Bd III, Karl Schumann (ed). M. Nijhoff, Den Haag, p. 119.

(c) These distinctions appear as a key to understand relations between a natural language and other, non-natural forms of expressivity, among them the *digital.*
(d) Research on linguistics as well as on fields of ego-positionings and their creation of cognition should unfold within the field of the 'non-naïve-natural'—including the border zones between the 'non-naïve-natural' and the 'non-natural' fields. That seems a major requirement of what is called the 'analog' language.
(e) All borderlines of the 'non-naïve-natural' remain flexible, undetermined, and articulated in natural/analog/digital forms of expression. But their processes of articulation remain problematic. Attitudes resp. positions that constitute the 'non-naïve natural position form a matter of continuous intertwining with others and thus adapt the properties of a flow. That flow is a matter of self-determination. In other words: *to achieve meaning, one needs attitude, i.e., ego-positioning.*
(f) To qualify analog- and digital expressivity in ordinary life seems a matter of positioning oneself in a non-naïve-natural region, its borderlines included. To mention the 'digital' in daily life is an act thanks to such a possibility of non-naïve-natural positioning. The 'non-naivety' of the terms we then utter is far-reaching. They often try to transfer meanings of non-natural expressions by means of suggesting parallels, through exploring metaphors or through creating oxymoron spheres or by means of words from another natural language.

The truth, that a word is not an act but an event, is derived from the wealth of expressive possibilities at the borders of the area we characterize as the 'non naïve natural' languages. We thus rethink the central issue of the positions that constitute our daily life on that basis. They lead us beyond the 'relations between types of language, resp. expressivity'—which is an actual expression that determines digital expressivity in our ideas and their daily conversations.

A misunderstanding is soon caused when we name the digital: 'a language'—even if one would consider the term 'artificial language' in this case. The digital must indeed be located within the non-naïve-natural sphere to be understood. But that does in no way determine the digital fully, correctly, technically, or philosophically; any understanding in that region does not represent the digital in its entirety, specificity, or total functioning. No, *the digital in a non-naïve-natural cultural context is the result of a process of specific conversion.* But how and what is precisely converted, remains problematic since the digital has finally to be expressed in forms of a natural tongue. The title of this book represents that insight.

6.2 Digital

The digital expressivity grows so quickly, broadly, and intensively that a new tendency can be observed. It embraces *the qualification of the digital as the new naïve-natural.* That requires deeper observations, in the first place the insight in cognition based on the fact, that digital and/or quantum domains are located *at both sides of non-naïve-natural borderlines.* A grossly formulated viewpoint remains therefore: the digital might not be a language, but we embrace the tendency to understand and manage it as such. What does that mean? What concepts support this insight?

The *digital* as a means of expressivity can no longer be understood as an *influential zone of the artificial* in a sense of traditionally analog languages. All tendencies of the modern world changed the dimensions of communication in a deep sense; its digital forms and foundations became a major component in that context. They changed almost *all* social denominations. *Being cut off the global digital network is a modern and never explored form of involuntary solipsism!* A characterization of 'the digital in modern days' is therefore of central importance. It seems that our knowledge and attitude became, as was mentioned, more and more related to *the digital as a new level of the non-naïve natural* which is perhaps on its way to embrace the level of a new *global naïve-natural* status. The question means ultimately: can one still define the digital as a sphere of artificial (but rationally understandable) features in our life? If one understands the artificial as a dominant feature, then the digital fabricates all elements for those purposes. That is valid for everything reaching from precious and intimate to technical and disheartening forms of communication.

A general discussion about *defining the digital* diminished during the third decade of the twenty-first century. It means, that a *theoretical* interest in this frame of thought formation and expressivity seemed to fade away and that a *practical* interest in applying and adapting these thought patterns unfolded considerably.[3] The digital was only in the first years of the twenty-first century subjected to definitions and epistemological notions such as 'naturalness'. It did not take a long time before the digital focused globally on quantifiable issues which related to the computer as its specific instrument. The latter functions in essence with two signals: 'on' and 'out'. Each signal is characterized as a 'bit'. Bits determine the texts. All information is ultimately expressed by the number of bits. And communication depends on the way in which expressivity is fabricated and for what it became engineered. That observation does not only imply changing perspectives on the function and tasks of language and expressivity. It also includes a reorientation of the traditional categories a language pattern embraces—no matter what kind of or type of mother tongue is concerned.

However, most challenging is the focus on *person forms* of lingual expressivity. They seem to show a process of dissolving grammatical categories and providing fewer determinate pluralities of positions.[4] An example of historical interest is von Savigny's term 'Volk', *people.*[5] The famous eighteenth century historian wanted to explore a term which was not permanently fixed but open to evolution by means of novel historical experiences and junctures which should support progress in the field.

[3] See *Footnote 7.*

[4] Edmund Husserl characterized them as 'ego-positions'.

[5] von Savigny (1814). See also: Broekman (2019), p. 96f.

But that could—in a truly exemplary manner—only occur when a transition from the grammatical first-person singular into a plurality of positions took place. Beyond the 'I' s, the 'You' s, He' s or 'She' s should a new plural create new forms of consciousness—not without changing the meaning concept itself.

The digital, one must understand and accept, is—in contrast to the analog—sharing such an insight and considers a new plural in revised expressions that function as basic terms of communication. One could say that *structuralism* already anticipated the developments of the *digital*. Both were striving for reorientation. Structuralists were fascinated by the decentralization of the subject as traditional category of grammatical nature; explorers of the digital share these whilst initiating even broader views. Both structuralists and digital practitioners argue that *there cannot be any first person without any other person, that is: a second, third, kind of person*. Saying 'I' *is* saying 'He' or 'She'; ultimately, a word has never *one* and *solely one* specific meaning! That is a key observation in the field of semiotics, which should never be neglected because of its immense social relevance. Words are always framed in a process of social change. They are continuously in motion; yes, they *are* motion. All these considerations play a role in the often unclearly determinable relations between natural languages and digital expressivity. Is the distance between the *digital* (which is formally characterized as 'artificial') and the form of communication usually named the *natural*, indeed unbridgeable?

It becomes acceptable to conclude, that: 'The digital world does not know any *subject matter*, since it cannot support the differences, concealed variations, and other irregularities linked with the term. It therefore manages digital matters completely withdrawn from any such interpretative color and speaks solely of *data* in this context.' This includes the insight, that semantic differences between *subject matter* and *data* are essential to understand the issue. Indeed: 'We are all aware of the connections of data, which in their harmony and togetherness provide daily information stemming from processes in the digital world (originally via datafication) and safely reaching us in analog terms. These data are like emails, SMS messages, TV images, and the like. They all relate to what in the analog language type is named a *network* or the *net* and they seem to be at home in every person's life—stretching from the outer banks of the Amazon or the southern meanders of the Nile to the inner streets of cities like Buenos Aires, Shanghai, Chicago, or London. But a digital understanding of the analog 'network' does not take into consideration any of the plurality of cultural, geographical, or sociopsychological differentiations that characterize the network's places of production and reception. The digital terminology teaches us to refrain from this wealth of human culture and expressivity, and considers the network or net as being the *interconnection of devices'*.

'The notion of the Web or 'www' has become as popular and as integrated as rain, sunshine or storm, money or gravity, love, and disgust. It is no longer an instrument but simply involves a move of the hand or of any other part of the body, not to mention the brain. The Web is the Network of Speech, often with but also without words. Its all-embracing function is mostly unproblematic, so that representations of social relationships seem a powerful effect of the Web as well as of related speech phenomena'.[6]

Cognition in the digital world changed our knowledge. *What something is* had in digital settings to be understood as: *how something must be used.* And that move is far more than a simple underlining of practice given priority over theory. *The digital spreads a utilitarian attitude not as a philosophical principle of modern days but as if that attitude were the leading role of nature itself!* No person, no individual, no 'I', no human existence fulfills this embracement entirely, but application itself appears as the main feature of modernity. The digital concerns therefore not primarily *cognition* in the sense of what or how something *is*, but it determines strictly how it *can or must be used*, applied, data-structured and delivering profit. Those utilitarian tendencies and principles do color the words, techniques, and data we encounter whilst consulting the relevant websites. There is a most challenging tension between a Wikipedia page offering insights in for instance *Digital citizenship*[7] and a simple e-mail directed to a casual citizen. The relatively few informative and scientifically orientated pages are a Web-minority in view of the millions of pages that function as an answer to questions, information sites or data-offering sites. The latter make our computers socialize our knowledge and insight in issues of contemporary interest without showing their true posture. They apply principles named communication indirectly but do ultimately support primordial interests of socio-economic and political tendencies. It may seem confusing, but we conclude that the many activities on our computer or smartphone must be characterized as a universal form of *instructional pragmatism*. No message, no read, no compliment, remark, or question in the world of communicative instruments can escape this dominant but seldom disclosed attitude of the digital. Its instructional pragmatism pins the user down by means of rules of appliance which are strictly to follow. They should be the sunlight for all forms of togetherness and color the lights of cognition. Does that bring us any elucidation?

This form of pragmatism became confirmed by means of contrasting the lingual 'analog' with the 'digital' expressivity. It seems as if all models, types, or surfaces of language and expressivity are still devised by means of the term 'analog'. That type of thought formation represents the patterns of signals and the ranges of values, it also delivers reliable transmissions in speech, audio, and video as well as an awareness of real time processing. It is therefore no surprise that in this light, digital types of language must apparently be re-positioned in analog patterns to become effective. It is very important to underline that digital expressivity exists only when the digital can be received and revived in forms and terms of the analog!

The most important question related to this view, is what the concept 'analog' (so seemingly different from the 'digital') has to do with language as definition. The first fragment of an answer to this complicated question should remain linked to the

---

[6]Broekman (2019), p. 294f.

[7]https://en.wikipedia.org/wiki/Digital_citizen. See also: https://en.wikipedia.org/Wiki/Digital_self-determination#Self-determination.

distinction between a 'naïve-natural' and a 'non-naïve-natural' positioning of our thought patterns. The phenomenon of language is in the realm of this differentiation in both cases understood as a 'natural' phenomenon. But its 'naturalness' is as complicated and varied as its major instrument called 'language' itself! The difference between 'naïve' and 'non-naïve' naturalness is therefore subtle and deeply influential. No wonder, that the formation of the 'configurations' which languages offer their speakers, writers, and all others (often classified as a 'first person singular')—seem to differentiate with the meanings and senses of the words one notices as major connotations in life. They are often 'naïve' as well as 'non-naïve', and this wealth of semantic possibilities determines our understanding of the term 'analog'.[8]

There is furthermore no simple one-to-one relation between any feature rightfully named 'analog' and 'language'. There is a powerful and enduring flow of signs and meanings unfolding as soon as a language is envisioned. Slowly becoming visible at the horizon is thus the idea that, belonging to the most vital components of language, words are continuously and at all levels in motion. All participants involved in the presence and practices of languages are continuously changing from 'naïve' to 'non-naïve' and vice versa. There is no fixated position and character, no borderline between the various positions—all are available for each speaker, author, thinker, or other participant in any activation of whatever language pattern. It means that differentiations in the naturalness of languages are part of the definition of a language.

That is a very important consideration about 'analog' in its relation to the concept of language. Our modern understanding of a 'non-naïve' positioning, and the ongoing expansion of the idea of the 'natural' within this term, is therefore important. Modern society's changes in naivety bring us newly conceived forms or types of language and cognition. One must consider why and how our digital moments in daily language and communication are qualified as 'natural': is it because specific human thoughts are foundational in the unfolding of the digital realms?

6.3 Self

The *configuration* of a Self does not solve the problem of the *identification* of a Self, and certainly not of any *plural* in this context.

Does one need a plurality of 'Selves' to identify one 'Self'—and does that view represent the more general need for any form of alterity to reach an identity? That question leads to a newly conceivable Copernican turn. Any 'ego-position' in a

---

[8] https://www.google.be/search?sxsrf=ALeKk00tyEfP62nTLyxaGQIK29w5dKigsw:1606904434277&q=analog+vs+digital&sa=X&ved=2ahUKE. See the difference between analog and digital formulated here as: 'Analog signal is a continuous signal which represents physical measurements. Digital signals are discrete time signals generated by digital modulation'. But the difference is apparently more than a matter of source or continuity.

'non-naïve-natural position' is namely in essence a form of self-determination. This initiates axial position-changing activities and elucidates how a methodological self-reflection on naïve as well as non-naïve knowledge formation turns towards other non-naïve and non-natural ways. Attitude changes represent in these perspectives a new type of philosophical theory. We speak, write, think, dream, or meditate at what we characterize as a 'natural' level of expression, which is often named 'analog' in contrast to 'digital' or eventually 'quantum-related'. 'Naturalness' is today growingly 'non-naïve', and that development accentuates the importance of the broadness of the 'Natural' as a concept. If linked to the spheres of the analog can the Natural (despite all difficulties) be defined precisely. It is, as if all actual problems of expressiveness and cognition are gathered in 'non-naïve-natural' thought patterns. Is that the case? There is no definitive answer to this question. There is no Self beyond a plurality of Selves. That insight leads to more than one illustrative and even cognitive context, thanks to the digital components of modern life. There is no Self anymore without an innumerable number of Selfies on the smartphone of individuals around me.

No wonder, that long before the digital Self-techniques Peirce was already skeptical and extremely careful in expressing the essence and cognition of the Self. Colapietro reformulates this viewpoint in his basic 1989 study entitled *Peirce's Approach to the Self. A Semiotic Perspective on Human Subjectivity.*[9] He quotes a Peirce formulation from 1868: 'The individual man, since his separate existence is manifested only by ignorance and error, so far as he is anything apart from his fellows, and from what he and they are to be, is only a negation.'

Our modern age has hitherto not produced any reliable alternative in understanding such developments and their history. Most attention is spent to a foundational exploration of the relations between perception (particularly the *visual* capacities) and meaning-creation in human consciousness. It was clear until the last decades of the twentieth century: the varieties of attitude resp. positioning relate to the diverse spheres of expressiveness, uses, types, and forms of communication. All were changing with these processes and cultural frames. A natural language could in this light be characterized as a mother tongue, an artificial language like mathematics, chemistry, or other non-naïve-natural tongues as scientific. But on the one hand is it most remarkable how those distinctions still mark our global view on language and expression today. 'Non-naïve-natural languages' are, despite their non-naïve character, understood as belonging to the family of 'natural' languages. In other words: the 'non-naïve natural' remains 'natural'. On the other hand, seems the sign-function of the Self to tower above all the differentiations Peirce had in mind. The semiotic relevance of a remark in this context is clear: Peirce was convinced that 'as in interpreting subject, the self must be distinguishable from any actual process of sign interpretation; that is, the self must be able to distinguish itself and, thereby, to distance itself from the stream of signs that at any moment of its existence uses the

[9] Colapietro (1989), Ch. 4, p. 61 ff.

self as a medium.'[10] Thanks to the pressure of digital expressivity we developed the insight today, that the mirroring of images is a determinative power in a semiotic framework. The became a philosophical and semiotically interesting issue that marks our modernity. Studying Peirce, one can conclude with Colapietro: '. . .if the self is a semiotic process, it is a complex type of such a process, one in which there is ramification and also one in which the various branches of the process act on one another'.[11]

Those who search for an essential feature of human cognition could find it: knowledge is the fruit of *a breach with natural evidence, which needs awakening*; in other words: is primarily an attitude change. Our feelings of natural evidence imply, however, a pertinent question: does that evidence exist as supposed in human cognition's awakening? In other words, is the 'being' of that natural evidence undisputed? That issue touches the fundamental structure of human existence. It says: does every human being, embedded in one of the cultures around the globe, enter social life by means of leaving a realm of natural evidence behind?

The issue is apparently embedded in a foundational narrative, which can be encountered around the globe. It says: do we indeed have to perform a step out of the realm of natural evidence to become perceptive individuals? This was certainly suggested by Peirce's whistle of the train or the sheriff's hand on his shoulder. They should be understood as signs of a breach with any pre-existing natural evidence, of which we were not aware. Awareness of possession and breach with evidence seem to co-exist and they engender at the same time in a process of epistemological awakening natural evidence. The latter is but one specific form of an immense variety of interpretations and experiences pertaining to such a breach.

This plurality touches philosophical problems. It has often been discussed how the scale of 'normal' phenomena of human life expands through 'abnormal' life situations and experiences. That was particularly highlighted in existentialism, philosophical anthropology, and existential psychiatry during decades before and several years after the Second World War. It basically determined the cultural climate in which Husserl tried to determine the multiple ego positions that were in his views philosophically important. They underlined that an existential theory about human beings based on a general ontology is contradictory and therefore not feasible. Heidegger pointed out that the philosophical expression 'ontology' should have a different meaning as soon as a human being and its existence are at stake. His interpretations in the famous 1926 publication *Sein und Zeit* [Being and Time] are in that regard understandable as interpretations of Husserl's *Lebenswelt* [Lifeworld] in a specific ontological positioning. In other words, the expression 'to be' and its neighboring concept 'natural' embrace a meaning, which depends on whether it is applied to objects or to humans. If there are multiple regions of ontology, as the Self experiences in our smartphone days, how then should we articulate the word 'to be'

[10] Colapietro (1989), p. 66.

[11] *Id.* p. 67.

and how do we discuss the question whether any pre-existing natural evidence should be awakened by a breach that ‘exists’ for all humans alike?

The relevance of these considerations is clearly detectable if one considers how a human existence is founded upon a plurality of ontological structures. Such interpretations are themselves embedded in a plural setting. A particular philosophical approach on its own may never be sufficient to grasp the dimensions of human existence or deliver any insight into the complicated dynamics of its subjectivity. *Human reality seems a universe of multiple transcendences.* In other words, the question pertaining to ‘the ‘being’ of reality’ relates to such a plural ontology in which multiple modes of understanding ‘to be’ are implied. That is basic for observations about the virtual and cyberspace. Natural positions change and thus remain connected within a plural ontology.

But do not forget that Peirce’s interest in any pre-existing natural evidence was not primarily ontological. His question was not whether naturalness exists in an ontological sense of the word, but how naturalness is philosophically as well as linguistically, and thus semiotically, understandable. Because that point of view is important, he proposed a breach with natural evidence as a major factor in the epistemological conditions of a human being. That caused his interest in what he called the indexical properties of such a state of being. If its foundation is an ontological issue, it is the ontology that founds human communication *tout court*—like a regional ontology that expresses how a plural ontology is needed for understanding each specific property at hand.

In all cases of considering the human Self is an ego-position focused. The naïve positioning is thus a form of knowledge, which does not embrace any reflection that creates a problematical sphere. That form is often described as ‘everyday life’. One categorizes this position as ‘a naive clarity’ in which life unfolds unquestioned. But is that indeed a successful way to access knowledge and reality? The ‘digital’ is defined as an almost unearthly perfection of a such a relation: it consists of all information, which a sender as well as a receiver must possess to create a successful communication. It is clear, that it will function like a mother tongue in the multiple types of analogue language. But the technicality of the digital includes a gap: the concept mother tongue does not and cannot exist in digital language—it is only a tongue in a non-naïve-natural positioning. Is the digital on its way towards complete naïve-natural features? One encounters here the global challenge of the digital culture when confronted with the necessity to express in natural/analog forms of articulation. Note, that it is a new and challenging thought to understand the digital culture as an issue to rethink the boundaries of naturalness of language! We must thank our computers and smartphones to bring this into our lives of the twenty-first century. The breach between a ‘naïve-natural’ and a ‘non-naïve natural’ knowledge is important because any Self performs communication within a continuous differentiation of naïve- and non-naïve natural forms of life. Different contexts play in that regard a decisive role and each of them has its own linguistic qualities to unfold and roles to fulfill. Two difficulties in that context ask our attention.

A *first* is, that words and names function in the naïve-natural position beyond spheres of stringent determination. The positions of an ego are hardly definable via words, grammar, or syntax. Even the characterization of the naïve-natural position itself is too broadly and not clearly conceived. It means that an important change of position can only take place after an awareness of a possible redeployment from a 'naïve–natural' to a 'non–naïve natural' positioning. This great breach 'saves us out of the naivety of a positive foundational function of truth', Husserl mentioned, so that 'we no longer need to experience the painful thorn of skepticism'.[12] And in this perspective, 'the depletion of the naïve natural position is the beginning of the path in phenomenology, which will at the end lead to a humanization of the human being.[13]'

A *second* is, that the performance of this depletion seems to be much more than a matter of terminology. There is always 'a drive to change one's position from the phenomenological backwards into a simple objective one.' This is essential, because Firstness is 'an unnatural habit' and as such as a 'complete change'.[14] This feature is perhaps (because of its importance) only fragmentarily presented in words or related technical terms. There is no precisely introduced terminology for the various ego positions in the generally outlined field of naïve-natural positions. We know in the field of non-naïve naturalness only three positions: the natural, the non-natural and the transcendental position. This is not enough to fully understand and master the entire flow of ego positioning. But it already shows the complexity of an ego positioning, which takes place either in a naïve-natural or a non-naïve-natural perspective. That insight embraces much more than the classical and almost dogmatic subject–object scheme.

It means: the natural, naïve and non-naïve-natural and have a function in the sphere of all non-naïve natural positions and at the borderline between naïve-natural and non-naïve-natural positioning. So, the question remains whether the outlining of these positions is sufficient. An exploration of one term in the sphere of another has often led to misunderstandings. In the non-naïve-natural context takes the change of position place on the way to a performance. It thus functions as a moment of the flow. No wonder, that the term itself was often debated as if it indicated a special loss of meaning and sense. In that context meant the term 'ego positioning' what in ordinary language is called 'focus', that is: 'particular interest' or 'specific attention and meaning'. Such terms concern life in two foundational contexts: one before, and one after the breach with naïveté. It also covers two types of meaning—at one side of the possible change of position. And each is at one of the borderlines of the entire non-naïve-natural position.

A light thus shines at two different semiotics layers. Both relate to observation, but only the non-naïve-natural region will lead to appropriate human cognition. It is the latter, which changes natural observation—a change, which is only understandable after recognizing the change of position leading to a renewed and newly directed focus on a different general epistemological issue. Observation is in that

[12] Husserl (1959), p. 27.

[13] Husserl (1954), p. 429.

[14] Husserl (1954), p. 204; Broekman (1963), p. 64 f.

focus no longer the observation of a some-thing: cognition changes according to the same attitude. Any Firstness is a 'general thesis': it is a step, which enables positions within the non-naïve-natural position to function on the path of nascent cognition.

Each naming process indicates the importance of linguistic steps into new forms of knowledge. It characterizes the impressive effects of the stream of consciousness, an insight that Husserl shared with William James. One encounters conjunctive elements (those who essentially belong together as the stream) and disjunctive elements (those who are incidentally implied) in the stream of consciousness. The Kantian desire to acquire exact knowledge about a 'pure' consciousness is tangible but not articulated. It yet revives in a third stage of reduction, which is leading to the transcendental ego position. The latter should finalize an intentional analysis, which takes its transcendental feature as the ultimate focus of the Self of a human being. It seems that the Self and the O/other can focus the pure ego on this road, to live the pure ego in the form of an 'co-presentation'. The two are always in togetherness—the co-presence of Otherness will never be a purely independent presence. A common world exists through an ego that can bring co-presentation of itself to the fore based on a crucial presentation. Only when creating an original duality of ego and alter ego might an ego position become related to a form of linguistic expression. Here is a view on the foundational and in-depth structure of all language.

Philosophy wants to be a discourse as an ultimate linguistic form to clarify the essence of being and cognition. *An ego is thus belonging to pluralities, which sustain the developments of human life*. In this light also unfolds a plurality of pluralities, in other words: the actual comings and goings of the ego in the flow of human consciousness. And there is the plurality of expressions, resp. languages related with those continuously changing life experiences. The latter are never separated—they always express each other and form a unity in themselves. This becomes clearly visible in the continuously varying show of ego positions, which function as expressivity and ultimately create a language character. The ultimate unity of all those ego positions must be emphasized. A consequence might be, that the 'I', the 'particular human being', seems characterized by the possibility to embrace various ego positions—which leads to a freely explored self-understanding and auto-recognition as essential component of the cognitive flow.

As closely as ego expression and self-determination are, so freely moves the ego in view of existential considerations such as 'who am I as ego in the world?' Any attempt to understand the ego as a crucial component of reality will meet the consideration whether an ego can stay away from any disturbing solipsism. That underlines the existential importance of the ties between a factual and a transcendental ego. The insights of phenomenology and existentialism encounter where language functions at the borderlines of multiple forms of egocentrism which are far from egoism. The central position of the ego leads to the close ties between ego and language (remember its grammatical form of 'first person singular') whilst contrasting an egocentric attitude and thus to sociability. The latter embraces a fascinating 'totality', resp. 'everything'. There is, however, no ego position possible without this position just being an 'attitude'). The latter underlines an exclusive valorization of a particular sphere of objects. Each valorization of the ego and its position embraces therefore (most fascinatingly) the praxis of plurality that determines the ego. In more general language, it means that every positioning is a matter of flow and thus of plurality—the essence of the ego as expressed in its subjectivity is in the plural of its continuously changing positioning.

6.4 Configurations

Simply noticing the plural in linguistic expressivity is not enough: the determinations caused by the types of language resp. expressiveness do count! Plurality appears to be decisive. The path to follow in the light of our interest in any lingual typology seems to lead from multi*disciplinary* to multi*leveled* features. The latter, implying new versions and visions, do not remain within the boundaries of one type of language or expressivity as was the case with the 'analog' or 'naïve-natural' type. No theory can justify its insights in communication while only relating to distinctions between for instance artificial and natural languages, or between digitally registered and converted languages. Plurality in the twenty-first century has a deeper sense: the relations between types of language and linguistic phenomena, such as communication, are more complex and richer in global culture than ever before. It means: more forms of lingual togetherness, its cultural observations and practices included, come together in their task to articulate events in daily life. The mutual forces in socio-cultural practices on the one hand and lingual experiences, insights, and practices on the other, are of global essence. Ego positions are more than ever linked to the major features of daily life. Their continuity, including its special focus acquired by reduction and comparable epistemological performances, makes effects like name giving, interpretation and translation possible—that means: the enabling of linguistic activities. Cognition and other functions of human consciousness should be understood in this perspective. It brings the insight that words embraced, and arguments accepted, terms trusted, and verbal reactions exchanged, are sustaining meaning, sense, and quality of communication. Despite the fascinating differences among the global variety of mother tongues, this embraces all language types, which are encountered like laws to capture human essentials. One cannot deny that this global and truly fundamental pattern is basic for humanity. The most central consideration touches, however, its historic character: is this language-tied pattern an unchangeable background of human life? In other words: does this pattern transcend any changeability or does it, on the contrary, underline the immeasurable value of change (and thus the flow character) in human life?

There is the generally accepted idea that any human being is the user of his or her language. Where that language comes from and how it became structured the way it is used is either a question widely neglected or solved by reference to a speaker's education: the expression 'mother tongue' is still effective in that regard. Those presuppositions, which are valid in all languages spoken around the globe, consider language as the most precious instrument of communication at hand. But the last two words indicate a philosophical problem that is gradually becoming visible. What is the meaning of this 'at hand' today? In our days we encounter digital forms of expression and articulation finding their way via analog forms, and vice versa—a situation that is in the above lines characterized as an 'interlude' and surpasses any idea of an 'at hand'. What is articulated represents seldom or never the rules for pre-existing patterns. This aspect is difficult to fully unfold, but at least two important schemes support us here. They are generally used to explain and exploit our knowledge and insights of language. We refer to the *speaker–hearer* scheme as well as the *user* scheme. Reading for instance Wittgenstein is often a subtle confrontation with the two in their interrelation. Our daily considerations, even as digital forms in analog language, repeat them continuously. It means that our reflections must relate to this basic feature in the process of 'thinking language'. The search for a guide in that activity is complex and does not bring us to re-read Wittgenstein, but rather to consider Walter Benjamin and his often-explored term 'Sprachgestalt' [lingual stature].

The latter could influence our thoughts on the linguistic processes at stake. The expression 'Sprachgestalt' functions already in his first essay on philosophy of language entitled *Über Sprache überhaupt und über die Sprache des Menschen*[15] dating from 1916. It concerns no rules nor grammatical regulations, but a specific entity with three specific features, which only suggest a proximity to the 'syntax': (1) language's often surprising directness, (2) language's exchangeable components (translation) and (3) language's abstract devices (word, sign, decision). Even in our days are those three considered as the major elements of language and lingual communication—especially where analog and digital relations are determining. But Benjamin treats them as a unity, which the word 'Gestalt' [appearance, posture, configuration] should indicate. They are thus clearly more complex and play because of their complexity a different role than the classical term 'syntax'.

The following background-issues are thus to consider:

(1) Translation is an act of understanding and enlightening a linguistic event as well as a form of corresponding critical activity in the heart of language formation. The most important components in this peculiar case are the German *'Sprach-'* and its counterpart *'Gestalt',* as well as their exclusive linguistic togetherness. Each of the three refers to specific tasks and meanings, functions, and fields in language. Their togetherness in one term does not constitute any repetition of already existing modes of expression. At the background of this idea remains the fact that sounds, forms, or meanings seem the basic constitutive elements of Benjamin's 'Gestalt', but also the way in which a language constitutes its verbal unities and sentences in general. The proximity of the expression 'Gestalt' and the technical term 'syntax' remains active in each translation. But the idea of a 'Sprachgestalt' is broader and more culturally encompassing than the expression 'syntax' suggests.

[15] Benjamin (1977), pp. 140–157.

(2) The component *'Sprach-'* implies any focus on a (grammatically determined) subject participating in a language-driven occurrence taking form. That focus was and is a major inspiration in Western philosophy. Its linguistic dimensions are not the coloring of static properties or the acceptance of a position, but in the first place an advancement of specific activities to be understood as linguistically relevant. In the English translation should the *'Sprach'- component* become understood as indicating the complexity of 'text' and of 'speech'; the choice between the two expressions remains a matter of creating lingual forms. The latter: 'form', does indeed neighbor the German word 'Gestalt'—an important translation issue on its own. But one should reconsider that writing, speaking, arguing, gesturing, or expressing a self, locates us in language. Things and issues around us (in fact everything) express their essence by means of language in many regards, including human existence. Language thus communicates a human being with its essence: not only with other humans but finally with life itself. There are many and often hidden issues in each linguistic theme and in each related activity. Traditional language, even today qualified as a mother tongue, emphasizes the role of a subject as the most essential component. That qualification seems not only to be respected by grammars (which include words as well as sentence structures) but also semantics and vocabularies.

(3) Each subject involved in language fulfills its task through creating a major social event. The naming resp. name-giving must be understood as a cosmic power of language—as already exposed in preceding pages, and the first lines of the cosmic history outlined in Torah and Bible tell us. No wonder it fulfills an axial role in Benjamin's essay. But that role cannot be rationalized or concretized through language as its sole and all-embracing instrument. This is Benjamin's point of reference: *what language realizes is always more than what can be expressed in language!* Language has a magical dimension from its first words on, its primary gestures or its encompassing sounds included. The many ways in which language mediates fragments of reality fascinates each speaker and hearer beyond the limits of their conversation. Any linguistic mediation is anchored in forms. The form will guide and prescribe us: they make us the reader of a poem, the viewer-visitor in a theatre or the reader of an essay. Thanks to that form, we 'know' what and how to express or articulate. They lead many types and forms of social episteme—even those who are chaotic, destructive, dysfunctional, or incomprehensible.

(4) This is exactly the meaning of Benjamin's 'Sprachgestalt'. Its essence must be recognized as a moment of the event, the flow, in other words: the ever-changing reality. It does not fit into a stabilized and fixated scheme or pattern such as the often-launched 'Speaker-Hearer' scheme. Even the concept and translation of the word language is colored by this insight and accentuated when the expression 'speech' is brought to the fore. We underline that the idea of a 'Sprach-gestalt' is not appropriately transferred into English language when it is understood as if it were a grammar, syntax, or any other static linguistic category—for instance a semiotic form. The antonym becomes apparent when the dynamic character of a 'Gestalt' is considered. In German is 'Sprache'

containing two meanings, which relate to two English words: 'language' and 'speech'. This difference between German and English is important in the act of translating the German 'Sprach-gestalt'. The complexity of meaning, often essential in a word, is indeed a central issue in translation and linguistic structuring. The question behind this observation is of almost universal interest: is each word we articulate either folded in a 'box' of settled meanings or a dynamic point of reference in an ever-changing field of linguistic signs called 'event'?

(5) The forwarding of expressions to function in a context of identity- or non-identity of meaning is today more difficult than ever. To acquire insight into the building and functioning of linguistic 'Gestalten' is baffling and puzzling, since it relates in today's normality to a differentiation and coordination of analog (often called 'natural') and digital language. For Benjamin was each spoken or written word a matter of participation in a language-driven event. Our insights today are more complex since we confirm through the application of multiple types of language that translating a word is translating a world. In other words: in today's language is no word thought, written, or spoken solely in the traditional analog, resp. natural language. Translations unfold meaning and sense in the shadows of analog, digital or sometimes quantum forms of expressivity and not of a basic natural language, as was the case in Benjamin's considerations. Tensions between the two points of reference belong to our days.

(6) The latter underline our modern multi-leveled understanding of interpretation and formation of language. Focus is on speech events that are no longer anchored in one single language pattern. Multi-leveled patterns rooted in various and different thought patterns and scientific disciplines ground our practices of expression and communication today. Benjamin's 'Sprachgestalten' are axial forms or figures of speech, which will not be recognized as grammar or syntax but rather as an open semiotic form. We know and master them, as beacons in multiple layers of expressivity, in analog resp. natural language together with digital and/or quantum layers. That has in all cases the primary function to recognize the basics of expression to be respected in lingual communication. The 'Gestalten', the forms, and figures at hand, are for instance recognized as 'poem', 'essay', 'address', 'lecture' or even 'tweet'. They indicate that that there exists not any formless or non-figured element of language. The latter observation implies two important dynamic facts: language and form belong together, and any linguistic form has in any case a flow-character as all human knowledge has. Only under the guidance of this insight is it possible to recognize our language processes as specific forms or recognizable types in the totality of lingual life. The flow of speech covers in this light our speaking as well as our texting, our thinking and imagining, which means: our awareness and the cultural determinations at hand including our memorizing.

All above considerations lead to the English translation of the German expression 'Sprachgestalten' as 'Configurations'. The 'con-' indicates the fundamentally social dimension represented by the analog/natural part of the word. The 'figure' refers to the form character treasured by all participating language basic creating the multilevel features of today's languages. The '-ations' warns not to forget the flow, the dynamic character at hand. 'Sprachgestalten' are, Benjamin would confirm, to the English reader 'Linguistic Configurations'. But do not forget, that translation is still a word or concept of natural, language—it does not clarify the complexity of the many *different* types in which an essential translation takes place, and it thus does not solve the question what the expression 'configuration' would be in a digital, i.e., non-analogically configured language.

6.5 Conversions

Our words do not belong to one, but to more than one type or category of expressiveness and yet must share meanings with unknown numbers of others during unknown periods of time. More than one type of language delivers the modules of a word or an expression, a term, or a concept we explore in our speeches and texts. That multiplicity and multilayered character is a new phenomenon in occidental history. It is sustained by the term: 'conversion' which thus needs attention when the characters and modes of communication are at issue. In the light of the preceding considerations will it become clear, that the term *conversion*, which indicates since the Occidental Middle Ages a 'turning around' or 'revolution', 'attitude change', or 'alteration', focuses in our days on a position which embraces one of the many levels of contemporary levels or types of lingual expressivity. We offer therefore some first and generally introducing thoughts about that concept.

Yes, indeed: our lives became a matter of multileveled languages and multi-aspect lingual forms of expressivity. Trusted words are today often surrounded by unknown meanings, which originate in worlds of unknown senses and thought patterns. The latter may seem to exist at distance, but they are coming closer and closer. Even if we already settled their names, their discourses and manners of exploration often remain widely undetermined. We call them 'digital' or 'quantum,' but we do not master them in daily life, let alone express or articulate them as trustworthy components. That should initiate research about *conversion*. It does not surprise anymore, that meanings depend today more on conversions than on grammars and syntaxes of a specific language. The latter belong to only one specific type of linguistic expression and do in general not answer the conditions of multileveled languages or types of lingual expressivity. That is difference in view of the term *conversion* which was one of the central concepts in the days of profiling the digital, for instance through discussions of the DAC (the Digital-Analog-Conversion) or the ADC (the Analog-Digital-Conversion). Today is conversion the term of the digital realm which can be compared to the concept of cognition, resp. knowledge in the earlier, analog world. If two expressivities are together in modern times, two concepts of acquiring knowledge are also form such a standard couple. More important is, however, an insight into the dynamics of both concepts: in days of an overwhelming influence and mental empowerment of one of them, the digital, is it important to mention how *conversion overtakes form and function of cognition.*

At preceding pages were already signs noticed of changes which show patterns of accelerating diversification in the realm of human thoughts, understanding and appreciating the human Self. Such changes find their expression in a global transition of the basic features that determine human knowledge: *from cognition into conversion*. Indeed: to *grasp* something that seems difficult or mysterious is always different from getting them *fit*. Those dynamics were characterized in preceding pages as an *instructional pragmatism*. The decisive pragmatic component is in the *fit*. There is not a 'something' anymore which is not already constituted by the power and insight of '*conversion*', which is such a '*fit*'. What was indicated by the expression knowledge' in its traditional and philosophical sense does not exist anymore. The dynamic realm of the digital reigns. The fit is determinable as knowledge at a completely different level of human experience and intellect in the case of conversion. In other words, there is no knowledge recognized in today's world without being marked as conversion.

One of the many consequences is, that the omnipresence of the 'word' is no longer valued as the exclusive component of cognition and behavior. First notions of that important change were documented around the opening years of the twentieth century. The *subject*—transformed by Husserl from component of 'subject-object relation' into 'ego-positions' including its feelings and language, its rational understanding, and its key function in all processes of cognition—became confronted with the *sign*. The latter was not solely a precursor of a new field of science and philosophy, named *significs* or *semiotics*, but also of the twentieth century tendency to change the concept of knowledge. What were changes in the twentieth century became replacements in the twenty-first century: *from knowledge to conversion*.

A 1904 letter of Charles S. Peirce to Victoria Lady Welby-Gregory should therefore be reread as a keystone in occidental philosophy. 'I wanted to write to you about signs, which in your opinion and mine are matters of so much concern . . . in mine, the highest grade of reality is only reached by signs . . .'.[16] The sentence seems epochal for our digital age and its multileveled experience of expressivities. Its consequences are seldom brought together with important cognitive domains such as understanding the universe, science, language, communication, speech, body, and text. These fields are components of the difference in accentuations within the concept of language that engendered during the first decades of the twentieth century.[17] They were obviously on their way to become multileveled and submitted to the techniques of conversion regarding meaning and sense. One must conclude that a technically correct and reliable meaning of our words seems in our days to be achieved by a stable and trustworthy conversion—wherever the incidental essence of conversion is found and becomes realized. The relations between word and sign are important; they have many undefined meanings and undetermined senses at work

[16]Peirce (1931–5), Ch. 8, Nrs 327f.

[17]Broekman (2019), p. 103 f.

within the one framework of speech or language in general. We thus repeat how human reality seems a universe of multiple transcendences. The 'being' of 'reality' always relates to a *plural* ontology in which *multiple* modes of understanding are implied. Indeed: *conversion* has in Occidental culture always been a component of *cognition*. But this changed in our days of digital dominance, so that we envision a total reverse: cognition is not anymore without reference to conversion and the latter is often predominant. So, we consider that only certain powers and factors make cognition possible (not everything can be known, as many individuals think) and others remain unknown and unknowable. For instance, we know what gravity is in its effect but never what it is in essence before it is treated by us as 'a thing to know'. Cognition is furthermore a process that is knowable only through its effect. But to know has today an additional problem: it is an issue of analog as well as digital expressivity. Each of the two must be expressed in one of them: conversion needs to be converted into analog knowledge to obtain a general effect.

So, the riddle is in the 'and'—are cognition and conversion comparable or what other properties make an understanding of their mutual relationship possible? An additional question complicates this matter: why is their relation in our days important and never researched or philosophized in earlier days? One of the issues at stake is the complexity of our linguistic expressiveness which relates to a traditional 'philosophical anthropology' and its various aspects. Subject and Self are the most important themes in that context, but what about their differentiating meaning?

But related questions come up immediately. Is within the global and far-reaching realm of expressivity a choice possible between the flow of meaning and sense on the one hand, and fixation together with determination on the other? That question concerns in essence a change in understanding and practicing language or expressivities—mother tongues included. Its observation contains indeed a broader understanding of conversion as a concept related to cognition. Do not forget: the 'I' in grammar of most Western languages, always experienced as the subject in relations, is a central component of what von Savigny already noticed in his critical studies of the 1804 Code Napoléon entitled *Vom Beruf unserer Zeit*.[18] He underlined the specificity of his own professional domain as a particular 'speech domain'. Each speech event confirms the plural character of language by means of the inherent multiplicity of that act.

Ego positions within the sphere of a naïve-natural and the much broader field of non-naïve-natural positions should clarify their specific way in which reality was conceived. But do they do that? Even the expansion of a 'non-naïve' positioning is not enough in our days. We articulate that fact through an extension of our traditional notion of language when we classify the traditional language as 'analog' next to equivalent notions of a digital expressivity and co-classifying the quantum positioning as another type of language. One should seriously understand that those extensions are only possible and brought into the field of communication within the reach and framework of a language classified as naïve as well as non-naïve natural.

[18] von Savigny (1814).

Even the most competent and all-round scholar, a citizen of whatever legally determined State on the globe, must cherish a natural language! It means that all cognition related one way or another to language still must find something like 'a place' within the reach of a type of linguistic naturalness. In other words: any complete, linguistically correct, and acceptable communication must be tied to some sort of naturalness of expression. Digital or quantum languages require therefore a minimal conversion to sustain any unfolding of knowledge. It is therefore quite understandable that various modern authors underline the actual need of translation, although they do not seem inspired to envisage the differences between translation and conversion.[19] 'The translator is translating a translation', Michael Cunningham remarked in his 2011 speech in Brussels.[20] His conclusion has an autobiographical character: 'I've come to understand that all literature is a product of translation'. Translation appears to be a continuous process in culture: 'The translator is simply moving the book another step along the translation continuum'. This insight does not take away that those translations always take place within the realm of natural language patterns (naïve as well as non-naïve). But we should consider that conversions are necessarily occurring between natural and (partially or entirely) non-natural patterns to keep that continuum intact. Indeed, Cunningham's remark has far-reaching consequences. Translation and conversion are proximate indeed, but they must respect borderlines between them. These might be a central problem determining cognition, especially in times of globally spreading digital features.

Peirce's insights in the importance of a sign are an inspiration to understand this, because in his option seem word and sign at least equivalent in rethinking language and its constitutional aspects. Both are at home within non-naïve-natural spheres of language, often at their borderlines. But on the other side of any naturalness are signs in effect, not words! It seems that a word is not a single and basic constitutive unit of language. At the other side of the boundaries of the natural are signs the partner of words, and conversion an activity to transfer them from one side to another. Thanks to that conversion becomes a non-natural language (or fragments of such a language) a natural one, and thanks to conversion become signs understandable like words. It means, that words, even if located at the borderlines of a non-naïve-natural region, can have a history of being-converted from signs as units of a non-natural region. This is very important for the important role of the digital in modern days and the naturalness of its languages.

So, even if the word as unit in a language is dominantly non-naïve, it can be adapted by- and become operational within existing natural languages. But they remain a parallel to the sign in a non-natural (naïve as well as non-naïve) language! A sign has also to be converted to become active in one of the forms of a natural

[19] See the difficult relations between translation and conversion in: Avanessian and Hennig (2014), Ch. II, p. 37 f. An example of contemporary focus on the general impact of *translation/transformation* is in; Stjernfelt (2017), pp. 117–141.

[20] Cunningham: Found in translation. PETRA Congress, 'Grand Hotel Europe', Passa Porta, Brussels, see: www.petra2011.eu.

language. To obtain a word-function, a sign should be converted: it means that its conversion makes it enter a field of properties, which are not present in a non-natural language. Its major components are threefold: the result of conversion into a word, underlines that (a) words are not dictionary-like fixations but life-events, (b) words depend on the inclusion and presence of another ego or the Other, (c) words need other words to be understood. The three provoke the far-reaching conclusion that a word has never one specific and unchangeable meaning. On the contrary: meanings are continuously participating in the flow, i.e., an ongoing process of change.

Conversions, which make it possible for non-natural languages or components of such a language to linguistically function (such as the digital language), have in the first place to do with a broadened understanding of the 'language' concept itself. Humans only understand digital language as 'language' within the realm of natural/analog components. In the naturalness of language exists the digital not as exterior to (naïve respectively non-naïve) naturalness. Conversion is thus given the precious and difficult task to have the non-natural function as natural and uses the expression 'language' as a co-determination for it. In other words: 'language' obtains by means of conversion features that seem to be 'translatable' from the natural to the non-natural and vice versa. A result is that readers of the 1's and 0's in the spheres of naturalness—the latter may be as non-naïve as possible—embrace by their reading the digital as if it were a natural language. Is its true character unveiled by this reading? Conversions overreaching borderlines between the natural and the non-natural create a dubious and challengeable awareness of the digital reality. It is as if the latter is continuously and harmoniously classifiable as real via the ability of exploring language as such—no matter whether that language is at the borderlines of its non-naivety.

But the question arises: what gives conversions priority in the total picture of lingual expressivity? They always pretend priority; they sustained for instance new techniques like 'digital technology' or a 'digital economy'. First portents were implied in fast Internet connections since the year 2000; the activity of conversions in the first 3D Printer became profiled in 2009. No wonder that notions of and about conversion reach from entertainment and artistic manifestations to sports and psychological therapy. They include furthermore economics, finances, and cyber-law along with property law—for short: their omnipresence is a recent cultural phenomenon. Focus is on computer sciences and computer technology plus Artificial Intelligence, whereby digital language seems most prominent, effective, and clear. We need convertors and accept their origin anchored in digital knowledge and practices because we live in a world of data. Data are made available and will be in effect by means of processes we call since 2013 with a neologism: 'datafication'. Data are approached as if they were an element of nature and accessed by means of human consciousness (in analog/natural expressivity). But actual problems concerning 'privacy' in the context of digital programs such as Twitter or Facebook, illustrate the vulnerability of the parallel between the relevant datafication processes and the activity of a human consciousness.

While manipulating and exploring data, conversions remain essential in all regards. But neither this activity nor the concept of 'datafication' (as an encompassing concept to analyze and consider modern life and its frames of cognition) is completely manageable. Even in the twenty-first century is our cognition much more than data-manipulation, as is suggested many times when the culture of the digital is at stake. The two concepts: conversion and language are axial in this regard. Converting interfaces are essential to the digital equipment involved in conversions as well as the devices, which will be processed to produce required operations. But an irrevocable fact is that all data ultimately require conversion to an analog signal so that they can interact with the real world of languages:[21] their omnipresence in all disciplines, techniques and thought patterns is based on that complex intertwining. The 'Digital–Analog-Conversion' seems to be the most central and effective *Conversion Type* because it presents the digital on an almost global scale in analog languages. This conversion extends effectively and transcends at the same time the non-naïve-natural regions of human cognition and linguistics. It produces shimmers of (analog/natural) reality to the digital, so that human cognition of the first decades in the twenty-first century is multilayered and in principle a plural fact: cognition is not only marked by natural- but also by non-natural types of language.

One should, however, not forget that the concept of conversion originally stems from digital types of language and forms of cognition. Important is the fact that each word does today no longer belong to one, but always and in all regards to at least two dominate types of language resp. communication: the analog and the digital type. Determinations of more types which could be involved, guide us immediately to quantum theories, their computers and techniques included. A new situation in the history of the Occident (even in global culture) thus establishes and requires full attention when modes of communication are at issue. They are decidedly different from modes in preceding centuries, the twentieth included. But the urgency to consider the two language/expression types and their social consequences determines only partially our meaning and sense of everyday lingual utterances. The existence of the two types already awakens a strong and powerful awareness about the importance of levels of linguistic expression, which overshadow any simple duality of the analog and a digital language type. Meaning and meaninglessness, their supportive normative context included, are rather caused by the expanding of grammars and syntaxes; but all still function only analog. Research on that field did not yet unfold because knowledge and insight into relations between analog and digital language in meaning-formation are almost incomparable with digital communication and its technicality at a global level. A generally acknowledged profile of 'digital semiotics' is not yet available, so we cannot answer the question, whether human behaviors are caused by a psychological (or psychopathological) mastering of digital-lingual meaning or are a pure consequence of the digital type of expressiveness and its global impact.

The issue is urgent, because digital language and its many forms of communication illustrate new forms of connectivity as if they concern inter-human

[21] Cf: https://www.elprocus.com/digital-to-analog-converter-dac-applications/.

communication. Norm consciousness and socio-ethical barriers seem not to exist in regions of digital expression; identities of actors are nominated by IT-ers and thus are only a technical issue. What is the 'I', or the traditional 'Subject' in our IT-ers' professional thought-formation? Related features of the Internet function do in that context also not further discuss the digital frames at stake! Disparity is a feature of all converters so that precision seems badly needed in the relations between them and all scientific and technological contexts. This goes with their impressive and hitherto philosophically un-reflected global omnipresence. Indeed: conversions are everywhere because they frame the definition of a word as a unit of meaning (analog) and of data (digital). But a simple formulation of this phrase, excelling in its 'and', is not enough! These and the related lines in the above text of this paragraph are no more than a first orientation about the central role and the many meanings of the term 'conversion'.

As a preparation for deeper insights, we re-examine a better orientation on what was documented and explained about conversion, and on what still must be unfolded in the forthcoming text. It should again be underlined that conversion takes place in every minute of modern society's life—but we do not have an appropriate theory to fully and immediately understand the process. Those who are confronted with conversion will often reach out to equivalent processes that take place in natural resp. analog language, such as 'translation', 'metanoia' or even 'poiesis'. But these do not respect the double anchor of the conversion: being a matter of 'non-naïve-natural' as well as 'non-natural' positioning. Its continuous move takes place from the latter to the first and can only find an opposite direction towards the non-natural after performance of the first! In other words: to say that the concept of conversion is originally a digital articulation is a matter of thought formation within the region of a non-naïve-natural and thus is also a non-natural positioning. So, what does this mean? The 'and' is our problem. In other words: this is an observation across the borderlines of two articulation areas, the natural and the non-natural language/positioning. But important is that *conversion is supposed to be in effect when conversion must become defined!* There seems an innermost repetition at work here, which is not easily clarified because one cannot speak two languages or utter two words at the same time—one that is natural and another that is non-natural—which at the very same time embrace a word and a sign.

So, we re-confine our major insight: *conversion seems the new cognition.* Be attentive, keep with the life-stream of attention, precision, and actuality. Be fit—your knowledge will be relevant even after your presence. Embrace the actual, adept to patterns spread out for you in the worlds of activity and attention. Bridge the gaps which are caused by the development of cognition—don't miss the stream which circulates around you. Be there and let the other be aware of your presence. Convert at the right moment—meditate later!

References

Avanessian A, Hennig A (2014) Metanoia. A speculative ontology of language, thinking, and the brain. Bloomsbury Academic, London/New York

Benjamin W (1977) Über Sprache überhaupt und über die Sprache des Menschen. In: Benjamin W (ed) Gesammelte Schriften, Bd II, 1. Suhrkamp Verlag, Frankfurt a. M.

Broekman JM (1963) Phänomenologie und Egologie. M. Nijhoff, Den Haag

Broekman JM (2019) Rethinking law and language, the flagship 'speech'. E. Elgar, Cheltenham & Northampton

Colapietro VM (1989) Peirce's approach to the self. A semiotic perspective on human subjectivity. State University of New York Press, New York

Cunningham M. Found in translation. PETRA Congress, 'Grand Hotel Europe', Passa Porta, Brussels, see: www.petra2011.eu

Husserl E (1921) Logische Untersuchungen, Bd II, Part 2. Halle

Husserl E (1954) Die Krisis der europäischen Wissenschaften und die transzendentale Phänomenologie. Husserliana Bd. VI, M. Nijhoff, Den Haag

Husserl E (1959) Erste Philosophie (1923/24), Zweiter Teil: Theorie der phänomenologischen Reduktion. Husserliana Bd. VIII, M. Nijhoff, Den Haag

Husserl E. Ideen zu einer reinen Phänomenologie und phänomenologischen Philosophie. Husserliana, Bd III, Karl Schumann (ed). M. Nijhoff, Den Haag, p 119

Peirce CS (1931–5) Collected papers, vol 8. Harvard UP, Cambridge

Stjernfelt F (2017) Diagrammatology. Springer, Dordrecht

von Savigny FC (1814) Vom Beruf unserer Zeit für Gesetzgebung und Rechtwissenschaft. Heidelberg, English Ed. at A. Hayward, (Trl) The Lawbook Exchange Ltd, London 2011: of the vocation of our age for legislation and jurisprudence

Chapter 7
Plurality of the Natural

Borderlines are everywhere. The suggestion that a digital culture, unfolding beyond any fraction, marks the transition of the twentieth into the twenty-first century, fascinates. Is there such a differentiation of meaning and sense which unfolds in parallel with the sequence of ages? That would be a background for the multiple attempts to characterize the digital one way or another. But it is difficult to accept the idea, that only a *virtual* reality—in our days named the '*digital culture'*—characterizes this turn of the century, this intense borderline.

One of the marks which enlighten that discussion is the suggestion that the digital is a 'new plural'. Its development is indicted by the introduction and study of the conversion processes and techniques from analog to digital and vice versa. Our attention is on these two processes, although today's dominant presence of the digital no longer brings them to the fore. But they mirror most questions, insights, techniques and thought processes of our digital culture and its focus on an unrestrained application. Since the culture of the digital became a global factor of interest is the technique of conversion an evident phenomenon and not a cognitive issue anymore! That astonishes: the digital does no longer interpret all dimensions of human cognition in view of the traditional and globally recognized duality of a subject–object relationship. A central digital occurrence of conversion took that place. No wonder that the techniques and performances of digital–analog and analog–digital conversions were of central interest in the beginning of the third millennium in which foundations of human knowledge begun to change and the dual relationship as creator of intersubjective patterns of life faded away.

7.1 Is Cyberspace Platonic?

But that question, that hesitation, is not enough!

It becomes clear that efforts to broaden the thought formation in the non-naïve-natural area never characterize the natural as a single and separate phenomenon. Yet,

J. M. Broekman, *Knowledge in Change*, Law and Visual Jurisprudence 8,

the latter seems an attractive and easy-going viewpoint. Michael Heim tried to elucidate the metaphysics of the virtual in this context almost three decades ago. He suggested in 1993[1] that one specific common and hidden power caused all sorts of changes since the origins of Western cultures. Centre of this flowing power would be the natural, which guarantees our knowledge and appreciation of changes. One reads in Mirton Kruger's Foreword to Heim's publication that 'for instance, Leibniz' vision of a community of minds precisely anticipates current data networks'. Does such a type of anticipation result from a continuity that features knowledge of virtual reality as well as digital culture? Doubts seem highly appropriate. For instance, a community of minds, thoughts, and knowledge, as imagined by Kruger, embraces very different thought patterns. These patterns are more different than our actual data networks and any background form of a digital culture. A deeper insight into the essence of knowledge in the twenty-first century shows that cognition expands significantly despite for instance the enormous expansion of techniques, which does not solely concern daily life. Our actual knowledge includes human insight into cosmic spheres and knowledge, for instance regarding planets that are millions of miles away and exist for innumerable ages. Concern our flying a drone since April 2021 in the areas of Mars!

Those insights are indeed accompanied by an intensification of interest and knowledge in seismic issues, which in their turn determine the character of human activity on the planet. And they are also steps to a renewed self-understanding, which correlate with those steps in actual human life. Heim concludes in this sense: 'As the interface shades into cyberspace (...) this interface brings with it a troubling ambiguity. The term interface originated with the mundane hardware adapter plugs used to connect electronic circuits. Then it came to mean the video hardware used to peer the system. Finally, it denotes the human connection with machines, even the human entry into self-contained cyberspace.' He finalizes the (re)construction of the development of the digital with the suggestion: 'In one sense, interface indicates computer peripherals and video screens; in another, it indicates human activity connected by video to data. The double meaning makes us pause: How peripheral is the human? How much of the system do we own when we enter the door of cyberspace? Where are we when software architects shape the data-scape into endless mazes of light attracting us like moths to a flame?'

Note, that the latter question is only understandable when a general absence of breaches in- or between types and areas of cognitive activities characterize the unfolding of human history. Is that, or has that ever been the case in human history? Heim indicates that the practices of e-communication (resulting from e-techniques and e-education) are a dominating form of socialization, of 'a re-education of human desires and interests. It entails a realization that what attracts us in the sensory world is no more than an outer projection of ideas we can find within us.' These thoughts lead immediately to a central thesis, which seems to be based on, and result from, a human fascination which suggests the existence of unbroken chains of histories.

[1]Heim (1993).

Heim astonishes when he formulates: 'Cyberspace is Platonism as a working product'. He suggests: 'The cybernaut[2] seated before us, strapped into sensory-input devices, appears to be, and is indeed, lost to this world. Suspended in computer space, the cybernaut leaves the prison of the body and emerges in a world of digital sensation.' He thus enters a very specific world, which is the world of digital sensations. The latter seems to require the sustaining of a Platonic attitude because a reality is at stake of which he knows very well that he has no full accessibility nor the physical and psychological status to access. Hence the challenging formula he proposes for understanding our managing a virtual reality with the remark: 'This Platonism[3] is thoroughly modern, however. Instead of emerging in a sensation-less world of pure concepts, the IT-er moves among entities that are well formed in a special sense. The spatial objects of cyberspace proceed from the constructs of Platonic imagination not in the same sense that perfect solids or ideal numbers are Platonic constructs, but in the sense that information in cyberspace inherits the beauty of Platonic FORMS. The computer recycles ancient Platonism by injecting the ideal content of cognition with empirical specifics.'[4]

What means 'Platonic' in this context, and why is this term given such a central position? We repeat the last sentence: 'The computer recycles ancient Platonism by injecting the ideal content of cognition with empirical specifics.' In other words, there are various steps to consider: (a) computer, (b) cognition and (c) empiricism are brought together—but do they fit, are they melted together, and if so, how do they perform Platonism on that basis? The question is in other words: *how is human thought able to grasp transcendent realities*? That formula shows the importance of trying to understand what is essentially different from a daily life and its human dimensions. Those transcendent realities are named with this classical philosophical word 'transcendence' because it concerns a level of knowledge and experience that is much higher profiled than daily communication ever can reach. Does that also have to represent the cyberspace and the digital culture of today? The question does clearly not mirror Plato's own situation. He wrote under conditions we hardly know, and his writings do not guarantee any precise delineation of his thoughts. Plato wrote, as far as we can understand, as if he was presenting fragments of insight in timeless truth. His words seemed to provide an outlook of enduring validity at a level we cannot touch. It means, we cannot judge the qualities of what seems a timeless truth without any insight into the human cognitive structures.

Platonism became a standard term which is allowed to embrace unknown and unreachable spheres of thought and knowledge. But the inner systematicity and the socio-political circumstances of its expression are mostly neglected in modern articulations. Plato's poetic as well as his philosophical dimensions were perhaps overwhelming. The question remains whether the circumstances of our actual digital culture can become understandable through quotation of Plato's thought formation.

[2]Today we would speak of an 'ITer'.

[3]Heim (1993), p. 79f.

[4]Heim (1993), p. 88.

The digital would in the first place be grasped by the power of human thinking. But how do we find a foundation for the idea that digital realities, supported by computers as their specific instrument of realization, do the same even though knowledge depends on the presence and global functioning of the computer? There seems no causality in the links between the constitutive elements of Platonism and the digital; perhaps only when we cherish the idea that the two mirror! 'Platonic' would in that case be a way of accepting and perhaps even understanding the digital via the riddle of mirroring. But even that does not seem to characterize our knowledge of cyberspace and the digital as Platonic. Its central subject, namely an implicit transcendence, is no more than a borderline concept of human knowledge. Underlining the limits of the qualification 'Platonic' in the case of cyberspace, the digital and its non-analog expressivities, has perhaps too far-reaching implications!

Consider the fundamental structure of human knowledge as far-reaching and as deeply as we can. Cognition is not only linked with thought positions and cognitive attitudes which can be weighed against each other, but also with those who bring coherence and evidence.[5] It seems that putting *the complexities of standpoints* into perspective could change the field of cognition and ultimately bring a new epistemology. But a renewal of that field is definitively based on structure and quality of human interaction, all informative techniques included. Human knowledge will never unfold apart from- and beyond a togetherness of knowing individuals. That togetherness is a central notion but also a riddle of the epistemological field.

This requires specific attention for our position as a participant in the actual processes of knowing and knowledge formation. And it shows a never-experienced plurality in what is beginning to be a new natural! It will never be the position of a someone who is *essentially and definitively different from us,* here and now: as soon as another human individual might try to become someone different, he or she will not be *another* human being anymore! This is valid although a certain desire to encounter an essentially different fellow-creature is never completely absent. In other words: *the real other*, who represents *an epistemologically relevant otherness*, is unthinkable although a desire to encounter such a well-known unknown other, remains alive. The real otherness is a myth, it cannot be expressed in words of a natural language, although the idea of such a positive otherness remains alive. Consider, that such a real otherness would be an otherness without the other—and that is impossible. It seems as if nature limits our minds and thus as if randomness as well as uncertainty challenge human life. They do so in all layers of human existence by means of cognition—that is the reason why it is possible that causes are not guaranteed to be linked to effects, and for instance an electron or any subatomic entity can be everywhere or nowhere unless a human cognition measures it. Here is Plato's image and its effects again: it is as if human knowledge can measure the unknown thanks to its technology, and thanks to its philosophy acquire speculative

[5]The word 'evidence' is linked to parallels in diverse European languages. The German expression *Selbstverständlichkeit* and the Dutch *Vanzelfsprekendheid* are most fascinating: they underline two constitutive components 'Self' resp. 'Zelf' and 'Verstehen' resp 'Spreken' in a meaningful manner.

insights based on unknown matters like the transcendence. It is as if we should not debate how to *explore knowledge* that challenge our categories of space and time, but that we should only carefully *listen* to what could become said about relevant otherness. It means, we should cancel the gaps and difference between listening and thinking. This is the challenge of digital thought formation and digital practices: one should encircle the unknown as well as the unknowable to keep our thought formation intact.

It is clear how considerations about a Platonic character of the digital culture and the explorations of cyberspace lead to deeply anchored philosophical thoughts. They are much more than a clarifying or classifying determination. They concern the entire process of human cognition and all aspects related to knowledgeable aspects of what is called 'reality'. The latter seems in the light of developments which pertain to the digital as well as the quantum theories and technology no longer on what we call *partition*. Our traditional creating and understanding of knowledgeable units should represent relevant fragments of reality. Our reference to a *totality* which precedes every partition should become the major theme of analyzing our knowledge. This leads to a deeper understanding of *conversion* as a cloud and as a process. A pressing question which belongs to a deeper understanding of conversion related to our cognition is, whether the unfolding of the digital culture and the major developments of AI or the quantum technology will not lead to more complex and richer categories of time and measures. It means that we should perhaps try to learn and accept ideas which were not thought before. This comes up when we read a quantum technologist explain how a single object can move as if it were two different objects at the same time under the condition that it is extremely small or in a lowest possible temperature. How can we bring such thoughts to the fore as acceptable? It hurts our own ideas about our Self, as explored in all variations of a philosophical and social anthropology. It could thus very well be, that *conversion* is the term which indicates a new view on human knowledge which is underlined in the digital age. Borderlines of human cognition seem to change when time and measure appear to differ in digital and quantum thoughts in comparison to the classical analog patterns. Conversion truly challenges our cognition in a most fundamental way.

7.2 The Plural in the Natural

Cognition not only challenges, but also changes in our days because of the continuous and variant pressures caused by conversion. Human knowledge remains one of the most important powers in life on the planet—but an unfolding knowledge transforms the wealth of human existence. Borderlines between determinable levels are never secured; they are continuously dynamized. In earlier days, they were the result of only one type of thought formation, which was a knowledge unaware of conversion. But our days unfold in the middle of all consequences of a reordering cognition. Keep in mind, that changes in human practices and thought patterns are elements of a continuity in the cosmos which is related to human existences. An actual conclusion concerns the absence of deeply rooted breaks and highly functional borders and limits, but on the other hand an awareness which Heim formulated: 'with an electronic infrastructure, the dream of perfect forms becomes the dream of information'.. Plurality and its determinations seem the major issue at hand. What are their effects?

We envision a metaphysics-of-the-digital, but does it enforce an understanding of the inner structure of human consciousness, cognition, and mind? So, do we accept the prevalence of a continuity based on a disregard of breaches, limits and boundaries in human history and its thought formations? Be clear: is the computer-nerd or today the IT-er who dived into digital thoughts and techniques, bravely following lines of Platonic thought? And what do we think or understand when we perceive that attitude? No, this does not fit to what was explained in the above pages—it would namely not be a sign of accepting and realizing what Voegelin named 'the flow'. The flow does not suggest that breaches, limits, or constraints are almost meaningless. On the contrary: the flow underlines that they provide us orientation, clarify our world, and stimulate new thoughts. For short: what was named 'the flow' is essentially the continuous process of change that creates cognition. Not only what Plato thought but how these thoughts were broken, changed or reformulated, experienced, and documented, limited and brought to new open horizons, determines our culture and existence. In that context is to consider that without barriers and breaches would not a single nerd with his knowledge and skills become appreciable in the twenty-first century!

Indeed, a flow without breaches, limits, translations, or transitions seems impossible. The soul of Platonism is only experienced at a moment of the multiple discussions about Plato's basic ideas, as are those of Descartes on an understanding of his ego or the stringent lines of reasoning suggested by Wittgenstein. By foregrounding temporality, movement, and other ways of knowing, we aim at the experience of what probes into the specificities of life and its various amphibious anthropologies. The varieties of the latter mirror the specificity of the multidimensional and temporalities surpassing flow. Our vivid interest in Plato or Aristotle pertains to the many moments during which new ideas or insights are unconsciously as well as consciously born. But such interest is never alone or just one precisely determinable factor in history.

A seldom mentioned example concerning the dynamics of the flow can be read in Max Weber's 1905 publication with the original title *Die protestantische Ethik und der Geist des Kapitalismus*.[6] Weber remembers that a newly conceived technique of administration was developed in the days of the theologian Calvin (1509–1564) named 'double entry accounting'! The new accounting technique caused important thoughts and events but above all new developments and appreciations of mastering capitals. The ideal and its need for a technical improvement were not condemned by any religiously anchored practices. And economy seemed not distanced from religious mainstreams. On the contrary: edge breaks in administration and accounting

[6]Weber (2002). Part 2, Ch. IV, a: Rationalization of the World.

lead—as this fragment of the history of modern capitalism demonstrates—to new patterns of culture. What looks like a process of secularization appears to be the moving and new direction of a flowing culture. The latter occurred via an appreciation of borderlines and the recognition of breaking edges. Boundary crossings might indeed create new dimensions of culture!

One question remains: does indeed '*an essence of history and cultural flow'* ever exist, and is it to be grasped in an unfolding cognition process? Voegelin suggested that philosophical analyses might not guarantee our attempts to define an essence of history, 'for the drama of history is not yet completed and thus not given as a thing about the essence of which one could state propositions; and the philosopher does not look at this non-thing as an observer but, in philosophizing, turns into an actor in the drama about which he wants to make statements.'[7] A few years after this conclusion, in 1966, he focused on 'political reality' as a framework within which we understand the functioning of noesis, the exercise of reason. This has in Husserl's thoughts been the subjective aspect of an intentional experience. A special intentionality is a major form of the drama in which all human statements must find their place. Voegelin concludes decisively: 'The realm of man ... is empirically determined (a) by the history of the knowledge of participation and of the phenomena of order derived from there, and (b) by the historically respective level of noetic exegesis.' He thus concludes that no theoretical construction from whatever origin can change those dynamics under the title of 'theory'.[8]

Wrestling to obtain knowledge of the flow and of all that exists within it, implies wrestling with its multiple edges, limits, change, varieties, differences, and other characteristics. The latter are understood as 'natural composites' of the flow, often in extreme non-naïve-natural contexts. They thus determine human knowledge, its self-knowledge included. These last words have an almost alienating effect: do edges and breaks determine specific limits of the non-naïve-natural region in which human knowledge unfolds? They do not, because there are in essence no such limits. *The 'un-thinkable' pertains only to a move in the human mind.* The term indicates that our thought formation is a historical process, so that its profiles remain determinable. But who is going to find and study them? The question leads straightforwardly to the functioning and managing of the noesis. But who is going to observe and maintain this order? Do we have to search such an order in the self-interpreting consciousness and its process of transcendence? Martin Buber provided a view: it occurs in the co-existence with the *other*. Lévi-Strauss wanted to find a reliable comparison: do not strive to compare with a single other individual, but with another cultural pattern so that a comparison would enrich each noetic grip. The thinking mind would embrace a mode to acknowledge and clarify sameness caused and enlightened by differing lights, as Goethe suggested. Or should we, not unlike Spengler or Toynbee, patiently wait up until the decay of Western culture takes place, so that another cultural pattern can take over? *Is the digital such a pattern?* It remains all in all

[7]Ch. 1, § 3; E. Voegelin, *Op. Cit.*, p. 116.

[8]E. Voegelin, *Op. Cit.*, p. 208.

fascinating how such thoughts develop and even overshadow the actual climate change problems as well as newly effective patterns of thought and experience, not to mention new forms of thinking like the AI or the Quantum theories show. Questioning the flow remains the major issue; the 'we' remains its riddle!

Our cognition as well as its noetic processing in which we are involved—mainly via thought and observation—seems above all an historic process. Any ego-position (particularly those belonging to what Husserl called the 'non-naïve-natural' position) is in essence a form of self-determination in the realm of history. This insight includes a view on plurality. The latter appears to solve a major noetic problem: all acts of self-reflection are in essence a change of attitude, and the plural is necessary for those acts to unfold.

Understanding the features of the flow equals an understanding of oneself. And the latter is a matter of changing attitude. Equality is in that light a moment in which the *actor* is understood as an *agens*. Self-understanding that makes the knowledgeable and above all the knowing subject an *agens* is a basic feature of the non-naïve-natural attitude. The latter appears as one of the most important zones of knowledge formation, we conclude. This is by no means a fixating move of thought formation, as the analog-digital dichotomy elucidates. Forms of thought deliver insight in other forms, no matter whether they are contrasting or harmonious. Human experience and knowledge show us a powerful and enduring flow of signs and meanings, which unfold as soon as language is envisioned. We learn that there is insight and new life through participation in the flow, although we often only think about it in terms of pure application.

7.3 Barriers and Bridges

Barrers and bridges are perhaps the most important elements of understanding meanings and signs, and therefore knowledge of any type and importance. Indeed: facing a barrier, being forced to use a bridge or accept and take a bypass makes us challenge the flow of life whilst uttering a sound: a *phew*, *ouch* or perhaps an *oops*. With them we place the barrier in the realm of language. The ego underlines language in all such barrier cases—but: oops! What does it mean? The words of the question are already part of an answer. The 'oops' leads to language which expresses a borderline, and the latter must almost certainly be passed. Its sound announces a transit, a transformation, a differentiation, or a renewed attempt, which seems very important and is therefore understood as a sign. We understand the 'oops' as a surprising and un-expected utterance of semiotic nature. The breach that causes the sound and its verbal expression is the sign that is put away in meanings of the word and its dynamics.

This interference of language and lingual expressivity in thoughts and knowledge has no dimensions. Hence our emphasis on words like 'breaches' and 'barriers' which are hardly knowable in the broader pictures of culture. Thy could have relevance for our in-depth cognition of meaning and sense, but they are today not studied in semiotics or any epistemology. That is no surprise: they mostly concern phenomena which unfold far beyond the limits of our expectations or perception. Unexpected presences of powers and signs from which we cannot decide whether they are produced by our device or from other instigations, appear in our laboratories and experimental settings. What is a 'frame of knowledge' or 'cognition in general' in this context? No wonder, that the answer 'they are data' became acceptable! But they bring the digital to the fore—a setting which does not embrace cognition but focuses on conversion and changed our 'grasping' of a reality into a 'fitting'.

Oops! Is it not a sign to be understood as the notification of the quoted noetic exegesis of consciousness change? In other words: a borderline must be surpassed and with it there is the actual recognition of difference: the realm of the non-naïve-natural appeared to have its limits! No wonder that we were obliged to respect and understand this complexity as our *noetic consciousness*. The movement of mind, which originates in existential tensions, transcends our consciousness, and expands the realm of the non-naïve-natural and its specific attitude. But the actuality, which was in the preceding pages given the name: 'The New Plural', should also be understood as such a meaningful sign. It is bound in expressivity and types of language, which indicate the 'objective lines.' Their stimulus is the difference between analog and digital expressivities! Not only the variety of fields that challenges the noetic process is important, but also the possibilities of transferring from one to another! Transition and transference are in the world of analog expressivities widely acknowledged in a form of translation, but when the plurality of analog *and* digital languages is at stake, then the translation appears to be limited by its analog patterning! In the case of the two expressions, we must cover our understanding of transference among types of expressivities and name it: conversion. Without deeper insight into that process is no understanding of the New Plural possible. Of all elements, fixated as well as changing, is one consideration of central importance. *The New Plural, as mentioned before, and the Self that functions in this Plural by means of creating and exploring its Selfie, determine cognition - all possibilities of conversion included!*

That determination is outlined in a remarkable manner when the *Digital* and the *Artificial Intelligence* are in effect; they appear to be different (but are not) when the *Quantum Mechanics* are considered. That relates to the fact that 'the non-naïve-natural' delivered hitherto unexplored lines of knowing and understanding reality related to human selves. They are to be understood in the digital component of the New Plural as *selfies*. In the case of the noetic position are, however, the barriers between the 'natural' and the 'non-natural' still the most important to envisage. Emphasis on the 'natural' fascinates, and borderline problems unveil delineations. A major issue becomes articulated: *is human intelligence operative on both sides of the barrier between the natural and the non-natural, and thus prepared for being understood in the 'New Plural'?* At the center of this consideration is the noetic position of the digital as well as the AI: do they have its origin in a 'natural' sphere? So, what is there to say about the qualities and meanings of the 'natural' and the 'non-natural' as independent qualities in life?

Our third millennium is, remarkably enough, opened by the three patterns (Digital, AI and QM) that reign knowledge in all regards. The three do influence relations among individuals—primarily between Selves and Selfies. The Digital does this more forcefully than other patterns that function in the New Plural. It focuses on data created through understanding and managing facts and practices of *intersubjectivity* as we highlighted in preceding pages. The AI touches correlated intersubjective data and thus creates facts and situations which are in the first place effective in *political* dimensions. In both, the Digital and the AI, are the dimensions of *knowledge* forcefully present. Cognition becomes realized by both in various ways but ultimately in the same way, namely through *datafication*. It is *data* which become known and the ultimate schemes that fixate them are represented by the activity known as *datafication*. In *Quantum Mechanics*, the third pattern of knowledge distinguished in the New Plural, knowledge seems folded technical dimensions, but the latter often remain functional in *intersubjectivity* through the presentation of astonishing facts of nature or of human technicality. An important issue in that context is the role and function of the measurement process, which brings natural issues in the realm of human judgment. The latter are always in plural, and contemplated in intersubjective, i.e., social contexts.[9]

Datafication is also in *Quantum Mechanics* of great interest, one must consider. But those data are at larger distance and less secured in view of our observation, Bohm states. He mentioned in 1980: 'if we try to use the prevailing world view based on the notion of particles, we discover that the 'particles' (such as electrons) can also manifest as waves, that they can move discontinuously, that there are no laws at all that apply in detail to the actual movements of individual particles and that only statistical predictions can be made about large aggregates of such particles. If on the other hand we apply the world view in which the universe is regarded as a continuous field, we find that this field must also be discontinuous, as well as particle-like, and that it is undermined in its actual behavior as is required in the particle view of relation as a whole.' He presents a conclusion that brings the Quantum Theory together with the AI as well as the Digital with the remark, that 'all that counts in physical theory is supposed to be the development of mathematical equations that permit us to predict and control the behavior of large statistical aggregates of particles. Such a goal is . . . a presupposition of most work in modern physics that prediction and control of this kind is all that human knowledge is about.'[10]

It is the link with human intersubjectivity which brings all three knowledge patterns which were mentioned as components of the New Plural together. But one should be aware that, despite the varieties of lingual expression, this unity is made possible by the activity named *datafication.* It is data that enrichen, and complicate human togetherness and it is the common interest in data that forms the Plural into a unity. The engagement with data is deeply based in cooperation with

[9] See Bohm (1979), p. 583f.

[10] Bohm (1980), p. xv f.

a diversity of technical means. Datafication is also much more than a simple digitalization. It shows that actual *cognition* in the frames of datafication and digitalization as well as quantum understandings, touches the deepest levels of the human mind. A game like *AlphaGo* shows that datafication is in essence a matter of data-*generating*,[11] and the related AI tries to achieve knowledge of that process of generating (in which conversion is inherent) beyond factualization. Playing the game is in that context not only a play but also an acquiring of knowledge. Two themes show the political dimensions of the Intelligence in the process of *Artificial Intelligence*.

A *first* is how in contemporary China are provinces and other parts of the State, towns and regions included, who developed an almost omnipotent power in the behaviors of citizens. They live under the dictatorship of data, must obey all data-processing, and possess no cognition or freedom which is external from the data-generation in which they must live. It shows the dangers of AI in its complete control of its political interpretation of *Intelligence* which embraces a large diminishment of individual freedom.

A *second* is in the fact that technical, social as well as scientific opinions became a direct deduction of parts belonging to a generalized data-technology, which took the place of cognition in all regards and perspectives.

Conversion is a central issue in the light of a full development of understanding cognition. Its special character is in our growing awareness of all epistemological consequences of the multiple ego-positions. In other words: this awareness has the role and power of a very central category in knowing the world and understanding life. It relates to the long living culture of natural (in the last century also named 'analog') languages and forms of expression, including their structures, their meaning creation, and related cognitive processes. Noetic insights are especially important in the realm of a recent interpenetration of digital resp. virtual forms of life. Basics for an elaborate understanding of conversion embrace several points of interest:

1. *There is no definitive and fixated contrast between the digital and the analog*—there is only a 'digital *via* (not versus) the analog' relationship in the New Plural possible. In other words: the analog is enforced to express the digital and the latter has the task to do the same for the first. But both unfold at different levels. Those differences profile and determine any reach of human knowledge.
2. A riddle and challenge are the fact that only signs, words, expressions, and comparable lingual *components of analog character create or support an awareness of digital reality.*
3. The infamous everyday language expression 'it is what it is' constitutes such a set of components. Note how it belongs to the *analog expressivity of awareness about digital reality.* The latter does not belong to the semiotic analyses of today,

[11] **AlphaGo** is a computer program that plays the board game Go. It was developed by DeepMind Technologie. See: https://en.wikipedia.org/wiki/AlphaGo.

although such an awareness would contribute to the unfolding of a modern epistemology.

4. insight in *conversion needs an acting subject.* It means, that the analog subject-object relationship remains functioning in common with the digital—or the latter will not exist.
5. The expression *'digital' is not a simple adjective in an analog language.* Meanings of adjectives are determined by the specific type of language in which they function. To reach beyond them is dubious. An example is the globally used natural/analog term, which should renew, reinforce, and globalize traditional features of thought patterns and actions. The term does clearly not indicate a dualism. The digital must be expressed in analog language. But their terms relate to meanings, which eventually reach further than the domain of natural/analog expressivities, even when they become used in analog expressivity.
6. The example of 'the digital' not being simply an adjective is also valid for the term functioning in so-called *computational linguistics*. The expression revises language and literature in the days of the digital. It should unveil the inner forces of the digital as well as its manifold and globally spread digital techniques—even when those are spread over- and integrated in natural/analog types. Their dynamics must be studied at the borderlines of both types of linguistic expressiveness, the analog as well as the digital levels.

The often-mentioned digital revolution was indeed revolutionizing because of its changes of linguistic components, its expressivity, and its forms of self-understanding of the human mind, dominated by the concept of the Self. The digital shift, already in disposition during the last decades of the twentieth century, created today major forms of social togetherness and equivalence, including an intensifying datafication of modern life. Its expression became: 'the Selfie'—an expression which seems valid far beyond any purely photography-like visuality.

Lovelli Fuad constructed a *Very Brief History of the Digital Revolution* based on comparing analog and digital features of attributes such as Adaptability, Continuity, Type of data, Wave types, Media of transmission, Types of values, Security, Capacity, Hardware, Data storage & transmission, Power consumption, Recording and Rates of data transmission.[12] In each of the two systems (or types) of communication is the managing of data essential. Their comparison is mainly based upon notions expressed in analog, i.e., in patterns of natural language. Differences and relations imply an analog character and do not seem expressible in/as digital types of language. But we do not acquire a deeper insight in the specifics of the non-analog lingual expressivity, let alone a comparison and epistemological clarification of these patterns.

One background question pertaining to 'knowledge' remains unanswered in this context: is a non-natural expressivity linguistically expressible *beyond* the analog

[12] Lovelli Fuad: *A Very Brief History of the Digital Revolution – Also Known as the Digital Shift*. In: HUB PAGES at https://hubpages.com/technology/digital-revolution-analysis?. See the basic 1995 article at https://www.ncbi.nlm.nih.gov/pmc/articles/PMC40721.

types of expression? In other words: should the *delineation* of a type of expressivity in essence be treated as a *limitation*? Such questions belong for instance to the interpretation of the brain as a creativity machine. One thus meets the link between cognition and consciousness in the context of conversion possibilities. That link challenges our cognition which seems our most important medium of communicative expressivity and is itself one of the most complex characteristics of human beings. Its complexity has fascinated the field of research from the 1950ies on and accompanied evolving notions of digital techniques and theoretical components. What was in the 1970s the 'Association for Computational Linguistics (ACL)' with emphasis on its task to elaborate 'computational linguistics' is today named 'Natural Language Processing' (NLP). That move is not without importance: the term 'computational linguistics' became replaced, but its components (the modeling use of human language) did not take distance from culture and practices of the digital. Our laptops and more sophisticated types of computers, not unlike our milliards of smart phones, tell us about the omnipresence of the digital in the New Plural.

The NLP suggests that one should study a language (or language in general) as if one enters a process and its object that is structured by nature.[13] Is that an attempt to formulate a newly to develop approach to human knowledge? Notice, how NLP focuses on data. It creates an appeal to the computer which should interpret human language for processing, analyzing, and extracting meaning from data stemming from natural language texts. It thus implies digital means to create (a) awareness of borderlines among fields of language and (b) unfold a capacity (natural or artificial) to focus on otherness—in the first place of languages—beyond borderlines. Both relate to the often-used term that outlines one of the most prominent features of our modern language: its multileveled character. Activities of 'Computational Linguistics' and the actual NLP with language- resp. expressivities processing as a technological priority illustrate the central role of the digital and challenge our understanding of the New Plural. One should not forget that Artificial Intelligence was already in the middle of the twentieth century a cherished branch in the USA. One of the most successful activities was the *automatic translation of foreign language texts into English*. The political color of that achievement became visible in the fact that especially Russian scientific texts became automated via English producing computers. Even when mechanical translation did not survive, the inherent digitally orientated linguistics became successful in its orientation versus intelligent processing of language data.

Borderlines are everywhere in this process. If two languages should be translated into each other, there should be a minimal mastering of their grammar, their morphology, their syntax including the semantics at stake, as well as the relevant vocabulary and traditional forms of expressivity, not to mention the internal differences between speech and text generation. It would be too easy to qualify those *deep functioning borderlines that constitute a human natural language* as unassuming or even irrelevant. On the contrary: they should be understood as belonging to the high-

[13] See https://en.wikipedia.org/wiki/Computational_linguistics.

level regions of the NLP and are immediately relevant for any unfolding of human cognition. The latter is in this context circumscribed as the mental action or process of acquiring knowledge and understanding by means of thought, experience, and sense-activities. It is clearly deductible from these correlations in what meaningful manner the digital became an element of globally understood and practiced human cognition—even beyond the borderlines between theory and praxis.

This meaningfulness should be sharpened in the case of a philosophical approach to modern cognition. Its sharpness, concreteness, and importance weights. The unique situation in which borderline occurrences confronting the natural with the non-natural as create new dimensions of plurals (which are different from adding new pluralities) are perhaps the most important building blocks. The understanding and even mastering of them is the major component of the 'Process' or 'Processing' in the NLP. But the NLP did not consider that all borderlines can change in the course of human cultural history. Envisaging these blocks appeared to be a constitutive element of cultural change. The unfolding as well as the understanding of the New Plural proves this in an unexpected manner. The study of the blocks and their functioning created such an insight. Conversion remains a major part of those P's—each of them being a ground word of knowledge. But one should not forget how the enormous power and global validity of each such word confirms the constitutive power of our understanding of what Searle once named 'the principles of possible expressivity' as components of speech of an 'I', a 'subject', a 'self' and a 'selfie': four terms which represent one of the most important lines of development of modern culture in world-wide dimensions.[14]

Again: one should not underestimate the importance of the borderlines or limits concerned. They became constitutive even in quantum languages. Once recognized as 'ground words', they appeared to be embodied as 'meaning' in types of digital expression. Their interweaving forms the network of the continuous flows, which words create. We call them 'speech' in daily life. Datafication seems impossible without this network; the digital thus reaches far beyond a pure functioning of digits. But an important conclusion can be formulated in the light of this multileveled character of language. If we can give a named position to boundaries, area borders, types of effect and insight or regions of research and knowledge—such as for example a non-naïve-natural region versus a non-natural—then we intensify our attempts to broaden the concept of cognition. With that attempt, we will also emphasize the many regions of transition between those areas. Cognition and conversion become in this light more understandable than ever. The area of computational linguistics will enhance that very modern understandability. It's important to remember and revalue how George Lakoff[15] underlined the insight that *Cognitive Linguistics* seem based on the fact, that *any idea, thought or formulation could always be understood in terms of another.* In the case of exploring one word, there is always a different word that can replace it or might provide a nuanced meaning. That

[14] Searle (1969).

[15] Lakoff (1999), p. 569 ff.

dynamics in- or around a word can bring us to metaphorical or other types of understanding.

Note that such an undeterminable partner has always to be of the same type: a digital term can for instance not function in the framework of a natural/analog language without losing digital features, effects and understanding. Lakoff completed these thoughts in 1999 by his observation that a word, a phrase, a sentence and even a fragment of a larger text can attribute a meaning based on information articulated before- or after that word or phrase. That is: *no word, phrase or other linguistic fragment will have a meaning exclusively on its own.* A word is never a word without other words, and that is also the case with phrases, sentences, texts, and other language fragments. It parallels the insight, that *no Self can ever be a Self without other Selves.* We are never ever able to think, speak or write without and/or beyond related lingual fragments. The general idea expressed in this rather simple consideration is, that language as such and is in essence multilingual, like the Self is a social phenomenon. No linguistic element can be in function on itself beyond- or at distance from its proper type of language, that is: without other words, sentences, texts, or images (as Benjamin's 'Sprachgestalt' suggests). This is one of the features of an 'open texture': language is in the adventure of its proper realization a continuum of phenomena, which stretches from expected to novel and unforeseeable articulations within the boundaries of a linguistic tradition and type.

Lakoff should have concluded that a human word is, not unlike a human person, in essence social, i.e., multiple. That multiplicity makes communication one of the decisive features of language and lingual research. It fascinates in this context, how for instance computational linguistics, NLP, neurosciences, or various forms of Artificial Intelligence (in their different contexts and circumstances) report about certain variations of this experience which are colored according to their field. But they have always to respect the *boundaries of their specific type of expressivity.* There is no strict borderline between the meanings of a word, other fields of information and data management. That is the riddle of these observations: communication awakens the importance and interest of limits and boundaries, in consequence for fundamental plurals. A fascinating conclusion is that neither the NLP nor AI or for instance linguistically orientated neurosciences, provide a relevant theory of implication in which borderlines between types of language (such as natural/analog and digital) are explicitly analyzed. Yet, one must remark that they are phenomena, facts, data, or issues of importance in understanding cognition and its relationship with conversion.

7.4 Conversion: The Story of the DAC's

We pay attention to a theme that would today no longer be valuated as an important pillar of the digital techniques and its global culture: the conversion techniques alias the DAC's. One must broadly focus on the contrasts between analog and digital expressivities to understand the concept of *conversion.* That understanding gives the tensions between the fields of analog and digital thought formation a new life. The two types, analog and digital, do not form a pair, a duo, or any other form of duality. The most important function and feature of the two is their intertwining which always occurs with a specific objective.

To formulate more precisely:

Analog expressions intertwine to create or sustain *cognition*; digital creations intertwine to adjust and configurate relations (everything related to everything) which create *conversion*.

This is reflected in the no longer foreground-story of the two DAC's, the ADC (Analog–Digital-Convertor), and the DAC (Digital–Analog–Convertor).[16] But several of the most important insights and developments of those DAC's are nevertheless important for a deeper understanding of the actual functioning of the digital culture which acquired global dimensions. Hence this paragraph under the title 'the story of the DAC's', which grounds several of the broader insights and experiences in our days. They could be brought together in a phrase which was already formulated in earlier pages and suggested the important change from 'knowledge is to grasp' to 'knowledge is to fit'. In other words: the *grasping* is a matter of the *subject as creator* in its role of causing knowledge; the *fitting* is a matter of the *subject as receiver* causing knowledge.

One should in the first place keep in mind, that a digital attitude does not concern every*thing* but also every*body*; communication is therefore a central concept (and effect) in the digital world. Those observations ground the meaning of this paragraph's title: *conversion* pertains to transversion, to communication between material processes as well as social individuals, and is therefore finally directed towards *cognition*. Be aware: we live in an analog world, and its analog specificities reach out to infinite facts and qualities. Our bodies are framed in infinite colors, numbers, tones, smells, judgments, questions, data, and signals. Possibilities created by them are infinite. And all of them seem in our contemporary world enclosed in either analog or digital expressivities. Their differences are multiple: Any analog signal is a continuous signal, it represents information, has many possibilities to create other relevant signals and is mostly occurring in real-time to provide a certain freedom of ranging issues.

In the second place, we keep in mind that digital signals are time-separated via digital modulation. They use discrete 0's and 1's to represent flexible information and implementation. They never guarantee that digital signal processing can be performed in real time. And their instruments never cause any kind of observation errors. This sustains the leading thesis of this book. A question 'why we need

[16] https://en.wikipedia.org/wiki/Digital-to-analog_converter https --and www.google.be/search?sxsrf=ALeKk00tyEfP62nTLyxaGQIK29w5dKigsw:1606904434277&q=analog+vs+digital Some two decades ago was the DAC a central topic to understand in the digital world and its techniques. Today is a DAC a fragment of the more general fitting, completion and streaming of digital elements and moments. The expressions DAC and ADC are hardly used anymore. The DAC was from the beginning of this evolution indicating *both* forms of conversion as a generality and the *one* specific Digital Conversion process.

conversion' is easily posed but its answer is a complicated process. One of the *first* constraints which are laid down by the digital world is, that the *subject* we want to approach must be transformed into *data*; a next step is to deal with conversion is therefore the *conversion of data*. The *second* is, that *specific types* of converters are feasible. Dominants are the analog to digital converter and the digital to analog converter. The *third* is, that studying, or other forms of approaching data requires a *practice* of these converting interfaces. They are essential to digital electronic equipment as well as to an analog electric device and its processor.

Today take human actions, words, insights, thought patterns and reflections place in an extended and mostly non-naïve-natural noetic sphere of convertibility. If there is no conversion, philosophers speak of a 'state of nature' which they qualify as 'natural'. But many 'conversion' occurrences are effective in very different circumstances and scientific approaches. That is inherent to our modern languages which are featured by a continuous intertwining of analog and digital expressivities—not by only one of these and separated from the other. This implies not only a *natural* but a *cultural* understanding of technical, economical, and socio-political features. *There exists no human understanding without an intertwinement of the multiple types of expressivities which are effective in the period we named the New Plural.*

Conversion is the marrowbone of the 'digital' in the contemporary New Plural. Internet connections exist since 2000; the activity of conversions became profiled in the first 3D Printer in 2009. Notions pertaining to conversion which evolves since the second decade of the twenty-first century are hardly systematized: they reach from entertainment and artistic manifestations to sports and psychological therapy. They include economics, finances, and cyber-law along with property law and copyrights—for short: conversions are truly a recent phenomenon. Their focus is on computer sciences and computer technology plus Artificial Intelligence, whereby the digital language type seems most prominent, effective, and clear.

Our omnipresent interest for data reinforces the conversion in general. Indeed, data are indispensable for digital devices. The in- and output of computers is always connected with formats, who belong to forms of digital expression and thus need conversions to achieve general performances. It is clear: we need them because we live in a world of data. They are effective in the social process we call since 2013 *datafication* and are approached as if they were an element of 'nature'. But actual problems concerning for instance 'privacy' in the context of digital programs illustrate the vulnerability of the parallel between datafication processes and the unfolding of human cognition. And moreover, conversions remain essential while we manipulate and explore data. An important goal of the digital equipment is to measure, filter or compress and send real-world analog signals. The concept 'conversion' received extraordinary meaning and attention because of its close ties with two standard expressions related to the ties between analog and digital types of expressiveness and lingual articulation.

Two conversion devices unfolded in the first decade of the twenty-first century and were treated as founding insights.[17] When studied in their individual technical and cultural context, they took a special place in the framework of the New Plural. Two practices were understood by the IT technicians as well as the social scientists as *a form of the binary character of analog and digital expressivity*. They were for instance perceived in a conversion process where an ADC conversion creates sound effects which a DAC will process back into analog effects as used by audio output equipments such as a speaker. All data ultimately require conversion to an analog signal to interact with the world of lingual expressivities:[18] their omnipresence in all disciplines, techniques and thought patterns is based on complex processes of intertwining. But their interpretation and managing as if they existed *as a duo,* or as *a pair,* remained in force.

The digital has therefore in the beginnings of the developing New Plural been understood as a counterpart of the analog tradition. And until today, the digital let not go any analog expression. This has certainly contributed to some one-sidedness of social and cultural insights in the culture of the digital, new dimensions of cognition included. But we should keep in mind that the history of the DAC and the ADC is a history *within* the more general history of the digital. Their expressivities integrated during the second decade of the unfolding millennium in the multiple problems and renewed technical as well as social features of the digital. The integration of the two conversion techniques proves how they are not a fixated dual but constituents of a continuously evolving process of significances, insights and meanings which create *cognition* in the broadest sense and are in what we named the New Plural. The specific role of both types of conversion became darkened and unattended during their integration in the new type of flow which the digital enforced. With this loss of insight in their constitutive roles were historical, epistemological as well as semiotic dimensions neglected. The understanding and evolution of the DAC concentrated primarily on sound and particularly music, whereas lingual expressivity, such as the meaning and sense of words, was less intensively noticed and practiced. Digital photography, digital cameras, or even pixels did not change that situation.

One must distinguish therefore in the DAC the 'Sound-DAC' (the S-DAC) from the 'Language-DAC' (the L-DAC). Verbal as well as non-verbal expressivity seems to be determined by this differentiation—the first do often approximate digital expressions more than the last. This should intensify *semiotic research about conversion* in general. The DAC is important in that regard: any DAC (the S-DAC as well as the L-DAC) is a twin brother of an ADC, the analog-digital convertor. An interpretation of signs and understanding of meanings belongs to the soul of DAC's. Their twinning and its implications should never be forgotten; any consideration that

[17] https://www.elprocus.com/digital-to-analog-converter-dac-applications/Unicode Technical Cie.: 2019. *Unicode Emoji Subcommittee,* subcommittee of–, Technical Committee Procedures, at http://unicode.org/emoji/

www.rohm.com/electronics-basics/ad-da-converters/da-converter-configurations https: www.en.wikipedia.org/wiki/Artificial_intelligence.

[18] Cf.: https://www.elprocus.com/digital-to-analog-converter-dac-applications/.

focuses on the DAC must ultimately unfold in the heart of patterns that format the daily world, and this formatting is mostly linked to analog expressivities. But the question remains: how? The analog type of language, technique and thought formation will always accompany the conversion process involving or even realizing the digital world! Verbal expressions appear as near and neighbored to digital expressions than non-verbal. That should intensify any semiotic research concerning conversion and the process of cognition which should also be socio-politically orientated.

Sounds are perhaps the most important factor of any DAC and its resolution through which the device can be defined. That is in fact the case with the S-DAC which is different from the L-DAC. We first concentrate on the S-DAC ability to precisely define the device in the case of musical players, TVs, and smart phones, which convert digital data streams into analog audio signals, and thus connect to screen drivers which display images on that basis. Any audio DAC (S-DAC) is a low frequency, high-resolution type whereas the video DAC (almost identical with S-DACs) is a high-frequency low- to medium-resolution type. It became the most important variation of all DACs and we thus experience how much this history of conversion is involved in our listening! That becomes confirmed with nearly all developments of contemporary music. Central meaning for musical effects has the digital music studio, the DAW. That digital studio is the location of a technically sophisticated and most effective mastering of bringing musical effects and human affects together.

This process replaces the traditional and analog inspired 'listening' and reverb, delay, chorus as well as other modular sounds. The *Dawn FM* livestream is a globally known example.[19] It is a studio album that does not provide the performance of one or more artists but organizes many contributions from a variety of authors. The ultimate totality of this Sound Product brought narrations, vocals and spoken words of English language origin together through the managing of several constitutive elements. Some were from the 'New Wave' around 1980, others from actual electronic dance music and funk sounds. Effects like reverbs, delays, or chorus did influence the final musical lines; they are a forceful example of the new digital techniques and attitudes in the realm of sound. Semiotically interesting is the emphasis on *organization* of the Sound. 'Organization' means here: the digitally structured togetherness of all components in harmony and fluency. Philosophically must be emphasized, that the *Dawn FM* is based on a powerful and inspiring *decentering of Sound Origins*. There is no Subject in the traditional sense of the word, no violinist, harpist or pianist, singer or songwriter, no reciter, even no dancer on electronic music. This decentering reenforces all sound presentations in accordance with digital principles and customs. Its presentation appears to be a matter of

[19] https://en.wikipedia.org/wiki/Dawn_FM ***Dawn FM*** is the fifth studio album by Canadian singer-songwriter the Weeknd, released on January 7, 2022, through XO and Republic Records. It features narration by Jim Carrey, guest vocals from Tyler, the Creator and Lil Wayne, and spoken word appearances from Quincy Jones and Josh Safdie.

organization, presence, and acceptance of the digit in rhythm and rhyme. The process shows how the digital does not interpret human cognition via the traditional and globally recognized duality of a subject–object relationship.

Fifty years ago, analog signals were pressed into record grooves. The needle on your turntable 'felt' them, created electrical analog signals, and finally transmitted them to your speakers. Today, all recording creates digital audio signals which need to be converted to analog signals. For that, you buy a DAC. They are offered on WWW sites from $25.- to $2.500.- and more (access the Yamaha Disklavier MIDI) because an outboard DAC delivers better sound quality thanks to their connections and cables in silver and gold! It all depends on whether you listen via your smart phone, your laptop, via more sophisticated Home Stereo Systems, or your own piano. The better quality the DAC delivers, the more you enjoy acoustically—especially sounds and music, but also spoken words in their musical contexts. Their quality is at stake, as embodied in the relevant data, which determine the area of sound and sound conversion, and unfolds at distance from all other constituents of the inherent conversion processes, such as emotion, attitude, or lifestyle quality.[20]

A general idea is that *one of the anchor places of conversion can be in the domain of sound*. Until the second half of the last century was sound understood and expressed in terms of analog language. Words about sounds were analog and their alterations resp. conversions, even the creation of new words, took place without changing that analog character. Appreciation, emotional reaction, and the qualification of sound were at stake. Music was evidently its most profiled field; it comprised all forms of expression, which articulated the desire to change, and thus to deeply master, sound. Conversions thus produced changes within the domain of analog expressivity. But what is their impact? Dominantly analog sound production brings tones that were sharpened or dulled, suggest distance or proximity, are darker or lighter, warmer, or even cooler, more apt for chamber music or for orchestral execution, and more inwards or more outwards directed. All those precisely mastered changes parallel with differentiations neurologists characterized as *emotional.* These could be related to smaller or larger regions of the human body. It is fascinating that *neurological studies parallel the S-DAC* in many regards although they do not refer to the specificity of L-DACs.

A 2018 study of Lauri Nummenmaa provides us a map of 100 bodies, which locate relevant emotions in various places of the human body—and it is remarkable how those played a role in the first conversions It should be noticed that predominantly positive feelings and emotions parallel musical sounds. That is the case with imagining, attending, recognition, remembering, surprise, relaxation, love, togetherness, warmth, closeness or feeling touch. But negative feelings are not entirely excluded; one also mentions dizziness, numbness, anger, hostility, disgust, aching,

[20]This makes clear, that *speech* is by no means a matter of *individual* drive, or of some individuals together—but a matter of *the polis*: the completely organized and equipped society. See: Vernant (1982), p. 49f.

hangover, or stomach complains. The map displays bodily locations as indicated by the participants, so that a unique topography of bodily-located sensations is available. Voluntary reproductions of bodily states are on that map associated with specifically named emotions and their subjective feelings. He thus explained how he 'used a topographical self-report tool to reveal that different emotional states are associated with topographically distinct and culturally universal bodily sensations; these sensations could underlie our conscious emotional experiences. Monitoring the topography of emotion-triggered bodily sensations brings forth a unique tool for emotion research and could even provide a biomarker for emotional disorders.'[21]

Effects of sound/music are apparently not *imprisoned* in head or brain! They form in their totality a background for AD as well as DA conversions and fulfill that function also when the conversions reached out towards Digital conversions, i.e., when the digital type of expressivity became part of the conversion domain. Effects of sound/music form in their totality a background for AD as well as DA conversions and fulfill that function also when the conversions reached out towards Digital conversions, i.e., when the digital type of expression became part of the conversion domain. The spotting of the emoji in the late 1990's and Apple's exploration as well as the USA Unicode in 2011 and later years demonstrates this close connection with the 2018 study of emotions.[22]

That situation is changing in the case of an ADC-type of conversion, in which digital notions intertwine with analog components to achieve digital results. These lead during the last decades to sophisticated technical instruments (merchandized to generalize sounds and types of music) that were compatible with the habits and requirements of digital culture, as the *Dawn FM* showed. Results of S–DAC conversion were at a larger distance to directly registered emotions, although focused on technicalities linked to sound and music, especially those of TV, discs, and smart phones. A background ideal was the widening and improvement of interhuman communication. That development was achieved when the entire conversion domain became perfected, economically active, and socio-culturally accepted. One concludes that this development represents a history of special types of conversion, from sound to music and from music to technology. But the most profiled conversion was the change from Analog to Digital types of expression, so that the DA conversion fulfills an axial role.

Conversions are today indispensable for global digital technicalities and the worldwide economics of digital devices. This is linked to the fact that computers only recognize digital information, so that in- and output is always connected to digital formats/types of language. But some devices realizing output will only accept

---

[21] A fascinating parallel is in a recent ECO-GEOGRAPHICAL APPROACH TO LANDSCAPES of Tieskens (2019) (7). 325.000 photos of landscapes were researched in their relation to emotional expressions in ordinary language, such as 'airy', 'mountainous', 'highland', 'sea', 'cloudy' etc. Not the idyllic pastoral landscapes but rather chains of mountains or coastal zones and rivers were appreciated as 'iconic'. See Nummenmaa c.s.: https://www.pnas.org/doi/10.1073/pnas.1321664111.

[22] Unicode Technical Cie.: 2019. *Unicode Emoji Subcommittee,* subcommittee of–, Technical Committee Procedures, at http://unicode.org/emoji/. Broekman (2020).

analog input. The use of a DAC is thus needed in all cases of any use of whatever type of computer! Numbers of its bits or its step sizes define a S-DAC resolution—but why do we need data converters? Ultimately because all computing is in essence converting! While manipulating data, the two converting interfaces of the ADC and the DAC are essential to digital electronic equipment plus an analog device. The irrevocable fact of the omnipresence of DAC's is that all data ultimately require conversion to an analog signal to interact with the real world.

This interaction has many colors and psychological aspects, which constitute the basic feelings of participation in a recent modernized culture. They lead away from what was even in the last decades of the twentieth century intensively connected with a *semiotic* underlining of human relations. The latter unfolded under the title of 'inter-subjectivity', which seems two or three decades later an old-fashioned concept that does not serve any consolidation of social structures or ideals, let alone *data*! No, today—in the first days of the third twenty-first century decade—one underlines the many constitutive moments of what today's interests mention as 'sound managing' in the developments of the S-DAC, its virtual economic structures and powers included. The latter are after all digitally engraved, subjected to continuous conversion, and related DAC activities *at large distance from sentiments or dual human relations*. In other words: the object of the S-DAC and its specific field plus activity became *sound as a state of data* with sense dispositions managed via digital insights, powers, and instruments! The latter became very important factors of a virtual economics in digital techniques as well as mentality in this framework in which the S-DAC appears as a primary instrument of sound management. The *DAWN FM* we discussed in the above lines is one of the clearest examples of the power of the mentioned factors at stake in these cases.

The most important specification of an S-DAC or and L-DAC is in its very precise resolution. For instance, the number of its bits is essential in defining each device. That is the case with the S-DAC, but it is different with the L-DAC. Improving a sound quality differs from new understandings of different types of language or expressivity, including the transcendence of barriers between analog and other linguistic types. Whoever studies patterns of daily language conversations will conclude that a precise defining of words, signs, and other components of spoken language (sound elements included) seems impossible and is in most cases irrelevant. Such an experience characterizes the phenomenon of human expressiveness and distinguishes possible uses of a DAC in the digital electronic world. There are hitherto only a few specific features that appreciate the L-DAC, so that *further research, especially in semiotics, should unfold*.

The insight that 'there is in our digital age no cognition without conversion' implies that *relations between S-DAC and L-DAC must be systematically researched as semiotic projects*. Of greatest importance in a general understanding of cognition are the borderlines in the non-naive-natural ego positions. Noetic components focus continuously on them. Their specificities involve a conversion, and the transitions in the non-naïve-natural position as well as those external to them are a key in understanding the appropriate semiotic dimensions of modern cognition. The L-DAC seems exceptionally empowered to highlight philosophical and semiotic approaches. But today's field of a DAC is mainly technical, mathematical, or scientific and related to electronic means and media or the field features such as Big Data and Apps in general, as the 2019 discussions about Facebook and its privacy illustrate. A special attention for highlighting the L-DAC seems necessary.

Any further research in the basic components of this L-DAC must be based on the observation that not only in the electronic world, but also in the world of our daily speech is the differentiation between analog and digital type of expression essential. In that light appear speech and electronics as parallel events of everyday life. Like in the world of electronics, is in the world of language and speech a conversion between the two types of expression essential. A point is already mentioned: there exist multiple electronic devices for a DAC conversion, but there is no instrument—not even a dictionary—that can be considered as a device specifically useful for an L–DAC and related linguistic DAC conversions!

This failing balance between *ordinary speech* and *ordinary use of electronics* does not inspire a theory or philosophy of language to consider this issue more profoundly. Emphasis is on the specificities of digital communication, which became familiar in today's so-called 'social media'. They created a new digital landscape in human communication. The question whether the digital character of such a landscape fulfills the central question of communication' to reach out to the other', is never formulated. Who is 'the other', and: what is 'communication' in digital worlds? That question is often raised but one aspect should be highlighted again: technological possibilities which the DAC and in particular the L-DAC witness, broaden the human field of expressivities. That broadening is much more than only an expansion of technical qualities and abilities. The L-DAC tells the S-DAC that expressions of human language are reaching far beyond single conversion technicalities. Introducing the L-DAC must keep an eye on two peculiar issues. An urgent question is how this attention can unfold. We underline a few issues of that context.

The *first* is that converters have in general many tools available. It would be of interest to find out, which tools are determinative, and which are excluded in linguistic DAC activities. Since there does not exist a systematic theory of the DAC in general, one must search for traces of the DAC structure in the multiple conversion effects—a semiotic research project that became hitherto not realized.

The *second* is, that DACs embrace many and various techniques, whereas the L-DAC shows a specific and characteristic pattern that relates with the S-DAC but is not identical with the latter.

A list of conversion tools is long and varied. They show for instance spreadsheet databases regarding macro packages or plug-ins. That is only one of the many examples where DACs reach out to mathematical, technical, or scientific applications. Their tools focus on varieties of factors, such as data characteristics, on length, surface, volume, angle, mass, time, speed of physical quantities becoming specific functions. They reach out to applications in various fields as mentioned via those tools. A DAC can take a precise number to convert into a physical quantity, such as a voltage or pressure, or precision time series data to a continually varying physical signal,[23] but there are fascinating limitations to register. None of the above-mentioned issues is useful for- or directed towards language or broader linguistic phenomena. Why is that the case? Differences inherent to the DAC structure related to language are difficult to sum up. One of the reasons is for instance, that the streaming of electricity, which is a basic phenomenon in the DAC (even in the case of changing output voltages), cannot be completely compared to the streaming of meaning and sense of linguistic elements, which is basic for language and speech. The same is true for the streaming of sound, which is inherent to speech, (cf. the difference between noise and sound) although Spotify has its own unique interpretation of meaning and sense. In the end, the function and meaning of significance is too different to function well in a comparison with any DACs digital basis. So, why, and how, would one try to grasp the effects of the DAC in the context of digital relationship? Several aspects seem to be important:

- The question comes up because of the profound relationship between digital conversation on the one hand and the double definition of a word in language on the other. The third decade of the twenty-first century opens with the global experience that no word of an analog language type exists and functions without its digital counterpart, and most probably vice versa.
- This new binary compound fascinates so powerful that the function of conversions between the two linguistic levels and their mutual influences concerning meaning and sense appears to be minimized. The effects of the two conversions, the ADC and the DAC, are nevertheless important: they master and manage analog speech and digital expressivity at their specific singular level as well as at their level of intertwining.
- To suggest that a specific Conversion can be decisive in qualitative forms of digital conversation does not imply that any conclusion about this type of conversion activity (humanly performed or machine-made) is independent and categorized as a single cause. On the contrary: here is again an intertwining of meanings and constitutive powers, among which for instance emotions play an important role. The latter emphasizes the importance of researching this topic.

It seems difficult to make the step from the conversion of sounds to the conversion of words. The loading of words with meaning and sense differs from loading the sounds of words. Questions pertaining to the conversion and transport of the latter in digital contexts are not solved. It was an immense culture shock when DACs (who converted sounds in all regards) appeared to be expanded by means of establishing new communication devices. They unfolded in the beginning of 2007 a multimillion dollars global market of smart phones, with Facebook (2004) and YouTube (2005) profiting. Worldwide patterns of unexpected connectivity concealed the reduction of linguistic communication and expressivity, which characterized the shock and still grows in each hand of a smart phone user today. But the links between language and a newly acquired connectivity are not sufficiently explored by a sole attention for this

[23] See: www.rohm.com/electronics-basics/ad-da-converters/da-converter-configurations.

aspect of the sound master. We thus distinguish the S–DAC from the L–DAC to pay in-depth attention to the latter. The first feature to determine in the case of the L-DAC pertains to the type of conversion, which is specific for this DAC.

We therefore consider any L-DAC conversion as a 'soft conversion' in contrast to the S-DAC effects. The soft conversion does not include the necessity (or even the technical opportunity laid down in the conversion flow) to change the items' configuration. It means that no increase or decrease of the precision of measures is required to determine a final, hard result. Nevertheless: all factors at stake in a soft conversion are understood and interpreted as belonging to engineering judgments. The engineers involved in that process are considered as free—they are as free as a speaker is free to communicate in whatever language, or in digital terms: a sender is free to perform. The freedom in soft conversion includes learning (acquisition and rules for using information), reasoning (rules to come to conclusions) and self-correction. The three are like the basics of AI: the softness of conversion creates for instance skeptical sounds about AI as being the 'most egregious misnomer in the modern age . . . nothing more than a superficial emulation of human-like responses to convince people into believing that computers are capable of thought, and . . . the fantasy that computers are capable of thinking and feeling.[24]'

But the soft conversion may at the end be a step towards understanding language, and in particular a text, as a narrative sequence of events, which is open to digital understanding. The question whether computers understand the text they bring to the fore might be less important than the question what effects the software environment has in broadening the patterns of our understanding beyond the 'naked eye'. The L-DAC might open new ways to explore our narrative impulses as a technique to unfold what meanings in the multiple levels of communication are sustained by our actual insight in today's dual typology of language. The latter determines our insights and our practices concerning the multiple language modalities we are confronted with.

It seems an important conclusion: the process of conversion between analog and digital type of language is fundamental for many new possibilities of lingual expressivity and the new forms of life created. It seems important that new areas not only result from new technologies—like originally was the case with the Sound-DAC—but also from new entrances into non-linguistic spheres, which today reach into social ethics: for instance, the appreciation of the LGBTQIA+ community or other regions of inter-subjective behavior, like the intertwinements of national and international politics show. Internet bullying and other problematic forms of virtual communication show the transcendence of purely technological grips and lead to ethical and inter-subjective accents and new insights.

Non-technical norms seem to become important again; they form sometimes an overwhelming contrast to technology-based criteria like precision, unquestioned completion, or exact functioning. Such evolvements recalibrate basic linguistic terms, which are often audible on the street and visible or audible multi-lingual

[24] See: https: www.en.wikipedia.org/wiki/Artificial_intelligence.

social life. Note, how they express hitherto unknown dimensions of our twenty-first century consciousness in which linguistic and technical forms seem integrated. The popularity of the emoji is an example for this broadening of expression. It is difficult to determine whether the latter is a linguistic expression or a newly standardized element of our modern virtual techniques. But one conclusion seems beyond any doubt: we go through new forms of social life. A major conclusion is here that ADC as well as DAC procedures create new grips on 'the other' as well as 'otherness'! One should be deeply aware of this development, which challenges to understand moral behavior as the result of conversions. And the latter challenge us in their turn to broaden the specter of our foundational concepts pertaining to mutual understanding and social communication. Do not forget how those are in essence analog drafts stemming from designs which are deeply intertwined with the world that realizes a growing culture of the digital. If non-technical norms seem to become important again, we qualify 'non-naïve-natural' areas, implicitly the barriers and bridges, which characterized this field of multiple positions. In other words: an important observation seems lodged in the contrast between the analog and the digital as well as the conversion the latter implies. The digital is never beyond or fundamentally free from what is classically understood as 'sociability'. Any subject embracing philosophical intentions must perform its aims with a continuous differentiation of non-naïve-natural forms of life—and the digital belongs to the latter!

To state the same in other words: 'the digital' is man-made. Ego positions belong to the creation of this attitude. They remain positions characterized by language—in fact always by analog language since digital languages are converted into analog terms to be understood. That concerns not solely a name giving, a specifically created terminology or any other correlated language activity. Description, imagining and ultimately cognition is integrated or being integrated as a linguistic function. Words, names, terms, and other noetic elements reach beyond spheres of stringent determination. Lingual expressivity is seldom (perhaps never!) definable via words grammatical or syntactical language forms. Even a positioning of what is either called the 'naïve-natural' or the 'non-naïve-natural', has been criticized as unclearly conceived. It means that conversions from digital to analog spheres of life and expression are only in effect after an insight in the possible redeployment from a 'naïve-natural' into a 'non-naïve-natural' position. Such a great breach is an anchor for conversions from digital to analog types of expression. That breach, Husserl suggests, 'saves us out of the naivety of a positive foundational function of truth', so that 'we no longer need to experience the painful thorn of skepticism.' Finally, 'the depletion of the naïve-natural position . . . will at the end lead to a humanization of the human being.'[25] This insight should be remembered for two extremely important reasons, which concern the process of conversion. First, it expresses how the today centrally positioned L-DAC conversion is not an issue of truth or untruth in human social life. Secondly, it evinces how translation and conversion are in their intertwining a moment of humanization.

[25] Husserl (1954), p. 429f.

We underline the strong ties between social (resp. socio-ethical) dimensions and conversion. Inter-subjectivity plays a dominant role in origin and practice of conversion—and analog thoughts remain constitutive. A surprised 'oops', center of semiotic power, is a sign of the analog's presence in digital contexts. Life never unfolds in life itself, but always in relation with other components, individuals, and pluralities of otherness.[26] We read and think about the 'natural' versus the 'non-natural' and the inherent complexities of the 'naïve' and raise the question what causes 'nature' to differ from 'data' in the face of technically overwhelming digital forces in modern life. The dimensions of this activity are surprising. Even the expression 'life' does perhaps acquire its meaning trough a general focus on the planet as one of the participating composites of the cosmos. It means, that the system we call 'earth' is observed in reaction to human action, spiritual activity included. Indeed: *how humans think, moves their planet*. The Occidental preference for 'the word' is too one-sided to accept as foundational in the relations between earth and humans. The same seems valid for the type of language either named 'analog' or 'digital'. This observation could be an element of an unknown and not yet existing philosophy of the quantum theories. What is named 'natural' is thought and expressed in analog language. It can in this context, a be understood as fundamentally different from what is named 'digital' in the same context! The correctness of the latter is unproven and challenges each attempt to unfold L-DAC activities.

It must be underlined that all types of conversion—especially those who are founded in practices of inter-subjectivity—are also closely related to semiotics in the widest sense of the word. There is no proximity, neither philosophical nor in social practices, which unfolds beyond the areas of meaning. A conveyance of meaning and sense is therefore not determined by differences between analog and digital type of language. On the contrary: relations between conversion and conveyance of meaning belong to the hard core of semiotics. It means, that a soft conversion differs from a technically perfect conversion in the S-DAC and is not based on a 1:1 relationship between analog and digital language. They do not interpret the latter relationship as a strict duality, so that a conversion in language is more like a translation and never a rigid application. This is expressed in the observation that *all lingual expressions are always in conversion*.

We encounter here a basic argument to acknowledge linguistic phenomena as a dynamic process, often named 'the flow'. Any DAC, especially an L-DAC can create links with a sign and delivers perhaps less functional precision but creates therefore space for emotionality and sensibility—for short: phenomena of intersubjectivity as a frame of ego positions. The approach toward the sign is important as for instance Charles S. Peirce opinioned that only signs can reach the highest grade of reality. A central issue in our considerations of conversion related to cognition remains, however, the relation between the digital and the sign. Are digits sensitive to signs? Do the properties of a sign fit to whatever property of the digit? In terms of Peirce's thoughts, and with him of any semiotic approach, one should not exclude a

[26] Broekman (2020), p. 420.

relationship between digit and sign. He claimed already in 1904 letters to Lady Welby that 'representation' and 'sign' are synonyms. The universe is thus the ultimate sign in which signs must be interpreted. That observation embraces the riddle of life in its entirety: the dynamic of understanding signs is the very image of life, so that the voice of reality can be heard in the significance of the sign itself. But all that is not possible without the human being and its brain, their often-narrow limits included. Peirce underlined the importance of semiotics in the heart of processes such as conversion: they never unfold beyond forms of intersubjectivity!

A final consideration about relations between human analog/digital expressivity and inter-subjectivity positions regards the constitutive power of the metaphor and the metaphorical processes a DAC seems to explore in its constitutive activity. They form the background of our 'digital thinking'—a notion, which is located at one specific side of the digital, namely the analog side. *We are unable to provide an access at the other side*. Modern computer programs further, fortify and direct human thought formation more than ever, but the divide remains important. Human intelligence unfolds at both sides of the divide, but the realization, quality and accessibility at each side remain very different. That is of greatest importance if one is aware of the fact, that metaphors characterize the dynamics of conversion. Grier is correct in noticing: 'The alarm over AD and DA conversions . . . appears to rest upon taking a notion of 'digital thinking' quite literally, as though it is something computers are actually doing when carrying out operations in digital languages, somehow paralleling what we are doing when we communicate in natural languages, but in a manner forever opaque to us humans.' Forms of 'programming' are based upon an exchange of metaphors, we conclude. That is observable when computers write programs for us, and even when they are programmed to write for other computers, one 'can in principle still work out the logic of the individual steps when necessary.' Only in the case of AI computers remains this logic unarticulated, because these are not programmed but rather trained, and thus are unintelligible to us.[27]

But a remaining problem is that we can only interpret and manage digital language via patterns of analog linguistics—and metaphors seem essential in this regard! The clearer the borderlines within the non-naive-natural realm are, the more the exchanges of metaphors are effectively functioning. But who qualifies the thought patterns at both sides of the borderline between two types of linguistic expressivity as 'metaphoric'? The answer is simple but full of complexities: we humans do, in only one type! It is indeed fascinating to observe that human expressivity is in effect on both sides of the borderline between a non-naïve-natural and a non-natural positioning. Metaphors are the carriers of meaning and sense: they also perform in borderline regions and never stop their semiotic activity in human thought patterning. Our computers and their bugs do tell us this in their practices of reading, writing and communicative understanding. Consider the often-quoted

[27] Philip T. Grier. Language and law: artificial and natural. Journal of Comparative Law, Wildy, Simmonds & Hill Publishing, vol. XV, issue 1, p. 302.

relation between word and digit. These are two signs: a digit belongs to an artificial discourse that IT-ers call 'the protocol' whereas a word belongs to what linguists call a 'text'. The first provides 'connectivity', the second 'meaning' and 'understanding' and both further 'communication' as understood in their field. A familiar key notion of the first is the cool and distanced 'inter- ', the second the warm and often enigmatic 'speech'. But if one concludes that the first has no place in the second, and the second not in the first (and who will accept this?)—are they then worlds apart? They were separated in the days in which a dual understanding of the terminus 'word' hardly unfolded. But at the end of the twenty-first century's second decade became this duality a fundamental issue in culture, science, and philosophy. Is that all there is to say? Anyway, the duality leads to specific transitions between the two layers of linguistic expression.[28] A vital question is whether they interpret 'conversion' as a term, which is correlative to 'translation' in analog language.

Relations between digit and word indicate the absolute need for a continuing conversion among themselves and their typical field of language. That conversion illustrates how there is no dialogue possible between the two; instead of a dialogue exists a maximal functionality of each of them as the reason for contacts between word and digit. There is no meaningful relation possible between issues of which one of the two has neither function nor knowledge of what the other calls 'meaning' or 'sense'. That insight is basic for any semiotic approach. There is nevertheless a relation possible among the two (if not meaningful), as the convertor illustrates before our eyes, but never under the condition that the meaning of 'relation' changes and completely fits with the understanding of digital language. Connectivity brought by digital functionality unfolds in the realm of meaninglessness—it can therefore never bring communication. That creates a truly problematic situation for analog terms engaged in relations with digital essentials, which profile the social need and particular structure of conversion in linguistic exchanges. Yet, digital connectivity remains linked to a norm-discourse when it expresses that it functions 'norm-free' or 'beyond normative- or meaning notions'. This seems a real post-critical position and raises the question about the true character of all DACs: they operate at infinite numbers of conversion levels but remain bounded by conversion in any of the two senses, either norm-free or meaningful! Their tensions are essential for a semiotic understanding of the issue. Conversion is in this light a striving for unity of word and digit, a unity which should be one of the essentials of human existence. It forms a challenge for those who see function as the most meaningful act that can exist, together with those who understand meaning in contrast to function as the deepest and broadest state of mind. The task of *conversion* remains difficult to fully understand. Components like word and digit are newly conceived and hardly definable issues with which one must live globally. That life seems the task of a newly challenged generation which is submerged in developments of cosmic relevance.

[28]This is despite the word 'language' (e.g., in the expression 'digital language') in digital understanding is an analog metaphor and 'digital language' in fact an incorrect expression.

The story of digits and the DACs was outlined in the preceding pages with the purpose to show how they unfolded in the first decade of the third millennium. It is most interesting that their description did not show any special subject or object or any elapsed period that causes the DACs to function. Where is their origin to function? Indications of any embracing constitutive factor are missing. It indicates that specific cognitive forms do not function in DACs—such as the traditional subject-object form—and are not given relevance concerning their generation and social or scientific function. In other words: the subtitle of this book 'Knowledge and its Semiotics in Digital Days' is immediately linked to a specific understanding of cognition within the frameworks of the practices of the DAC. To study them shows how cognition in the thought patterns of these practices reaches somewhere else than in any subject-object relationship. This 'somewhere' as well as the 'else' underline the missing of an awareness of knowledge in this newly conceived context. Instead of knowledge reigns process, flow, streaming, adaptation, fitting data. Cognition has no longer any interest: everything should fit. Conversion seems the name for that fitting and replaces knowledge. That is the essence of the story of the DAC's. Ultimately represents that story the replacing of cognition by the perfection of the conversion, i.e., the *knowing* by the *fitting*. The seemingly endless differentiation between the analog and the digital reality has no other purpose than the transformation of the known into the fit, the story of the DACs illustrated.

References

AlphaGo, See: https://en.wikipedia.org/wiki/AlphaGo

Bohm D (1979) Quantum theory. Dover Publications Inc., New York; originally published Prentice Hall, New York 1951

Bohm D (1980) Wholeness and the implicate order. Routledge Classics, London and New York, p xv f

Broekman JM (2020) Like your emoji — a philosophical context. Soc Semiot 30(3):415–429. https://doi.org/10.1080/10350330.2020.1731991

Fuad L. A very brief history of the digital revolution – also known as the digital shift. In: HUB PAGES at https://hubpages.com/technology/digital-revolution-analysis? See the basic 1995 article at https://www.ncbi.nlm.nih.gov/pmc/articles/PMC40721

Grier PT. Language and law: artificial and natural. J Comp Law, Wildy, Simmonds & Hill Publishing, London, vol XV, issue 1

Heim M (1993) The metaphysics of virtual reality. Oxford UP, New York/Oxford

Husserl E (1954) Die Krisis der europäischen Wissenschaften und die transzendentale Phänomenologie. Husserliana Bd. VI. Martinus Nijhoff, Den Haag

Lakoff G (1999) Philosophy in the flesh: the embodied mind and its challenge to western philosophy. Basic Books, New York

Searle J (1969) Speech acts: an essay in the philosophy of language. Cambridge UP

Tieskens K (2019) Cultural value of European landscapes: a quantitative approach. VU Amsterdam

Vernant JP (1982) The origins of Greek thought (Tr. From the French Ed. 1962). Cornell University Press, Ithaca, New York

Weber M (2002) Die protestantische Ethik und der Geist des Kapitalismus. In: Archiv für Sozialwissenschaften und Sozialpolitik. Bd. XX und XXI; see the modern English version: Max Weber; Peter R. Baehr; Gordon C. Wells The protestant ethic and the 'spirit' of capitalism and other writings. Penguin

Chapter 8
Rearguards of Subjectivity

Mimesis was derived from the Greek verb *mimeisthai*, which means 'to imitate', has been an important and surprising feature of man—no matter in what cultural or social context mimetic activities are encountered. This observation is an important fact of the ongoing rearguards on subjectivity which strongly characterized philosophy in the middle of the last century. However, to walk around and experience the importance of human mimetic abilities remains a prerogative of all of us, even today! They relate to a philosophical understanding of the human subject, its history and social function included. Rearguard battles over the position and quality of the subject always emphasized its characteristics. Almost all philosophical movements of the twentieth century approached *mimesis* without analyzing their overall and often global context. The concentration on this issue was explicitly confirmed by mainstream thought patterns of the twentieth century, such as phenomenology, Marxism, existentialism, structuralism, semiotics, positivism, analytical philosophy, and others.

Walter Benjamin contributed to this thought pattern at the occasion of his many walks in Paris during the thirties and forties of the past century.[1] He confirmed that each Self is mirrored by its hands which keep hold of any type of Self-image! Today is that literally and figuratively the case. And what is more: the subject became a Self during those walks by means of an articulation that considers an all-embracing mirror process. One concludes that mimetic gestures confirm and pay attention to the lively Self of each individual person. Benjamin experienced a remarkable and hitherto undetermined dynamics behind this identification of a Self which tells every individual: 'show your Self, so that you can be!' He knew that those words articulate an *instructional pragmatism*—its limitations included. One should be aware of the fact, that in our days this pragmatism seems no longer based on our education, history, or tradition, but above all on the forceful appearance and key positioning of mediating techniques—analog, but often primarily digital techniques.

[1] Benjamin (1972) ff.

J. M. Broekman, *Knowledge in Change*, Law and Visual Jurisprudence 8,

8.1 Mimetics and Modernity

Any visitor's appeal at the entrance of the temple of Apollo in Delphi was formulated by a serious 'gnothi seauton', a 'know thyself'—a valid slogan to remember[2] by each visitor of Parisian Passages in the twentieth century. The experience and philosophical formulation of the human capacity named 'mirroring' seemed a modern coloring of the earlier Greek, Jewish and even Buddhist call and at the same time an interest for our foundational knowledge of the human self. His oeuvre is like a Self: versatile, richly structured, layered and certainly not open to a straightforward interpretation. Yet it concerns one of the most challenging and in-depth philosophical thoughts of our century, a source of inspiration for critical theory and other thinkers who were attracted to such a similar problem.

A surprising observation is that almost all definitions, determinations or characterizations of the Self look as if they were the fixation of a singular item, named a 'Self'. The latter seems a unique essence far beyond streams or flows of thoughts. But on the contrary: each Self is the component of a development, a multiple identity, an extremely complex 'I-You-Us' occurrence—a plurality which is enigmatic in essence and concretization. In other words: the 'I' as well as the 'Self' is not to be thought or experienced in whatever singular is possible. All that is expressed and realized in classical approaches to understand the Self as determined by any Other—but that does not seem to be enough!

This is nevertheless the absolute normal, the evidence, the generally accepted basic view: there is no Self without a contrasting or otherwise related Other. Contrasts or other types of relation are indeed basic for understanding Otherness. But that is no longer the acceptable theoretical or philosophical basis for a contemporary understanding of the Self. Notice, that there is no literature on the Self which does not embrace the duality of Selfness and Otherness and yet, an exquisiteness of this duality is no longer to be accepted. Why? The simplest form of answer to this complicated question is, that Selfness or Self are not a distinguishable issue in terms of individual components because they determine parts of a continuity which is to be characterized as a process. That continuity could be an important riddle!

A surprising and most general observation is that almost all definitions, determinations or characterizations of the Self look as if they are the fixation of a singular item called 'a Self'. The latter appears to be a unique essence that reaches far beyond streams of thought or any other determination. On the contrary, each Self is part of a development, a multiple identity, a highly complex 'I-You-Us' event—a plurality that is enigmatic in essence and concretion. In other words, both the 'I' and the 'self' may not be thought or experienced in whatever singularity is possible. This is all expressed and realized in classical approaches to understanding the Self as determined by an Other.

That is the absolute normal, the proof, the generally accepted basic view: there is no Self without a contrasting or otherwise related Other. In other words: contrast

[2] Green (2017).

relations are fundamental to understanding Otherness. And yet that seems no longer the acceptable theoretical or philosophical basis of the contemporary understanding of the Self. Note that there is no literature on the Self that does not embrace the duality of Selfhood and Otherness and yet this duality must no longer be accepted. Why? The simplest form of answer to this complicated question is, that Self or Otherness are not a distinguishable matter in terms of individual components, because they define parts of a continuity that must be characterized as a process. All these considerations lead to the proposal to look *behind* the popular Selfie and name the Self as the central subject of the digital culture the *Self-E.*

This conclusion is not only of historical importance, but also applies to the formation of the work of contemporary thinkers. What, for example, would Jürgen Habermas' theories on communicative activity (which largely determined the center of the twentieth century) have looked like, if they did not consider such a step to change a fundamental naming in philosophy?[3] Not only the work of Max Weber, but also that of Walter Benjamin was a source of inspiration. In Habermas's processing of that thoughts, the theme of criticism is central. 'Saving critique', a specific concept of Benjamin, is then juxtaposed with 'Ideology critique'. This implies a particular knowledge-theoretical relevance of the concept of 'modernity'. It is incorporated into the prevailing paradigm of communicative understanding. And it is therefore difficult to escape the impression that all this is ultimately about a paradigm shift. Such a step concerns the manifest and paradigmatic idea that an all-embracing *knowledge* of objects must lead to a new paradigm. Knowledge always concerns the *relation* between linguistic actors. Thus—as outlined in preceding chapters—the paradigm of a philosophy of consciousness has been abolished and the paradigm of connectivity activated.

In this way, an opposition is sharply delineated between Benjamin's 'saving critique' and the more traditional concept of 'ideology critique'. One could say, that in this the latter opposition between a philosophy of consciousness and a philosophy of social understanding is already present in the last decades. But the latter was nevertheless often described as another form of philosophy of consciousness. The argument for it was, on the one hand, that the idealistic roots of this form of criticism still function and, on the other hand, that the difficulty remains of clearly answering, who or what exercises this criticism. Habermas therefore attempted to rework the concept of ideology into a communication theorem. It is clear, that several problematic transformations occur.

It concerns first of all a moment of polemics. It is a respectable and intelligent reading together with a reductive, perhaps even mutilating reading, when *the mimetic* character of modernity is insufficiently elaborated and the connections with philosophy in general neglected. In other words, mimetic thought and modernity are already deeply problematic and polemically connected in the second half of the 20^{e} century, as the critical thinking of Walter Benjamin and the social philosophy of Jürgen Habermas indicate. What is interesting in this context is how the influence

---

[3] Habermas (1981).

of Th. W. Adorno can be detected. Reading him is determined by a polarity that goes back to Gershom Scholem's interpretation: a polarity between Marxism and Mysticism. That idea is adopted by Adorno and it is extrapolated into the work of Habermas and his assessment of Benjamin. But this polarity is not fully apparent in Benjamin's work. Benjamin's work is necessarily incomprehensible, and that it can never be reduced to a few basic assumptions in a comprehensible manner. So, the necessity of a disparate operation follows from this should be repeated. The polarity between Marxism and mysticism becomes an all-embracing tool to encounter problems of Benjamin's work. The reflection upon his work becomes mimetic. Through this activity will the *here and now* of the reading be recognized, and the images, texts and situations of the *past* be rescued in the *present*. This is especially true of the central theses considering a mutual understanding as a new paradigm for philosophy and social science.[4]

F. H. Jacobi spoke as early as 1775 about *the unity of I and Thou* and the need to take this unity as a philosophical starting point. His statements belong to the so-called pre-history of dialogical thinking. However, this theme was prematurely redirected to a more sociological, especially macro-theoretical approach to communication. As a result, the philosophical foundations have not been further developed. 'I open eye and ear, or I stretch out my hand and feel at the same time inseparable: You and I, I and You' Jacobi formulated, and 10 years later: 'Without Thou the I is impossible.'[5] Similar statements which all express an experience that wants to be taken as a philosophical starting point can be found with Hegel, Fichte, Schelling, Hölderlin, v. Baader. Later, with Feuerbach, the same accuracy regarding the importance of social connectivity as the basis for philosophy is very great, and implies a critical distance from German idealism. It remains widely problematic to envision *mutual understanding* as constitutive in any relationship between autonomous individuals—even if these individuals are conceived as participants in the same language!

One could underline that thought patterns directed towards modernity—accompanied by the differentiation of active mimetic forces in perception and intersubjective contact—are deeply inspired by *dialogical* insights. It appears that the recognition of the Thou in dispositions of the I is often difficult and almost always bound up with paradigms and theoretical positions that are rooted in the culture of each 'present'. Mimetics, modernity, and dialogic insights constitute a stable and challenging thought pattern and cultural view. But one finds, remarkably enough, never a remark concerning any form of *cognition and the role of the other* in that process. The connection between dialogic forms of life and cognition remains a riddle, despite all aspects of paradigms determining otherness and cognitive positions.

---

[4] Adorno (1980); Scholem (1957).

[5] Jacobi (2009).

8.2 Culture and Criticism

Even in the years following the First World War, is it not easy to detach oneself from that dominant idealistic principle with the central, all-important place and function of the subject. This applies to Herrigel, Grisebach or Ehrenberg just as much as to Rosenzweig[6] and Buber—also to Benjamin! Thus, the turn to the non-individualizing, dialogical moment is a reversal, which concerns the goal of knowledge and philosophy. This experience is not always precisely reflected in the formulation of the paradigm of rapport.

Therefore one has to ask, whether Benjamin's implicit paradigm shift is an example of the 20^{e} century to turn radically against idealism and philosophy of consciousness. A deepening of this questioning leads again to a discussion around the concept of critique, modernity and history, with as its main theme the opposition between a 'saving critique' and an 'ideology critique'. A central question is in that case how to understand saving criticism, which is contrasted with ideology criticism. In doing so, one experiences how art criticism (as a theory of experience based on a mimetic philosophy of language) relates to political praxis just as any conception of history does. These connections cannot be made known by a superficial analysis. Indeed, for this one must introduce specific criteria for a *theory of progress*. All conservative, i.e., mainly past-oriented, anti-evolutionist and surrealist aspects of thought are pushed into the background.

All of this gets a renewed actuality in 20^{e} century discussions on modernity versus postmodernity. It is called the philosophical exponent of aesthetic modernity, which stretches from Baudelaire to surrealism and later movements of that century. Any modern consciousness of time is directed to the disruption of tradition and the anarchic blowing up of the continuity in history rather than to the construction of the future. That is a constructive, emancipatory rationalization which the philosophy of consciousness counters by a paradigm shift. The subjunctive object model of consciousness, which until the middle of the 20^{e} century represented reality, is replaced by communicative rationality.

This paradigm shift comes up again around 1985 in the discussion between modern and post-modern philosophy. Are the post-modern attacks and critiques of the project of Aufkläring insufficient? A critique on reason and metaphysics is formulated from Nietzsche on and has been called the 'dial of the post-modern' through Adorno to Heidegger and Derrida to Bataille and Foucault. It culminates in aporias and ultimately remains stuck in the old paradigm! The solution to this state of affairs, in which 'postmodernism' is seen as the catch-all word for the exhaustion of the philosophy of consciousness, is in the notion of 'rapport,' and thus a deepened and expanded form of dialogue. The postmoderns fail to solve the basic problems of the modern: namely, the problem of an age that must seek its normativity within itself—the same issue was already addressed by Hegel. Postmoderns work with a concealed normativity. They are faced with the paradoxical task of finding their own

[6] Rosenzweig (1921/1930).

standards for the contingency of a merely transitory modernity. They do this by seeing past and present (but also present and eternity) in a *mimetic constellation.* Thus the tendency to read history as a radical inversion of an exclusively future-oriented time-consciousness—against the fixation of time-consciousness on modernity—is strengthening. All this, of course, is closely related to *the problem of criticism.* There are some themes which are inseparable from this criticism: the theme of culture, of modernity and of history. These are intertwined and form a complex network of considerations.

A most relevant experience is also a fundamentally critical one: *all experience is distance.* This idea breaks the proximity which is generally ascribed as a property of experience. The feeling prevails, wrongly, that experience always brings proximity with it. It is precisely this feeling that is being questioned! Criticism breaks the often mythical proximity which makes experience a closed experience. Language has always a double reference, it is everyday language and the superhuman (sacred) language. *A* language is at the same time *the* language. Criticism and distance thus go together with familiarity and closeness. Speech and silence must always be thought of together. No form of communication can be thought to be separately from this. That is why every criticism (which cannot take place without language) is a component of the history of the culture which includes the language in question. It is not outside culture. The critical point of view, insofar as it is a point of view at all, must always be seen as a determined and determinable immanent point of view. No wonder, then, that the self-determination of the critical standpoint is always a problem. Whoever does not take this on is guilty of an ideological distortion. He is then unaware of the content and the experience of time which history is given with this criticism. Homogeneity and the emptiness of time are, in fact, the consequence of this in all conceivable variations. Culture, as far as its decline, belief and development are concerned, can only be seen from within. Such a determination never has a merely historical-philosophical relevance, but always also a knowledge-theoretical one—it concerns especially the point of view of the subject of history and knowledge. Because of this fact, the concept of 'modernity' also acquires a knowledge-theoretical role in this context.

This critical self-determination takes place through the documentation of culture. Here too criticism and distance are essential: what one reads *as a* text and *in a* text is always more than it says. What is written is never just a statement of facts and fictions, but always also a reference to the state of culture. The reading that takes place here is more than a metaphor. Such a reading reads the meanings that have been laid down in people's attitudes, their fashion, their architecture, their behavior, their movement, their laughter and their weeping. Every reader in is that respect a special historian. Every reading activity can be identified as a saving moment of history. Faced with oblivion as catastrophe, the work of the historian is indeed akin to a rescue operation. The fleeing, fleeting moments of truth are saved by deciphering them, that is, by synthesizing them into a text. This, however, is not an addition, not a conservative preservation and augmentation of the written texts with the unwritten. Diametrically opposed to 'history as text' is 'culture as inventory'. The position of the psychoanalyst should be mentioned in parallel. To consider history as a text means also: to be alert to the concealed, to the gaps, but above all to the defense mechanisms, to the fact that every text is a defense speech. Thus 'salvation' and 'criticism' are contrasted with 'apology'. The latter leads to a further questioning of the status of criticism. How should one determine such a discourse? It would perhaps be obvious, to become aware of a distance between that discourse and a critical discourse. But what then is the place of the reader and what does his or her reading matter in this position? Is that reading indeed exclusively a moment of the critical discourse? And, one has to ask oneself in the face of the outlined background, can a theory of communicative action really separate itself from the producing discourse, since a theory of communication will never bed separated from language? A critical reading presupposes not only that there are documents which are read, but also that a reading activity is developed which is interpretable as a moment of communication. This connection is not given with the notion of rapprochement or rapport, since communicative action is exclusively between constitutive and individualized subjects! No wonder that a notion of 'rapport' is ultimately understood as the basis of the 'speaker-hearer' relationship, whereas language and human togetherness form a much richer and more differentiated pattern.

In all this, another question remains difficult to answer. What are the 'documents of culture' that must be read according to an epistemological-critical attitude? To pose the question is to raise the suspicion that one is seeking an answer that should be at the level of the totalizing rationality of knowledge, culture and science and the embracement of a rationality that everything that is can or must also be thought of as property. It is perhaps not without significance that the problem of *criticism* is often so strongly related with that of an *artistic criticism*. Is this because there is a suggestion that the 'documents of culture' are ultimately works of art after all? Works of art would be documents to be read if history were a homogeneous structure, so that the normativity of that history would also have to be understood as homogeneous. Valuations then remain focused on what is generally classified as 'art'. Works of art are then the property of a critical subject, ultimately: of the subject as historian. But how can criticism be made central by first reducing it to art and then elevating it to an epistemological question? This state of affairs appears as a reductive tendency, which wants to make visible via an aesthetic experience, what cannot be made visible via discourse or any other rational reasoning. The relation of art to general rationality is then thought to be parallel to that of silence to speech—a main problem of the 'speaker-hearer relation'. In that latter relationship, silence is of greater significance than speech, because language is considered an unreliable means. A critical agency is attributed to that silence. The idea is, that this silence as a moment of criticism brings us to the limit of the experiential, i.e. to the limit of rationality. That boundary indicates that the ultimate functions as the actual, the essential.

This is already a moment of silence and as such a moment of being dependent on revelation. Experience is form of revelation. This also becomes relevant when one realizes that the question of the 'documents of a culture' has by no means been answered. But are they really so indeterminable? That depends on the rationality in which one wants to place this determinability or indeterminability. Documents of culture are by no means determinable a priori. But that leads precisely to a theory of reading! Documents of a culture must be read—this also implies reading what has never been written. That reading is imbued with the passion of determining the indeterminable. Fashion, gesture, attitude, behavior, figures are just as many examples of the indeterminable according to our technical rationality. But in view of a theory of reading, are they very determinable documents of a culture. They are indeed in danger of being lost or short-changed in any historiography. This explains Benjamin's interest in the street, the urban perishable image. In this transitory image the constant emerges, and in that emergence is the definition of aesthetic modernity concealed. In this vein, Baudelaire is the painter of the modern. The 'physiognomy' of a time is in danger of being lost in its demand for continuity which characterizes such a historiography. Perhaps this transience is the paradigm for the (endangered) tradition. In that sense, every construction of history, and every philosophical reflection on it in the sense of a philosophy of history, touches not only the author, but also his time! Finally, it must be remembered that the mimetic moment, to which a leading role is assigned, is anchored in the indefinable mimicry of people among themselves. The superficiality of people, spheres and things is a senseless equality in its ephemeral character.

It brings us for instance to a closer look at the theme that was referred to as 'art and criticism.' It is central to all philosophical thinking and, as a result, all philosophy is bound up with the place and function of the subject. For example, the weeping play in the Baroque places imagery against the individual specificity of the work of art. In this language-bound way it expresses experiences of suffering, oppression, the irreconcilable. This creates a contrast with the art that pretends to bring freedom and reconciliation, fulfillment and harmony. Is that still aesthetics or a philosophically grounded consideration of art? That question is fundamentally critical. Art is being ripped open from within, and this is a process in the moderns, which is precisely why they are taking their place in the history of the 20^{e} century. As said before: the concept 'modernity' gets in this context a profound epistemological meaning and function. It shows moreover, that in this context the ideas are the real object of philosophy. They can never be represented directly. They depend on mediation by concepts, and to these concepts the things are then subject, as con-figuration.

This position is not immanently aesthetic: it concerns the legibility of works of art as elements or documents of culture! The answer is therefore anything but traditional. In fact, art history is not concerned with the works of art, but with the substance or form of those works. In this respect there is a parallel with the history of philosophy. There, too, the philosophical idea itself is hardly discussed. It concerns always the history of systems, dogmas, philosophers or problems. A philosophical interpretation threatens to locate itself in what can be called a 'timeless and empty continuum'. Only then does the question dominate whether there is a progress in art, science and philosophy. Whoever asks this question must first have renounced the work of art itself, the thought in itself, the knowledge as such! It thus becomes clear that what is missing needs to be clarified. Criticism must bring up the missing, must 'save' what can be saved. 'Saving' thus becomes a key concept in the theory of knowledge—an unprecedented qualification. But let us be careful about concluding too quickly. Note: it is always about *rationally* justifiable knowledge—it is always bound up with that of interpretation. Only in such a form is knowledge possible. Two important limitations are thus given. There is (1) *rationality*, which is itself a limiting design of all possible knowledge, and there is (2) *interpretation* as a form. Note: both play a role in the determination of subject and subjectivity in philosophy: both are important fields in the rearguards of the subject.

Rationality is a form, and every form is a well-determined rationality. Both are mainly characterized by the fact that they show a coherence in all relations. The term 'constellation' is in modern twentieth century philosophy often used to describe the concept of 'coherence'. Constellations of works of art are not dependent on one work of art versus another but concern the result of every interpretation of the many different works. They occur independently of one artist or one art critic. They are forms of rationality, interpretative units, models. But the assumption is obvious, that the coherence of works of art in every aesthetics is an image concerning a constellation of ideas. Ideas are in relation to things like the constellations are to stars. But these are neither the concepts nor the laws of the stars! The epistemological position is interesting here. For philosophical idealism, ideas are the concepts of things, and so is Kantian transcendentalism, where ideas are the laws for things. Representation of the ideas is at the same time criticism; representation and interpretation run into each other. Notice how the language-philosophical component takes once again center stage. That thought movement is, as already mentioned, central in every reading: as a text and as a word. Everything has to be named again and again. Thus reality is added to reality: that is the dynamic of the 'salvation of phenomena'. Philosophy must constantly do what should be done in aesthetics: collect the creative life in the idea, bring it about, concentrate it. The word is released when philosophy takes up its naming activity again. However, it constantly searches for a method. The latter concerns immaterial relations via naming, that is: naming needs materiality. Knowledge, presence, phenomenon, time, visible coherence, constellation, text thus exist *as name*! What can be said and thought about the subject?

8.3 Knowledge and Truth

What was designated as 'name' thus seems to focus on the concept of 'critique'. The latter would in such a case make criticism axial to knowledge and truth. Language would then eventually retreat into an epistemological concept of criticism, from which political practice can only be considered by means of philosophical interpretations and positions. Is the 'saving' critique (often mentioned in the above, which indeed focuses on missing meaning) adequate for understanding a political reality? When legitimate violence is in political reality contrasted with structural violence, is that probably just an optical illusion. Structural violence is latent in all institutions. Both forms are opposed to another violence, namely revolutionary violence, which re-establishes the 'saving critique'. This constitutes the access to a dimension of direct understanding of social structures as the basis for a universalizable theory of knowledge and its foundation in criticism. Every background of criticism is knowledge, and especially historicity of knowledge. The internal time structure of knowledge is especially important because it is a *mimetic* moment.

Any reading makes clear, that a traditional understanding of knowledge is aimed at insight in a homogeneous and empty time continuum, in which an additive and therefore linear process can be used as a methodical principle. 'Progressive faith' is the 20e century a keyword for this attitude. But it turns out to be a juggernaut: ever new theories of progress are developed and generally accepted in the name of progress, and every original innovative and even 'saving' movement is swallowed up in the emptiness and homogeneity of the internalization of progress. What critical potential can survive here? Against the knowledge structure that serves the progression, there is always a saving critique, indeed the saving of the Phenomena in Being! This is no futility, but is it enough? However, this question raises a counter-question: who will judge, whether it is enough or not? Certainly not he, who keeps the gaze only forward, for that gaze alone serves . . . only progress! But criticism is stagnation in the hurricane of movement! The question, what political consequences and implications a principle has, is not essential. Such a question does not involve any disturbance of the dimensions of time and place. The question is still thought in terms of application, in other words: it is still directed to the relations between norm and fact. In the words of Nietzsche 'One should be very light' (Man muss sehr leicht sein . . .) to philosophize. One's own weight should not impede the change of point of view. Indeed: *metanoia* is at stake.

This also requires unprecedented powers for philosophy. A contemporary conception and praxis of 'deconstruction' is consequently to be found as a background for 'critical' concepts (especially the relation between truth and knowledge). Deconstructive moments consist here not only in learning to name the hidden moments, but also in taking initiatives to demolish them. These are primarily theoretical moments and not revolutionary tactics which give rise to street terror. Thus in 20e century philosophy one encounters the demolition of the idea of a universal history; the elimination of epic elements; the refusal of a critic and historian to even experience the position of the victor. Abstinence, especially in knowledge-theoretic terms, can bring about change. In this regard, the opposition between truth and knowledge must be recalled. Knowledge demonstrates, writes down—especially from result to result—and is bound up with systematics, with a goal. Nevertheless, all knowledge takes place in the sphere of the realm of possession: *to know is to appropriate.* We will have to revisit this theme and its expression. Namely truth, on the other hand, is by no means bound to modalities of *objective disposal* or availability. In this sense, truth is not a manifestation of the subject-form of our thinking when knowledge appears to be fulfill its possessive form. No 'I' is privileged in the face of truth; it cannot be grasped with a concept—only in the representation itself. The latter is decisive: a representation is not an imagination brought about by an intentional subject. I must wait for a representation; a representation can bring about an 'I', yes, even force it. But in the representation something is given to the subject, the subject experiences that something is given to it: so one must conclude that truth 'gives itself'. That is why truth is not knowable as knowledge, but as image—especially as 'dialectical image'. It follows that truth is not characterized by immediacy but should be seen as 'roundabout way'. Nevertheless, there must always be a well-defined and determinable subject in order for this dynamics to take place. How is this dependence on a subject structured?

Note that in the light of the foregoing considerations, knowledge always has a textual character—even in unwritten forms. Also if an abstinence is at issue which turns out to be of the greatest importance in the theory of knowledge. It is the abstinence from possessive knowing, the abstinence from initiative, from centering on the intentionality of the subjject, from taking the road or possessing a theory. Thus, in the end, there is a waiting for the phenomena, for their self-reception, for the moment when they allow themselves to be represented and thus break open the empty and homogeneous time of knowledge to make a meaning appear in it. Note, that meaning is given, it comes—its coming is expected. The vision, the engagement, the construction, the knowing of the different dimensions of time—especially the contrast between the empty and homogeneous time and the fulfilled time, an interest in inalienable and meaningful as well as rationally meaningful social connections: all these are elements of the theory of knowledge which unfolded in the last decades of the last century.

Epistemology is therefore a theory which takes all doxa and ideological distortions into account. It always concerns interpretation as a reading of reality. Theory unmasks that this truth can be *possessed*. It also unmasks that a knowledge can come into being which would be different from homogeneity, emptiness, and alienation. Theory is affected on all sides by such dislocations. All this apparently involves a critique, which has yet to gain a foothold. A 'saving' critique must first of all still be admitted to the order of discourses in science, knowledge, and society. It is important, to perceive and accept this. On the surface of our stabilized and socially accepted discourses is scarcity; there is only a limited number of places available. What social valuations should allow for new occupations of places? And if that has already happened, so that the conquest of places has been brought about—has this dislocation then come to an end, has it then come to a different kind of social harmony, and ultimately of what in the social context is called 'truth'?

The text of history is linked to this consciousness, yes, it becomes a readable constellation thanks to this consciousness. Therein lies certainly rooted what Habermas called the 'time-consciousness of modernity'.[7] The historical consciousness of the moderns always pits the 'newest age' against the 'new age': the present thus acquires a special place and value. A censorship is always constructed, a self-determination is always documented in the present. That creates a continuity—a continuity which is characterized as a bourgeois virtue, but which can be disrupted philosophically. A present time is full of presence. Apart from the question of the foundation of the modern era, is the question how that foundation founds itself in itself. Any past modernity founds itself in the past. This is not an incidental

[7] Habermas (1981).

perception: there is a mimetic relationship here. After all, the present and the past stand in such relation to each other that they can be crystallized into a mimetic constellation. One cannot 'liberate' oneself from the past by internalizing it reflexively, but by making it a moment of transparently reading, and thus realizing it. *Mimesis and realization unfold together.*

But there is more. Reading is a true event, the historian a good reader, a true reader. That reader, however, is not necessarily the reader of truth. 'What was never written, read' is an expression repeatedly used. To read is to render. This involves not only the history thus read and experienced, but also one's own work. Theory and experience interlock. A method unfolds in the mimetic event (which can thus be conceived as a methodically founded event) that strives for mediation and immediacy, insofar as reflexion and experience are thought together. This applies especially to reading the non-written: history, or more precisely: the event, the occurrence.. This combination of reflection and experience is important. For example, it may never be possible for me to have the textual fabric of Marcel Proust's *A la recherche du temps perdu* clearly in mind after reading the last sentences of that work. Is there even a last sentence of that work that can be labeled as such, one may ask, and hasn't the reading already begun long ago, long before the reader approaches the end of the text? Is the text still an example for me, while it must have become a model for the translator if the translation is to make sense? Benjamin's ability to read was completely different from mine. His time of reading was fundamentally different—not only because I live in a different cultural period, but also because the immanent time of reading among readers is different. Thus the dependence of different readers is different. The same might be valid for understanding the history of a life, a commonplace, a literature, yes, ultimately for history itself. The translatability of a text ultimately depends on that type of history. It becomes suddenly, or not completely, clear. What applies to a moment in the relationship between original and translation, between language and language, must likewise be considered significant for history itself. The all-enlightening and synthesizing event of the moment of reading and understanding is an entering of time in a vertical way, against all horizon-intentionality imagined to be a constitutive consciousness. But that entry is again very different according to time, circumstance and psychological constellation. Those moments do not *measure* time, but *make* time like being connected, different according to their depth structure. History is general. Yes, it is. But history is extremely individual, without being individualistically definable, without being locked up in an aesthetics or a theory of knowledge, an ontology or a metaphysics.

In the core of 'materialism' is the mimetic seen as the core of representation. *The text is its own quotation*: how can textuality and quotation be discovered in each other? The art of citing is only momentarily discoverable. Any attempt to characterize the quoting ignores a main principle of knowledge, namely the representation which a work offers. What remains is an abstract classification of text fragments in a conception of time and history. The difficulty is, however, that every page of reading is understood without being able to prove what is read in a positivist sense. Every ending of a text is non-quotably present in the entire text, so there is in it no end supported by a beginning., The text is consequently not an object of proof, not an object of criticism or a testimony of it. If a reader's ability to quote is insufficient, he or she is dependent on a flash of understanding. But that happens to the reader, it does not concern a concept or a reflexive act that is predictable and methodically provable on the basis of which an argument can be built. So, is all this after all a matter surrealism? Astrology, and not a work of science? 'Knowledge and Truth' are continuously at order!

8.4 The Decay of the Aura

The opposition between saving criticism and ideology criticism is always put into words. For example, Peter Bürger relates his reading of Benjamin and Habermas to a critical hermeneutics.[8] His critical viewpoint also concerns the function of art. Marcuse analyzes ideology criticism in connection with the autonomy of art. Benjamin sees the decay of the aura, which transforms autonomy of art into other forms which can be instructive and critical, and from there can lead to new experiences.

This refers to the fundamental change concerning the structure of the work of art—but only as an example for broader philosophical issues. This reference is based on the fact, that today the organization of perception (and thus also the perception of art) takes place in a different way. The autonomy of art was once aimed at truth (i.e., the ideal of beauty expressed the desire for happiness), but this claim has now been lost, and with it the authenticity, uniqueness, and inviolability of an artwork. It has acquired a different status, and thus also a different reception arises. It has disappeared from the sphere of special appearances and can no longer claim authenticity or inviolability. One is tempted to say that the work of art thus acquired a new function and entered the market—the market as a specific form of socio-economic organization—and gets its most important expression in the exhibition of the artwork. Then one becomes aware of the mass reception of art and the role of the non-analog means of expression.

Benjamin tested this position already against the film, and another theory is then connected to it. New experiences arise, generally spoken, from a shock: a shock sets such new experiences free and thus creates the basis for a new vision on knowledge and politics. But note the nature of those experiences. They are not new experiences that can be added, so to speak, to the old, so that the whole slowly processed and transformed into a transferable (inheritable) good. This is what is called lore and/or tradition. The technical reproduction of the traditional work of art and, in particular, the new arts of reproduction (such as photography and film) demonstrate their cathartic side in that manner. This feature is based on the fact that authenticity is affected in every reproduction. Who touches authenticity, touches tradition. In that cathartic position one has to reform autonomous art experiences into new

[8] Bürger (1979), p. 166 f.

experiences. The creation of new structures of perception and the organization of new modes of experience is after all not anchored in liberating actions of a revolutionary subject, but today more than ever the development of new (reproduction) techniques. The fact that modes of experience are set free by the techniques of reproduction is their actualization, and that is the 'positive form' of these techniques. For the degradation of each aura is a renewal possible. That brings a positive moment in the negative to the fore. Adorno will call this the culture industry, which is not just a reification of art. It is also an actualization.[9] The claims of an avant-garde to intervene in everyday reality and thus close the gap between art and life—indeed, to dissolve oppressive autonomy—is realized through the techniques themselves. One can call this not only a positive but also a utopian reading of the signs characterizing our days.

It is the task of any new art to open automated modes of perception and create new avenues for art consumption. This is usually materialisticall done by a change in the technique of reproduction and not by the hand of the artist himself. It is clear that such techniques as Dadaism and also Surrealism foreshadowe artistic possibilities that are eventually realized in film. As a result, a one-time historical situation has been created. Not only a one-off situation in the Western European culture is accentuated in that case, (the concept of modernity) but an aesthetics is developed which treats creating artist and consumer equally. In this respect is a scheme created that no longer verifies the traditional subject-object relationship. The breach of existing relations of production by new developments is interesting in this respect. Parallel to this process is the change of all social and knowledge relations pertaining to art. Thus it is once again visible that ideology criticism concerns the reading of what has already been written, but not yet been read. Yet the question is justified, whether this really focuses on a *false* consciousness, that is: a specific conscious and a distorted representation of the facts at the same time. The object of 'saving' criticism is always: meaning. Ultimately it concerns knowledge as an expression of social relationships. In this way moments are sought that have not been absorbed by their own history. Ideology criticism is always a disjunctive reading, a 'productive criticism'. It concerns an act of knowing, which always implies components of each presence.

Against this background can be said, that the process of decay of the aura is equivalent to something that cannot solely be the result of a description, but implies *the unlocking of new possibilities*. In this respect is even an attempt to understand the concept of critical hermeneutics and its implications too limited. What is at stake is the problem of critique as a descriptive of the process of the decay of the aura. Only from the boundary between speaking and silence, between the word and its blank, can be understood why non-affirmative forms of art and ultimately the allegory itself can be understood as forms of criticism. They are opposite to the individual totality of any work of art. So, it is not quite clear anymore whether *the aura* as a figure has a place *in the philosophy of art* or perhaps *in the philosophy of language*. This

[9] Adorno (1980); see also: Habermas (1985).

ambiguity continues to exist and function as such, but one must face it. After all, any aura expresses experiences, which cannot be given a representational character. An aura expresses suffering, oppression, a missed opportunity, the irreconcilable, the negative in contrast to art, which normally claims to bring freedom, reconciliation, and fulfillment. In this respect are aura and allegory an equivalent to criticism. The aura contains all the sadness and protest. Even the distance on which criticism is based seems contained in it. Should criticism still be made conscious out of allegorical motivations? Or is the allegory itself already so strongly accruing that it can function as criticism almost without further definition or transition? What does one read from sadness, from melancholy? Perhaps the most concrete, because concretion must be saved in allegory. Not the intangible, but precisely the most concrete is in danger of being lost. The decline of the aura and the disappearance of art in society are not identical with the loss of culture. On the contrary, both belong to the history of modernity.

The power of mimetics should be found in experiences which are anchored in a mimetic theory of language. But that involves more than just a foundation of the relation between language and experience. That relation is after all mimetic in nature. Notice, how language as the basis of experience belongs to the mimema of experience, just as experience as the basis of language belongs to the mimema of language. The semantic potential of language is determined by experience, just as the semantic potential of experience is determined by language. Experience has the epistemological structure of interpretation. For interpretation, however, exists no final moment in which adequacy and finality are determined. The dialectical image is to experience what the text is to interpretation. Both are moments of verticality and both break the scheme of thought of the horizontality of consciousness. The basic structure is that of perception, not that of autonomous speech. This answers the question who can be considered the author of the liberation which the saving critique should bring. Everything comes down to a correct understanding of the specificity of the relation between language and experience. At various points should one see, how philosophy must submit to this necessity. The answer is therefore not given directly; that would not be adequate in the face of the problem. Philosophy, after all, in the view of the last decades of the last century, is directed towards *knowledge* and the concept of *truth* connected with it. Representation, method, tour and detour are concepts that one encounters all the time.

It becomes clear in that context, how:

(a) *truth* is not obtained through analytical knowledge, but can be grasped in *representation*. The 'in' means not in an instrumentalist way 'by means of', but 'in medias res';
(b) *sense and meaning* are given. They are both, despite all the strength, concentration, and wisdom of the philosophical method, delayed. Their coming must be expected by the philosopher. To this end he must learn to see and read, while
(c) the *mimetic relation* is the basis of seeing and reading. It is the central motive for types of textuality—both those, which have art and nature as an important point of reference. The same seems true for historical texts.

The mimetic relationship frames the possibility of getting to know the 'theory of ideas' belonging to texts, their way of reading and their way of seeing. Mimesis is quotation and presence in one. Time concentrates the image in itself and to itself. The object of this quoting, which implies criticism and philosophical method, is *meaning*. It is primarily that meaning which is lost in history. As an example Benjamin takes the history of modernity, the 'Urgeschichte der Moderne', his Passages–study, which is a study of an 'almost forgotten meaning', modern semiotics would add. Their dialectic includes quote as well as presence in one. This creates the emancipation of experiences. It is why meaning and significance must be understood as *given*. They must be awaited. Open places are filled, and that is already a struggle, yes, even of class struggle which enforces meaning and significance. The autonomous word of the poet or essayist turns out to be the mantle, with which the dependency is proudly covered. The word only breaks through and only acquires meaning, when it is revealed and makes the extent visible to which it conceals a mimetic power which is bound to time and place. History as progress, as homogeneity and controllability by means of rational constructions and reconstructions is such a cloak. Struggle, scarcity, deconstruction, breaking open the dismantling of continuity seems a mimetic event.

The following consideration should be added. It is, as if meaning and sense were not a reproducible commodity. And it is, as if the experiences of an intercourse with nature as well as with one's own self could by no means be extended at free will.

One should in the *first* place acknowledge that, myth is not the vehicle, the *ochema* of humanity, or the preferred instrument to transmit meaning and sense from one generation to the next. The myth is itself meaning, and as such subjected to the rules of semantics. Myths are not repositories but units of meaning expression.

It follows, in the *second place,* that the statement, according to which the potential of meaning itself is limited and can only be transformed, can hardly be founded. It is not that potential is limited, but relations among the mimema are finite. The units of meaning are limited because the 'open places' (in the surface of language and text, time, and history) are limited. The myth, too, must be placed if it is to potentially unfold its meaning. So there is no decay, but salvation concerning history.

In the *third* place is that concept inscribed in a general idea of philosophy. It is aimed at *representation*, and its mimetic force can only count on a limited availability of topoi. There is scarcity, and where there is scarcity, there is contestation, indeed, struggle.

The mimetic force thinks the extraordinary, it discovers regularity in the irregular in the true sense of the word. By extension, it perceives how the ordinary and the extraordinary coincide. But on the basis of what unity? Thinking together with the extraordinary implies a thinking together of the regular and the irregular, a wild existence that cannot be domesticated. A wild being: if any experience then springs from dealing with history, that experience is fundamental. How can that be? The question dominates the issue of mimetic ability. The perfect mimesis is no longer mimesis: to produce and to see equality is founded on historical mutability. From here, the decay of the aura, the positioning of modernity, and the power of mimetic ability are one and the same unity. Of great importance is, that the mimetic needs not only a place, that is, a syntactic moment, but also a carrier, that is, a flowing unit of meaning that functions as such. This dependence, too, is not primarily a limitation, but an expansion of possibilities. 'Reading what was never written', writes Hugo von Hofmannsthal after his reading touched the oldest: from the stars, the bowels, the dark dances, the hand lines. That reading is an evolutionary thinking. What is read from the parables is the future. This is true not only for the astrologer, but also for the true historian. It is this reading of the future from the signs of the times a hidden concern of the man, who shortly before his death wrote cryptic-looking metaphors about history?

Language, name and word come together here. What communicates itself in language is evidently a spiritual being, not language itself but something that is distinct from language, dependent on it and in a constant referential relationship with it. The 'spiritual essence' of something is thus not its language. The difference between the spiritual being and the linguistic being, in which it communicates itself, is of great importance here. The difference is in language but not causally, graspable by language. Ultimately, it must be said that every language communicates itself. The linguistic being of things is their language. Everything communicable from a spiritual being is immediate, in its language. The communicable is immediately the language itself. Every language is the medium of communication. Hence the linguistic character of man is precisely, that he names things. Here, too, viewpoints diverge.

The 'bourgeois conception of language' will aime at conceiving the word as a means, especially as a means of communication. The object of that communication is the matter at issue—descriptively—and its addressee is the human being in the position of the hearer. This is opposed to a different conception of language. For that view, neither the mediocrity, nor the object-orientation, nor the bondage to the speaker-hearer scheme is central, but the NAME. Language draws itself together in the name—therein lies the *mimetic* energy and the problem of the *aura* in the most concentrated manner. Even 'history' is a name! Communication in the sense of: sharing, belongs to the essence of that language. In the end the mimetic theory of language finds its limit in one image, which is not and should not be one. Every text is an *empty place*—otherwise no meaning is possible. Hence the pictorial prohibition as the topos, where the word of God and the name of man are virtually coherent. Both constitute a finite boundary in relation to an infinite language.

The name is the unbroken image—every symbol represents a break: a name is never a symbol of the untranslatable language. In untranslatability the sentence no longer holds any analytical function, because there can in that case no longer be any difference between utterance and expectation. The value and dignity of a text as an image has not yet been established in any theory of ideas. The essence of the mimetic becomes, however, experienced through textuality. The mimema bring all of which they are mimemas into being. There is no object in the mimetic relation that has ontological priority. In other words, there is not first a naive-ontological determinable object, which can then be said to be taken as the object of the mimetic relation. Every construction conceives itself as an 'image', by first creating a 'pre-image'.

Every representation is thus determined by an *authos* which grounds it. Every mimetic act is therefore always filled with origin and beginning. Thus one writes a text and experiences that one has written a translation/interpretation. The battle of philosophy is indeed about: *words*. But which ones! It concerns always those words, which retain their origin as a mimetic force. *Origin* has hardly anything in common with *genesis*. Therefore the word cannot be grasped as having immediate meaning. The name refers to the before and after history of each word, and thus presents the mimetic power today. This before-and-after history of the word determines itself in the face of a failure of meaning, which can perhaps succeed. The history of failure is mythical—it is the history of the Fall. Since then, we can give names and confer meaning in a broken relationship to reality. But a force has remained, recalling paradise. Every meaning and sense we confer had to remind us of it. This force is the mimetic moment, which shows itself in the before and after history, how it serves as an example for itself. He who, like every human being, stands in history, fills a full 'now-time'. Man understands himself as time in a vertical way.

8.5 Complexities of the Plural

The rearguards focusing on reality, position, and function of the subject—as broadly reported in the above paragraphs—did not embrace important new insights or mind-turning ideas in today's thought patterning. This was not because new insights or viewpoints were in that period not discovered, formulated or unveiled. On the contrary: many revolutionary views were presented and articulated in a fascinating variety of native languages. But at their background—and often underground—unfolded also new and more complex forms of interhuman communication. Those caused unexpected difficulties. One of the central problems could be formulated in a traditional expression: the fact that the very traditional and basic 'speaker-hearer' model got lost. Only a hitherto unpracticed 'sender-receiver' modality was left to replace and remained available. In other words, what a hearer or receiver deciphers or uploads since our days, seems not to belong to the materials of what in earlier ages was considered as the result of the activities engendered by an individual speaker.

One must conclude that modern communication results from a very different framework and from a special interface model. In other words: the authenticity and understandability of messages on which the rearguards in the last decades focused was lost during their very reporting. That characterizes philosophical messages from the last decades of the twentieth century. They were not only determined by what an actual philosopher was thinking, writing, and publishing at a certain moment in the 20th or in an earlier century. No, they were also differently received and understood because of the changing patterns of our twenty-first century's reading and understanding. This touches, of course, the actual situation of human cognition as well as the basic patterns of a modern self-understanding.

So, the question arises, in what manner we characterize this fundamental change of what our precursors left us in today's world. One of the most widespread observations makes clear that all reports about the issues which were at stake in the rearguards of the subject were deployed in *only one* particular and all-embracing system of thought patterning and expression. It appeared, that occidental languages had at least during two and-a-half millennium this specific feature in common, a feature which is since the nineteenth century classified as *analog* language. It is remarkable how relating to or using signs and signals of *information* represented by a continuously variable physical quantity such as spatial position, voltage, or others, is proven to be essential in this context. The idea of an *analog language* appeared to be strongly tied with a culturally diversified concept of *information.* The innermost features of such relations and their practices create the character of any analog exploration. But the innermost function of analogy is the *plural* which determines the philosophical essence in this context. That seems reasonable, because any analog meaning or sense is something that *is like* another meaning or sense in design, origin, use, etc. as the result of a comparison, a parallel, a mirroring, or other cognitive processes. Notice that in our world of today exists always 'a something that is analogous to something else'. It is therefore evident, that today one does not circumscribe the analog without referring to the digital—as a differentiation, a distinction, a something else, an otherness which functions constitutively in the determination of the analog and became cultural evidence.

Reality seems in this light a totality of differentiations in a most extended outreach of numbers. The degree of otherness (or of non-identity) does not seem to be of any importance. Understanding the 'analog' as a characterization of language thus implies that language is understood as a set of meanings which are comparable among themselves. One of the most pro-active is the idea that language is a collection of operational *signals*. Their practices give cause to a variety of social *values* in which the process of interhuman communication unfolds, focusing on *information*. The latter seems the founding factor of a socio-cultural plurality. Be aware, that analog signals, resp. language, are often perceived as a natural form—even if their natural character remains undefined. The correlative meaning and sense of plurality is seldom or not clearly at all in this specific context. The mirroring between the analog and the digital remains at issue whereby their plural remains the riddle.

Re-presentation (essential in conversion) is a major part of the process that creates an analog signal being a continuous signal of physical *measurements*, like digital signals result from *modulation*. The difference between them is that in analog technology information is translated into varying amplitude, whereas the digital technology translation of information occurs exclusively into binary format (zero or one) where each bit is representative of two distinct amplitudes. In an analog language are meanings determined by a *speaker* who uses grammatical or cultural practices for his speech, whereas in a digital language are meanings the product of the *topic* that is organized binarily.

This observation includes the fundamental fact that our understanding of the analog language embraces by necessity two issues who look like a plural. We suggest that any analogy concept embraces on the one hand an *epistemological* and on the other a *socio-cultural* flow of comparison. The task of the first does mainly concern our *knowledge* of the pattern at stake: we embrace in any constitution of an analogy two components which each need to be embedded in an activity of contrast and differentiation. The second is broader and pertains to the *axial ideas of our days* which are expressed in general scientific and cultural ideas and their social format, such as the Digital, the Artificial Intelligence or the Quantum Theory. Whether those two comparisons are correctly interpreted as a *plural* remains an unanswered question. Is the double of the first and the second component of the comparison a *plural* or just a *mirroring* with the purpose to profile.[10]

In that context and especially in an ad hoc contrastive sense is understandable how one is simply taking the *analog* as the natural antonym of *digital*. That antinomy does not decide the question of its character being a singularity of a plurality. But naturalness is never and nowhere a simple socio-cultural given! The digital does in our days always mean a characterization of information (the third factor in the mirroring process), which is appropriately represented in that specific form and operations named *the Digital* and socially embraced by that nomination. In contrast to the *digital* seems the *analog* just another, less sophisticated type of information, which is not so fit to perform interface operations. The question of the difference and co-existence of the two concepts (the analog and the digital) is in general a matter of socio-cultural practices and not a matter of applying well-founded definitions. The role of nominating one of the components in the above context as *plural* remains problematic, and never a simple issue of name-giving.

Notice, that plurality is a deeply rooted philosophical issue. It is crucial to understand plurality in a sense which engages us to grasp it as a factor of the new normal in the twenty-first century. But our grasping the plural is in this case an understanding of a knowledge-related issue that founds our epistemology on the one hand and a socio-cultural plurality which determine our positions in life, culture and society on the other. Those two do function everywhere and in all possible contexts of human experience. They underline the axial functioning of any plural which is the social and individual context of our judgment whilst we explore language in all aspects of life. That judgment uses the expression 'analog' as well as 'digital' as if they were a persistent plural.

But there is a problem to mention. It must be underlined again, that the functioning plurality which characterizes the *analog* embraces *two* components. One is generally accepted and the other is generally neglected. The first concerns our knowledge of the feature we denominate, and the other is the socio-cultural context within which that knowledge exists. For maintaining the concept of analogy as a mark of linguistic typology are *both* aspects essential. But the problem is that only the first seems activated and the second remains generally unnoticed. So, we describe the following basic observation: *in our exploration of the term 'analog language' is one plurality present and the other almost completely absent.* That is why this paragraph suggests indicating a specific complexity of the plural. If an analog signal is concerned (including eventually a 'word'), then the latter is

[10]See this Chapter §1.

understood as a *continuous* signal which *represents* physical measurements. Therefore, one must keep in mind that such a representation is understood as an act of human cognition but *not* as a socio-cultural element which was introduced in the preceding text as 'The New Plural'.

This one-sidedness does not solely concern the single expression 'analog'. It embraces a large variety of names and expressions related to the differentiation between the analog and the digital in our computerized world of today. To formulate the issue in a different manner, one asks: when

1. **'a'** is the term 'analog' and **'b'** the term 'digital' 'and
2. **'a'** seems partially or entirely determined by **'b'**: is **'a'** in that case any form of **plural**? Notice that
3. the specific determination will be qualified as a special form of **communication** between **'a'** and **'b'**. That communication (even understood as 'interface') is a form or format which both, **'a'** and **'b'**, accept, and both are submitted to the conditions under which knowledge of the two terms exists.
4. The final answer will be, that neither **'a'** nor **'b'** are a **plural** although both may participate in a functioning plurality.

This is very important for the term *conversion* which is closely linked to our modern understanding of *cognition.* One should underline that *conversion* is the expression for understanding how the analog functions—not only in analog contexts based on knowledge or awareness of the digital, but in all cultural mainstreams of actual science and thinking, the New Plural included.[11] The term and actual enforcement of conversion implies diverse harmonies and disharmonies in contemporary culture and regards a fitting of important components as well as the necessity of changing contents and functions in the Occident and other regions of today's worldwide activities, the *www* as well as the *Interface* contact regions implied. Conversion determines and stimulates the fitting of analog understandings and thought patterns in the entire world of digital as well as non-digital interhuman contacts. The fitting which belongs to the internal structure, and to the external powers of cognition in modern times, determines new semiotic structures. It means, that we should not live with the idea that analog thinking disappeared during the first decades of the new millennium. On the contrary: it just became in those years one of the important components of a hitherto unknown and complexity named The New Plural. It thus renewed its proper attitude in view of plurality as such. The question is hardly resolvable whether in that context the analog is a singular or a plural issue, or what other qualities are at stake in the analog thinking patterns. Insight in the latter replaces today what in earlier Occidental ages was entitled a study in 'human history'—embracing norms, ideas, meanings, and signific as well as other particles of human language and behavior.

The inner structuring of the 'analog' is an indication for a more general problem of human history, which should be understood as a worldwide process of *living with*

[11] See Chapter I,6; Ch. III,1; Ch. V,3; Ch. VI,5; VII,4.

meanings as a way of *giving sense to life*! It all focuses directly to the thesis of our preceding chapters, that *conversion* is the most recent *dynamics of cognition* thanks to the New Plural's context. The latter plays a crucial role in our understanding of conversion, which has effects in various regions of human behavior—from religion to law, from physics to philosophy, from mathematics to linguistics. No wonder, because most of those fields take part in the continuous flow of socio-cultural changes in life! Only in this flow can cognition be understood as becoming identical with conversion!

The latter is in our actual literature understood as an attempt to grasp the many levels of human activity which are in change. Human attitudes, software platforms, marketing and related economic fields, chemistry, law, logic and linguistic appear altogether in that light. This is a remarkable fact, because most of the essential factors which played a role in philosophy and broader thought patterns of the twentieth century were *not* issues in constant change. But in the days, that the New Plural unfolded became this feature generally known and applied as sciences, politics and philosophy show in our days of digital nature.[12] In that light—from the New Plural as well as the Digital—seems the rearguard concerning the subject intensely important. One of the basic factors is indeed the position and the power of the subject in this newly developed twenty-first century's setting. The latter is determined by a New Plural anchored cognition, which unfolds in relation with the analog and is at the same time chained to the digital and influenced by AI and Quantum thought patterns. This complexity results in *cognition without (resp. beyond) subject-driven control hierarchy*. The role of the subject in that flow of control was in the preceding pages indicated as a *triple character* which includes the Subject, the Self and the Selfie/c. q. *Self-E*. The latter is more than a digital image of the Self: it is the digitally functioning Self, which is proposed to be indicated, resp. understood, as 'a Self-E'.

A conclusion fascinates: *the process of conversion is nearer than ever to the process of cognition*. The Subject's exclusive and central role in cognition has diminished during that unfolding proximity of the two. Its role did, in practice more than in any theory, transform into *a triadically structured potential* which is linked to all components of the New Plural and has all the spiritual as well as social space which is necessary to unfold emotionally. The latter is truly revolutionary; this becomes clearly visible if one compares the processes of conversion which played a dominant role in the period of the DACs and the ADCs as described in the above Chapter VII. The latter remained limited to the special task of correctly and profitably adapt certain techniques or instruments from the analog to the digital spheres of research and activity. In the recent period, characterized by the employment of the New Plural, became those two processes submitted to wider and more general socio-cultural processes. One of their features is an intensified understanding of data and dates that operate in the self-zones: these are, as mentioned, linked with what was named 'the S-triad' [the Subject, the Self, and the Self-E] in their multifunctional

[12] See: https://en.wikitionary.org/wiki/conversion.

settings—(*emotional* dimensions, which are seldom skipped from the knowledge process) included. Such a diversity of signs is characteristic for the actual world and its multidimensional meanings. Conversion became in that light a most natural and generally accepted procedure to keep meanings at the level of understandability.

Consequently, one must confirm that our twenty-first century's view on the world became different because of the New Plural's plurality—which has vested itself in our mind as 'the new normal'. Visions and practices of the analog world were changed within precisely that context. The Digital, its dominance and social importance included, became in the New Plural's context a *sign* of that change! And that newly signaled sign has the 'S-triad' as one the most relevant cultural and social axes one can discover. No, it is not like we must discover the passion and impact of the Subject, as was the case in ages since the Ancient Greek. On the contrary, we should rediscover the tensions between the different parts of the multiplicity which the Self brings us in these 'post-analog' days. One of its components reminds us how the traditional Subject lived from the ability *to grasp* what must become known and appreciated as a substance of life in this world.[13] That attitude brought 'possession' as an almost holy part of our knowledge and condemned any relevance of it as a factor that determines cognition. Is the 'S-triad' a formula to overcome this attitude, which enjoyed economy, law, psychology as well as mathematics and other sciences as the eminent protector of life and goodwill on earth?

Is it impossible to answer that question with a 'yes' or 'no' beyond doubt or hesitation? The components which make our knowledge into an obsession to *possess* what we like to know, and those that make it solely a drive to make the essential components *fit* are by no means delineated. We accept and read *signs* of them and are not aware of the semiotic complexity in which we live. Is knowledge today dominating interacting minds? That is never unmasked, even not in the tendencies which dominate the multiplicity of the Self, which was left after the enduring rearguard troubles of the subject. The Self became a mask for another Self, as the digital concept of *interface* made clear. Such types of newly conceived communicative dynamics seem essential for conversion, which creates a deeper and more actual understanding of cognition in our digital days.

But there is a surprising conclusion to add. The relation between cognition and conversion contains much more than the simple word 'and' as written in the title of this book. Their relation is foundational for men and society, for human nature and cosmos, and especially for 'I' and 'You'. The three are so often considered as a key to our knowledge and understanding. It shows how the simple addition as enclosed in their 'and' to combine cognition and conversion, became in our days replaced by a complex pattern of the dynamic 'S-triad'. That replacement seems an important *sign* which is broader than any *filling* or even *fulfillment* in a semiotic context. And what is more: not only the character of such an 'and' between cognition and conversion seems at stake, but also, and perhaps in the first place, the *inner world* of the general order we are gifted to endure in our digital days. They understand the world as an

[13] See Chapter I, §3.

infinite receiver and container of a human *logos*—a rationality which is embedded in reception and application of rational as well as irrational implications that form life's well–fare conditions.

Neither cognition nor conversion seem to be a final determinant. The 'and' that brings the two together, appears as the vital *sign* that ultimately transcends each semiotic attempt to awaken the appearance of core elements which function in man and cosmos. This is what *conversion* pretends to *contribute* rather than to *be*: it wants to transcend positions such as cognition and conversion, their 'yes' and 'no', because both are no more than fixated positions. But they should belong to the flows in cosmos and human mind. That feature should be understood, so that the 'and' between the two (the cognition as well as the conversion) will bridge the 'yes' *and* 'no'—a bridge on which the leading voice of human life can be heard as a two-part song. The 'and' hides an unexpected and hardly understood power, which reaches far beyond the power of conjunction: *the power to meet the riddle of the plural.* In that power is the energy of art and design enclosed, in full: the form and format of human life. The 'and' seems to embrace as well as deliver; Rosenzweig named for that reason the 'and' one of the primeval words a human language could encompass. Thinking cognition includes what today is called conversion through that word and its flow. In other words: 'the wealth of the 'yes' and the 'no' is enclosed, bridged, and protected in the 'and'. The latter expresses a unity of cognition and conversion which seems reborn under our actual digital conditions of multicultural lives and thoughts. This unity appears to lay the foundation for a Mondial Ideal: a cosmic understanding—an interface of hardly imaginable dimensions which could become in essence the language of humanity as such.

References

Adorno TW (1980) Negative Dialektik. Suhrkamp, Frankfurt a.M

Benjamin W (1972) In: Tiedeman R, Schweppenhäuser H (eds) Gesammelte Schriften. Suhrkamp, Frankfurt a.M

Bürger P (1979) Mediation - Rezeption - Funktion. Ästhetische Theorie und Methodologie der Literaturwissenschaft. Suhrkamp, Frankfurt a.M

Green MS (2017) Know thyself–the value and limits of self-knowledge: the examined life. Routledge & Kegan Paul, London

Habermas J (1981) Theorie des kommunikativen Handelns. Suhrkamp, Frankfurt a.M

Habermas J (1985) Der philosophische Diskurs der Moderne. Zwölf Vorlesungen. Suhrkamp, Frankfurt a.M

Jacobi FH (2009) Lettre à Fichte (1799): Lettres sur le nihilisme. GF-Flammarion

Rosenzweig F (1921/1930) Der Stern der Erlösung, 3rd edn. Lambert Schneider, Heidelberg

Scholem G (1957) Die jüdische Mystik in ihrer Hauptströmungen. Suhrkamp, Frankfurt a.M

Chapter 9
Conversions Convert Us All

Abstract Once they were contrasting: the concepts of cognition and of conversion. Today, they became synthesizing and bridged by the 'and' we created for them. The pain and difficulty of that creation is a moment of philosophical thought formation—which was never a completely independent and self-employed power. It might be the greatest challenge in this context to consider that no component of that insight could unfold without the Self considered as the omni–factor of this entire flow embracing mind and world.

After all considerations in the above texts are tendencies to register, which require further consideration. The preceding pages showed how we are positioned in perspectives that are very different from earlier days, especially when the complexities of meaning and sign are at issue.

(a) The most influential type of cognition is the Digital *amidst* and *related with* Analog, AI, and Quantum approaches—a type named 'The New Plural'. Stable and traditional patterns of cognition reigned since Plato and Aristotle, but today exist new forms on Humanity, Life, Self and Cosmos which enforce new forms of cognition. The human Self (introduced in these pages as 'the 3-S triade') does still play a primary role in those transformations—but that Self is never a fully determinable entity like the Subject once was. In other words: all of us are involved in digitalized processes of conversion.
(b) These considerations challenge us to connect with a further understanding and more radical differentiation of the traditional Subject—even in most intimate regions. We focus therefore on the structure and activities of the mentioned 'S-triad' as well as the 'semiosphere of the Self' and suggest the new term 'Self-E' to indicate the Self as Master of Digital Activity.
(c) This leads to a further analysis of dissolving borderlines between cognition and conversion. That dissolution characterizes our days of digital thinking and living; the process itself creates a bridge between the two C's and offers new forms of integration.

J. M. Broekman, *Knowledge in Change*, Law and Visual Jurisprudence 8,

9.1 The Self and the Self-E

Self and *Self-E* are terms with meanings introduced in the preceding pages. The term *Self-E* is destined to function as the new expression for the Self when it functions as the Subject of- and in the digital world. It thus indicates the knowing and knowledgeable Subject or Self when digital signs and meanings unfold. Emphasis is, most interestingly, on the special character of the Self as a center of digital activity—including those occurrences which concern the digital self-determination of the actor in digital contexts. The preceding pages proposed the term '*Self-E*' as a special indication for *the Self in Digital Spheres and fields of Meaning*. That term indicates spheres which also played a role in earlier descriptions concerning this type of ego-positions. One encounters such ego-positions for instance in the last century's phenomenology: Husserl showed how that philosophical understanding and exploration of the issue already had a history of many ages. But criticism since those days focused on the *'subject-object' frame* of such ego-positions, mainly those who were worked out in mechanisms of what Husserl proposed as a 'phenomenological reduction'.[1] He articulated how a human existence is always founded upon a plurality of ontological structures, so that all our interpretations seem embedded in a plural ontology. A *subject–object frame* on its own will thus never be sufficient to achieve a sound insight in human subjectivity. But nearly all utterances of the past centuries were related to types of cognition which were founded upon that frame, and especially on the 'subject'. They were all viewed as fixated by a 'Self' and did not focus on a 'Self-E'. One could really write a cultural history of the links between Subject and Self when they originate cognition—and would never truly finish that text![2]

It is in this context of great interest to keep in mind how the term 'Subject' became already relevant in the sixteenth century, the concept 'Self' in the 17th, the concept 'Selfie' in the 20th and the proposed 'Self-E' in the twenty-first century. A Selfie embraced primarily an *incidental smartphone photograph of oneself* (its concept originated 2002 in Australia by Jim Krause) but was soon involved in a worldwide exploration by means of today's digital techniques. This process confirms how signs are given meaning, and those meanings function as the often most important component of culture! That forms a philosophical background for the need of a *continuous fittingness* among the three: the Subject, the Self, and the Self-E. That dynamics is basal in the process of *conversion* and might for many researchers also be a key to understand the concept of *semiosphere* in relation with semiotics. Activities in a semiotic sphere might namely be culturally differentiated, but they are never an exclusive matter of any specific cultural pattern! The mutuality

[1] Broekman (1963). See also this book Ch. III, §3.

[2] See: Singer (1980), p. 485f. See also: Colapietro (1989), p. 99f. Id.: Charles S. Peirce: *Collected Papers of Ch. S. Peirce, Vol 7,* Cambridge Massachusetts: The Belknap Press of Harvard University Press, [A. W. Burks, Ed.] 1958, p. 591f. Mangieri (2022). Cfr; Torop (2005). https:// www. ceeol.com/search/article-detail?id=14989.

of Subject, Self and Self-E is not identical with culture itself, although it will sometimes be validated as a culture-founding process. A new qualification must be contrived in relation to the often proposed 'New Plural'. That is a task ahead whenever the coherences of Cognition and Conversion are studied! One should not refer to the three whilst contextualizing them in the traditional meaning and sense of 'culture'. This cannot be accepted because they are engendered and functional in patterns of Analog, Digital, Artificial Intelligence, and Quantum Mechanics thought formation.

Mutuality thus determines our interest in *meaning and sign* which creates the Self and the Self-E. Their creation is observable in the very moment in which a Self-E signalizes how it completed the Self's sphere through becoming recognized by itself as a Self-E! It is important to focus on the fact that this mutuality between Self and Self-E is closely related to the roots of daily life in its global context. The clouded sky at the horizon of our knowledge indicates that cognition became problematic in the days of 'the New Plural'. Its anchor-point, for centuries understood as a Subject, evaporated in a Self and a Self-E (apart from the Selfie which was never fully accepted in digital knowledge patterns). *The adaptation of those three anchor points sustains our worldwide network of digital knowledge.* Our gaze and our hand often reach in vain for a highly needed identity, but this seems to disappear with the fast flow of those sustaining components.

These thoughts and ideas are not distanced from real life experiences in past and present. Imagine for a moment the year 1888 and its September 10th, the 49th birthday of Charles S. Peirce who just in that year bought a residence in the USA's Pennsylvanian village named Milford! He had explored already the connections between Epistemology and Logic: the latter was in his eyes (and according to the tradition of his days) a form of the first. One of his most recent ideas was the 1886 discovery that 'electric gearings can perform logical operations'—a rated version of the digital performances our computers deliver today.[3] But long before he already positioned the problem of finding the locus, identity, unity, and continuity of the Self in the steadily changing stream of science and consciousness which embraces all of us: for him was the Self not an individual organism, but the result of semiotic thought formation. 'Great'! 'Wonderful'! Peirce would have fervently enjoyed reading the term 'Self-E'. As explained in preceding chapters is today's rise of the digital culture based on the application of earlier DAC-techniques and their later performances of conversion. This impresses because—as we explained—it is as if those techniques concretize the realization of Immanuel Kant's 'split ego'. Our actual consciousness (related to 'the I which is becoming a Self') evolves herewith into an unknown future. An important aspect of its future and function was named 'Selfie' and should now become even more independently and appropriately named as 'Self-E'. That change is studied neither philosophically nor semiotically.

It seems precisely in this context important to underline how *conversion* functioned as *a silent power of semiotic articulation of the Self and the Self-E* in the heart

[3]Burks (1978), pp. 913–18.

of all those changes! Notice, how the concept of speech is absent here, although the Self-E seems to free us from fixated patternings of knowledge and provides us a hitherto unknown enjoyment of cognitive freedom in- and through digitality. Yet, the three (subject, self and self-E) remain equally determinative despite the concurrent strong priority pertaining to the digital type of thought and action. So, observe the Self-E in this regard! No, that concept does not represent a 'modernistic view, which can hardly be given a grip'. The differentiation of a Self and a Self-E might be actual, but its possibility was foreseen in earlier years and perhaps even ages. One has therefore to ask, what in that light means 'the *continuous* adaptation of the three'? And how do we understand the Self that produces the Self-E which creates a self-understanding at digital distance from the classical subject's Self? But there is more to say: what about the insight that formula and practice of the Self-E became in the digital culture of today the only possible manner to format social relations? The Self-E seems to create The Other in what became in our days the 'receiver world' thanks to its digital character. But how do we express the importance of the digital in processing that Other? We mostly do not know, and what occurs is no longer to understand as the consequence of a well-determined action of the Subject which we believe to be! Yes, indeed: take your smart phone and click one of the many options the instrument offers you. With each choice you change into a somewhat different subject and perhaps also a different *Self* because of the multiple consequences of your click. All clicks make you responsible, participating, liable, and making law: via your usage, because you are in the patterns of your phone a subject created by law that creates law—and will be named 'Self-E'!

You may have wanted to do something different with your smartphone: to photograph a nice situation, a portrait of you walking with others or amid wonderful flowers: your face framed by great roses. But be aware that with all of this you created a 'Self-E', as we propose to call it today and as it originated as a portrait of your Self in a specific situation and was called a 'Selfie'. All this is based on the forceful medium techniques in your phone, which deliver the impression that the world should be understood as if it were a composite of Selfies! In that world we live and look—here I was, look at it! And there it looks as if I was attentive: look at it. Give it a glance: this position I had yesterday here! You see me now, but that is only today—it all looks as if, but if you take a closer look, you change your impression. The entirety of the Self becomes a sign in all visual contexts. It is offered here and now by the smartphone remembering yesterday's positions; therefore, you cannot accept or think of a negativity, a plurality, an unethical scenery, or a heartbreaking plurality. The Self is *here and here*, it is not *there* and will never submerge in an unknown composition—it is here, and it is Self creating a Self-E. The world is the result of an infinite mirroring, Walter Benjamin would have remarked during his walks in *Parisian Passages* which composed his Mirror-Town. Remember Colapietro writing: '...if the self is a semiotic process, it is a complex type of such a process, one in which there is ramification and also one in which the various branches of the process act on one another'.[4]

So, these are the 'interacting minds' in our lives: not only the view, the picture, the portrait, the calculation, but even the alphabet itself and its analog contexts fulfill a role in our emotions: and life encompasses even more than those contexts! It confirms the insight that knowledge and understanding are not straightforward effects of a logic of the mind.[5] Feelings are important factors in semiotics, even if they are hardly traceable! We all depend upon our enculturation processes and their plural character. Today, in digital thoughts, do we for instance associate and encounter the E- as it were an index for the electronically generated and digitally mastered cloud in which we shape our minds, ideas, and intellects. We experience fundamental issues of the world of everyday with that letter. With him are we often at an important distance from barriers we experience as indications of our normal limitations in life. However, those limitations form in their overwhelming togetherness a unique and forceful process. This experience of today's digital power underlines the meaning and sense of a *process*, which might become endlessly more powerful than any sum or other form of togetherness of Selves, resp. Self-E's. Meaning begun to shrink, and the meaning of meaning seems to disappear from our sight as well as our insight. Deleuze and Guattari formulated in their well-known *Anti-Oedipus* that 'there is no such thing as either man or nature now, only a process that produces the one within the other and couples the machines together. Producing-machines, desiring-machines everywhere ... the self and the non self, outside and inside, no longer have any meaning whatsoever!'[6]

One suddenly remembers the small statue of the famous author Gertrude Stein[7] in Manhattan's Bryant Park, next to New York's Public Library. To explain her readers the essence of a rose, and ultimately of life itself, she coined the words 'a rose is a rose is a rose is a rose'. Stein's struggle was to overcome prejudices vested in our language and in all linguistic articulations. Language, she formulated, is a real thing in itself and not the imitation of sounds, colors or emotions. I think, she suggested once, that in that line the rose is red for the first time in English poetry for a hundred years! Her suggestion encloses the awareness that language is an everlasting activity in the life of humans, including almost all forms of intellectual recreation.

Yes, your phone allows you even larger and more distinct forms of your Self's image of yourself—in ways that could not be imagined some 20 years ago and which are still not completely identical with any self-image you cherish today! Mind and

[4] *Id.* p. 67, 136.

[5] Kandel (2012), p. 185 ff.

[6] Deleuze and Guattari (1984), p. 2.

[7] Gertrude Stein, (1874–1946) was a well-known American novelist, poet, playwright, and art collector. She was born in Pittsburgh, Pennsylvania, and lived from 1903–1946 in Paris. Modern painting had a profound effect on her writing. In her prose poems, images and phrases came together similar in manner to Cubist painting. Her use of words characterized associations and sounds rather than meanings, and received considerable interest from other artists and writers, although they did not find a wide audience.

self were reduced to moments of your brain's activity before your phone and its digital world existed. Today, subject and self come together again, but in new dimensions. It is, as if this togetherness creates a new social and cultural event—and yet: a letter is a letter is a letter! But the Self-E (produced by the togetherness of Subject and Self, thus transcending the barriers between analog and digital thought formation) is only a fraction of the Self we know and thus accept as component of the consciousness of our identity. My smartphone makes me into a complicated and above all multiple personage: I am a subject in its social as well as legal sense, but also a self to finally be introduced in social relations—and all that transcends my being subject! But is that sufficient to understand the letters this subjectivity embraces?

Especially the latter observation is problematic in a digital context and its frames of understanding. 'To be' and 'to have' became different issues in the digital. Our terminology which expresses and supports feelings, emotions and awareness created a distance between face-to-face relations and messages on E-mail and other digital means. The letter E- indicates an important focus on a different world. Roles of speaker and hearer change constantly in modern culture, the reciprocal relations create a field of tensions among them, there are no two separated specialized fields at issue. Those tensions are thus never possessed by only one of the two. Speaking subjects are de-centered by their speech-activity, as your smart-phone indicated. Their function is in the field they partially constitute by their simple presence. Your phone should bring communication, but it can only function thanks to well-defined and well-fitting positions in that field. The latter do not create a domain, a communication field or community. Your Self-E is an attempt to de-center what needs to be a center in order to function. For example, try to discuss a sensitive situation via your iPhone. You cannot, since that instrument is not a component of the situational sensitivity and does not offer lingual structures at stake. No: *the E- is a newly conceived cloud that colors how we experience the world of every day*. It is hardly possible to express what particles, what substances, what spaces are constituting that cloud. And yet, the E.- remains a letter, which is but a letter! Are we able to join everybody's struggle to articulate the essence of one's own life? What about our letters?

The question is by no means nonsensical! It leads immediately to the newly introduced expression 'Self-E' and especially the in this context hitherto unused 'E'. Indeed, the 'E' is no more than a letter, but what is the meaning and sense of this one moment of our alphabet? That question challenges us to find a way from apparently innocent considerations of the digit to deeper layers of understanding. The Self-'ie' is just a moment, a fleeting mini-image, a flowing nil, a shadow-possessive pronoun linked with a smartphone picture which just catches a short moment, a 'here' which is hardly a 'now'. The letter 'E' is, in contrast, a serious affair. The Self-'E' is the Self, indicated by the letter 'E' to indicate a center of digital fields and operatives—which are perfectly comparable with the Subject functioning in earlier fields of knowledge and understanding. Writing a letter is no longer an innocent activity. They direct us to long lists of concepts and expressions which dominate our world as well as our activities in that global domain. On could perform and go on using the entire alphabet and check which words are already partially or even completely determined by the 'E-'letter. Others would be on the edge of that position and several but not many did escape! Only a few speakers made clear in their speech activities how they remained distanced from the 'E-'world!

Notice, how E- is

> experience, e-commerce, e-trade, e-bay as well as e-business, e-communication, e-mail, e-information, e-electronics

which leads us to

> exceptions, extensions, explorations, externalizing attitudes, to extremes, exults and exuberances

as well as to

> ecology, e-programs, e-devices, e-environments, e-teachers, e-centers,

not to mention

> european, eventualities included!

One important eventuality among many others is the fact that conversations of all kinds play a role in the e-world. It is apparently not the devices but the exchanges of lingual nature which seem essential. So, if one analyses an e-conversation of whatever nature, there seems to be a central cluster: *the you and me and the world of E-*. Is that a newly formatted dialogic context? Difficult to decide is that there seem to be two real and one virtual partner in an e-dialogue. Two real persons are accepting the third, which is represented by the presence and effects of E-. So, is typing your e-mail or writing a text on your laptop a form of E- including speech? One should take serious how the e-world upgrades your writing—at least to speech levels and perhaps sometimes even higher. What privacy is at stake when you deliver a speech with your smartphone in your hands? What are you doing in your parliamentary discussion with your handheld E-device on the table, next to your hand-written notes? Where is the borderline between private and public in such cases? Don't forget that written and spoken words possess small and very limited reach compared with the global reach of e-written words!

Indeed, if we follow these thoughts, we become aware of the important fact that any *sphere* implies a definitive recognition of the importance of *speech*. The latter is not an issue of individual utterances, of letters, words, numbers, ideas, and the like, but of a particular activity sustained by special composites. We mentioned how spheres are based on con/texts rather than on texts. That can be gathered from the social influence of for instance certain numbers or letters, including their function as well as feelings and indications. That is also the case in the growing influence of digital expressivities, which are also noticeable in human speech. In the days of the answer world (Welby), which in subtle and complicated manners changed into a 'receiving–world', transferred the relation of a human being that unfold in *speech acts*. The speaker as actual moment, as well as the hearer, were urged to fulfill the role of client as well as delivering party in any speech activity. This double sense is in all regards mirroring the position of a human being at the level of philosophy. A human 'being in speech' is in essence an eccentric being. Every thought, move, activity, relation, word, understanding is resulting from a 'point over the shoulder' and never the result of whatever fixated totality one could imagine being anchored wherever. A human is deeply, firmly, and existentially 'what he is not', namely: not complete, continuously growing and changing, in search of another identity, committing itself to other norms and values. There is always freedom and space to be different, to create the unexpected, the surprising or the alienating, the addictive, the dark side of the light in speech as well as in general language. You take your phone to convert or to confirm your situation? No wonder that otherness and alienation, the other person, that is: the beloved as well as the hatred, seem to outlive sameness in the concept of a self!

Here we are back to the Self and the digital Self-E! Both are a metaphor for the wealth of inner positions, which are created during the self's continuous positioning in life—even if we do not consider the inner dynamics of the specific position of the Self or Self-E for a moment. This creates a special precondition: one should no longer embrace views and thoughts within the boundaries of Hegel's concept of 'Sittlichkeit' or any comparable norm system, but put an eye on the terrestrial formations of human experience, insights and spiritual presences. Accepting a moment of discontinuity determines the flow of life on the planet—its globalization, climate change and interstellar positioning included. It occurs today, that our sciences do no longer embrace special relations with unities of norms and values made in located townships, world cities or laboratories. The same goes for modern democracies: several EU democracies seem in fight with nationalist tendencies; but they are not fully determined by local problems and insights! On the contrary: the profiling of the human mind mainly focusing on democracy is at stake. Whoever limits his or her observations to political boundaries will be the jester of terrestrial regions with different names, sounds or contexts of what we experience as a Self. Whoever brings features of individual words or speech in question as data, challenges the limits of analog norm systems ad reaches out to abolish any ambiguity of morals. Bringing such features back to the world of analog expressivity is not and should not be the same as restoring a constitutional legal system and its coherent state concept as the basis for a post-critical democracy. The digital culture creates flows that operate at distance from a litigious society: one 'diké' fights another—that's life! Subject and Self are enjoying it in their uninterrupted mutual conversions. Yes, we all became a *Self-E* in the digital days of today!

9.2 The Semiosphere of the Self

Introducing the 'Self-E' expands the *Semiosphere of the Self.* But language, text, and culture are not apt to fully grasp the *sphere* within which the *seme* fully functions. A sphere is linked to flaming and sensitivity, and that seems neglected when the semiosphere is understood as a parallel with the biosphere, the noo–sphere, the logo–sphere or even with v. Uexküll's German concept 'Um-welt'—all together parallels which should characterize our experience of reality! Notice that any 'bio-', 'noo-' or 'logo-' does *not* explain how *the sphere of the Self as such* could cause and create forms of life through meanings. The latter should cause the Self to unfold a meaningful life. Indeed: *spheres enable cognition*, but they do so through feelings of togetherness, sharing, and social orientation beyond economic or political calculations. Such components of spheric character are based on a mood, on shared sensations or on a readiness to commonly accept, judge, perceive, acknowledge, or decide knowledgeable issues at hand. So, the art to retrieve meanings and signs is coloured by a subject or a self that is able, willing, and even successful in *looking beyond* any cultural structuring and is open for the multidimensional dimensions of our grip on reality and its multiple meanings! One should therefore repeat the question at hand: how does one understand the concept *Semiosphere of the Self*, including the *sphere* that harbours the Subject, the Self, and the Self-E? One aspect fascinates: a sphere is never without a well-designed subject but on the other hand never fully determined by it. Any question concerning the term *Semiosphere* should therefore not in the first-place focus on the '*semiotic'* dimensions but on the '*sphere'* character, including the social and psychological features of its 'Self'.

In that perspective are for instance Juri Lotman's and other studies of the Tartu-Moscow School fundamental. However, their suggestion that a semiosphere and its rational structuring should primarily be understood in the frame of cultural dynamics, does not suffice—even when those dynamics are considered to imply constitutive 'language/text/culture' relations or the 'creation of general culture studies and understanding methodology'.[8] A new sphere of meaning and articulation thus seems observable. Notice, how the concept of 'sphere' is hardly functional in the rationalities of the discipline called semiotics. Spheres are impressions, vague determinations which offer a meaning on the base of con/texts rather than of clearly determinable and fixated texts or speech phenomena. It was mentioned but not analyzed in the preceding paragraph: spheric meanings can be gathered from the social and often also emotional influence of for instance certain numbers, or letters of the alphabet, including the place and function as well as feelings and indications of an 'a', 'b' or 'y', an 'E', an 'Y', a '5' or a '7' and others. That is absolutely the case in digital expressivities and their growing influence. Peirce has already exemplified this emphasis on letters and numbers when considering the meaning which the First, the Second and the Third obtain in his own philosophical approaches—his words formulated literally what he called a *guess at the riddle*! His inner struggle became expressed in words of that riddle: 'Perhaps I might begin by noticing how different numbers have found their champions.' Not the numbers but the search for numbers seems important, he underlines. 'Two was extolled by Peter Ramus, Four by Pythagoras, Five by Sir Thomas Browne, and so on. For my part, I am determined foe of no innocent number; I respect and esteem them all their several ways; but I am

[8] Lotman (1998); Lotman (2005), p. 205f.; Lotman (1990); Lotman (2009). See also: Torop (2005). See also: Hartley et al. (2020), p. 591f. Mangieri (2022). Cfr; Torop (2005). https://www.ceeol.com/search/article-detail?id=14989.

forced to confess to a leaning to the number three in philosophy. In fact, I make so much use of three-fold divisions in my speculations . . . ideas so broad that they may be looked upon as moods or tone of thoughts, then as definite notions, but which have great significance for all that.'[9]

And what can scientists, specialists, philosophers, psychologists, or educators explain us so that they present their understanding as an elucidation of the E-sphere? Is this requirement reduced to electronics, cyber techniques, electric cable systems and networks, or to the business of providing new communication facilities which embrace the leap of the century and ultimately new realities?[10] A virtue of any answer to such questions is the widening of our experience concerning the touch of all E- 's which affect all of us in our daily activities, plans, wishes or works. The E- is not only an instrument or an essential part of a complex coherence of various instruments but rather the central identification of today's bio-sphere, life-sphere or sphere concerning essence and globality—no matter whether computers and smart phones are available or used. It fascinates how one must write those words down, because their institutional acknowledgement seems widely absent in the new formats of our worldwide thought-formation with- and without computer networks around globe and spacecrafts.

We repeat our earlier reference to numbers. Peirce is not hesitating to mention that for him the ideas of First, Second, and Third '*may be looked upon rather as moods or tones of thought*, than as definite notions . . .'! The three are fundamental in his ideas about a new foundational cosmology in which numbers fulfill a central role—a positioning so characteristic for the digital culture of today. 'The First is that whose being is simply in itself, not referring to anything nor lying behind anything. The Second is that which is what it is by force of something to which is second. The Third is that which is what it is owing to things between which it mediates, and which brings into relation with each other.' And Peirce adds as a sneer: 'what the world was to Adam on the day he opened his eyes to it (. . .) that is first, present, immediate, fresh, new, initiative, original spontaneous, free, vivid, conscious, and evanescent.'[11]

What was suggested here? It is like a description and at the same time a construction of the *semiosphere* which should unfold a continuously changing, floating, formatting, knowing and knowledgeable Self! For that reason, we introduced the Self-E. Seldom does one encounter a clearer attempt to describe a proposal concerning triadic logics which in its deepest sense is a sphere! Rethink the difference between a sign in a *sphere* contrasted to a meaning in *discourse*—would Peirce have thought, and Foucault after him. But Peirce remains emphasizing the exemplification of triads (i.e., numbers) of ideas instead the spheres of semiotic accentuations. And that seems a final distancing from the indeterminacy of *sphere* (which remains central and essential for us today) and an insight that guides him in the

[9]Peirce (1992), p. 247f.

[10]See Kurzweil (2005).

[11]Idem, p. 347f. (My Italics. JMB).

infinite calculative differentiation which features knowledge. So, *in leaving the sphere behind, Peirce opens his thoughts which pertain to our actual features of cognition*. In other words, he chose to redirect his points of departure. The latter appeared to be a change from conversion to cognition and he tried, most astonishingly, to find its foundations in a change from cognition to conversion!

Is that still possible? The development of a human character in cyberspace is difficult to circumscribe, or to analyze by means of the cognition patterns we cherish. Our conclusions about the triple character of the Self seem to confirm that observation. Apart from the special *character of a human body and its psychological space* should the occurrence of specific *character marks of cyberspace* be mentioned.[12] The existence of cyberspace on itself relates deeper and far more influential on human beings than any classical mind-body theme ever could suggest. Note the linguistic formulations at issue: an immersion in the digital and in its cyberspace brings us a double meaning of the word 'space' the *human* space and the *cyber*space are by no means equivalent. One should keep this distinction in mind because it plays a role in all second thoughts and speculations about the virtual and its digital features. What is made visible, tangible or perceptible is implicitly made to abolish some of the most impeding differences between human space and cyberspace. A basic argument is that the mind's eye and the physical eye should be regarded as working closely together, so that the eye can be determined as possibly wired to the brain via a computer. We should, in effect, interface with our own thoughts, experiences and ideas! That is not only at stake in the digital techniques and cyberspace but also in what is called today the AI, 'Artificial Intelligence'—an important component of today's 'New Plural'. It seems interesting that in this case the human body seems to be understood as the birthplace of this interface, in other words: a carrier of extra-sensorial awareness, since it combines *sensorial* and *artificial* awareness. Is that insight a reconfirmation of the complexity we named 'semiosphere'?

The combination of the sensorial and the artificial presents the riddle again how the activity of a human mind and a human body integrate. Notice: this includes explanations concerning the body proper and above all the in a body enclosed *Self*! A *sameness* of cyber space and body space seems in this light one of the most important suggestions to unfold human cognition. It is important to accentuate that this suggestion is not possible without the digital's dynamics of conversion! Embodiment and disembodiment are both determining human knowledge. They do so in an exemplary manner through their appeal on embodiment as a constitutive moment of human relations – which finds ultimately its confirmation in the digital expression 'interface'.

[12] Broekman (2004) Ch. IV, §2: *The Body in Cyber-Education*, p. 116 ff. See also: Turkle (1985), p. 309f.– Id.: Rosanne Stone (1991), p. 81ff.

9.3 Are Interfaces Facial?

The question is of importance, and directly relevant for the relation of human beings to the dimensions and properties of the digital as expressed in the many forms of cyberspace. The central interest humans are spending to their participation in the universe was always mirrored in a positioning of Mind and Self which strived for congruence with universal patterns. The triadic structure of the Self is a complicated addition in this view. Metaphorical features of the human face are an enrichening addition but not a fundamental issue. Does cyberspace need human faces so that it can function? Perhaps only to enter and to effectuate that space as a cognitive instrument, but not to create or just understand existential profiles! One should notice how human profiles are in the latter more intensively related with *metaphors* than with *data*!

Data must be engaged in a form of communication if they can become accepted as data! Interface is one of cyberspace's privileged expressions of such a global requirement. But what is an interface in a simple definition? Or does another word for interface exist? Several verbal expressions do indeed indicate interface, despite its clearly artificial character. Think of terms like such as port, configuration, graphic, device, workflow or functionality—not to forget face book! *Face* is an active metaphor and at the same time is cyberspace and its interface(s) a privileged place for *disembodied communication*. So, there exist deeply hidden contrasts between components of the cyber-dimensions, although a face seems to represent the human body beyond problems. But the contrasts between face and space are outstanding here! The expression 'cyberspace' is apparently a metaphor which conceals various meanings—all such meanings are a parallel to 'face.' *It is remarkable how many body-related expressions are at stake in the process of articulating the digital and the cyber-thinking, resp. cyber-activity!* Does a communication without bodily activity exist? That reality seems to reign the definition of the digital and its techniques. Do the latter function thanks to a hidden metaphor as their basis? Is, despite our general impression of the cyber reality as being at a decisive distance to the human body, the latter the final and exquisite metaphor for human communication? Is the human face its most concentrated and fundamental metaphor in that regard?

A possible insight in such questions which can lead to an answer is in *communication in se and per se* which is the striving for all elements of our digital culture. The most explorable factors for communication are speech (resp. language) and face. These are constantly present and leading metaphors of the cyber world. An all-embracing feature of the human body in digital techniques and thought patterns is its abstraction. The distance between the portraited selfie and actual social togetherness becomes worldwide in effect thanks to cyber techniques based on abstraction from the human body! The same is true for speech: words as elements of cyber-communication reach widely and bridge barriers between spoken languages.[13] Why is all this so important for the cyberworld, why are these fulfillments sometimes technically as well as socially difficult transportable and transformable (conversion) elements? Because not words or faces themselves are directly at stake: they are only important for cyberspace via its metaphorical uses as a basis for communication. Notice, how the latter is not important because of transhuman considerations but of the technical limberness of data. They are globally at stake and form the platform of exchanges in all regards: economically, scientifically, socially, religiously and philosophically.

Cyberspace is in this light a marketplace, a place of unlimited exchange and disembodied communication. Metaphors of the human body fulfill a major role in that context: they claim an enduring proximity of the market and its techniques of communication on the one hand, and the dignity of the human being on the other. In that way seems the highest quality of proximity to be reached at distances which are hitherto unknown. E-communications thus strive for correctness and validity of social practices which are only social in their metaphorical context. They fulfill at a technically high level in linguistically changed dimensions which were already in 1936 formulated by the English linguist and philosopher I.A. Richards, who wrote: 'The processes of metaphor in language, the exchanges between the meanings of words which we study in explicit verbal metaphors, are super-imposed upon a perceived world which is itself a product of earlier or unwitting metaphor, and we shall not deal with them justly if we forget that this is so'.[14] Richards could in the year of writing those thoughts not have imagined how in his days non-existent cyberworlds would underline these words. It is today clear how metaphors structure our perceived world, our bodily existences included—they even do that in the center and full activities of the digital culture. They create sameness and similarity needed in the twenty-first century for worldwide communication and cyber exchange regarding data of global interest. The question of a foundational background of all these processes is shriveled in the background descriptions of reality delivered by the digital.

It is therefore not surprising, that we are interested in the consequences of the *artificial* character of faces.[15] They are meaningful because they are *given* a meaning long before their activities unfold. Their artificial aspects lead to at least three philosophical implications. One should primarily never lose interest in the *mental* components of facial phenomena. A second feature is all-embracing: the effect of faces in human life are neither understandable nor perceivable without *abstract* dimensionalities in effect. This should be understood as a constitutive moment of the generalizing power which inspires everyone who perceives a face. Comprehending the meaning of a face needs powers and forms of abstraction to understand the essence of facial features. A third feature is the existential dimension, which underlines the fact that facial expressions aways need to be interpreted. A

[13] See Chapter VII. §3.

[14] Richards (1971), p. 109.

[15] Broekman (2009), p.45ff and: Broekman (2010), p. 41ff.

'blank face' is not an exception in that regard. Those three dimensions find their common ground in the fact that a bearer of a face is never the only one to create meaning. Every face is the result of a social correlation and an interpretation of an Other who participates in the encounter: there exists no natural and solipsistic autonomy of facial expression. Faces relate to bearers as well as observers which are at the same time interpreter. The sign quality of any face depends on those three, which are in their turn necessarily involved in interactivities.

An individual autonomy is thus never the privilege of any face. The Roman Deity *Janus* demonstrated that one face is never enough—he needed *two* faces to perceive in different and mainly opposite directions! That specialty brought him insight and knowledge concerning the past as well as the future. He thus represented the most powerful possibility of interactive life, which became for centuries a symbol of change and transition. The face, much more than any part of the human *corpus,* is a *sign* of a human life's dynamics.

A special moment is when someone sees another in the face. Do they mirror each other? No, because they would in that case not see anything and were just mirroring. Any face beyond interactivity has no expressivity and is therefore semiotically irrelevant. Faces are in essence interactivity, and they cannot become a sign outside that realm. In other words: a face is never in itself an entity, but it is always encapsulated in a meaning process, which is in a clearer formulation the creation of an entity becoming a sign. The deepest conclusion is that faces are meaning in the context of recognition. These dynamics are at stake if one looks in a mirror. One experiences in that case how interactivity gives life to that mirror image and to how others might perceive it. The Janus-experience repeats itself and articulates itself as if its words are: 'I am the one I was and will be!'

But the leading question 'Are Interfaces Facial?' is, however, not sufficiently answered by these considerations. One of the major reasons is the mechanistic self-supporting character of cyber techniques in which the term 'face' occurs. They are in fact forms of reality experience without an overtly accessible, rational or intuitive understanding and practicing. They try to function without the creative interference and variability of the human mind and related human activities. To watch, to observe, to act via the computer in the virtual spaces of the Web, the Internet or Cyberspace seems an act beyond borders or techniques. That act seems secretly anchored in metaphorical powers—even beyond linguistic barriers. Facial features of the Interface suggest a close and formative relationship with such powers.

Behind all this could a much simpler observation of the face and facial occurrences be enlightening. Keep in mind, that the first Selfies were a picture of the proper *face*! A text which presents the words of a politician, an artist or a scientist together with a *facial* image of the person in case is more attractive than the same words presented as a quotation in a general text. And within the frame of a photography is the face much more attractive than hands, coiffure, legs and feet or other parts of the human body. That entire differentiation is only enforced when human communication is at stake. Faces are the strongest components of the encompassing mirroring which strengthens human cognition. They do mirror themselves in each communicative act—and thus in each face that participates in that act.

In that context is it evident that we speak of a 'Facebook' or of 'Interfaces' in cyber techniques. The 'face'–terms are even not translated into other languages, not in French, German, Spanish, Portuguese or Chinese—they remain globally understood in the language of cybertechniques One must change the entire setting of one's computer to introduce and apply for instance Mandarin Chinese or other types of non-cyber language. And a German 'Gesichtsbuch' or a French 'Livre de Face' or a Spanish 'Libro de Cara' simply does not exist!

So, the answer to the question *whether Interfaces are truly 'Facial'* is complicated. Their description by means of the expression 'Face' is in two ways different from the sense and sentence of what is questioned. They are (a) *like* what is *metaphorical* in a natural language but (b) they are only *metaphorical* in what a natural language calls: an *artificial* language. This is what can happen in cyberspace being such a setting: the face can recognize itself as an artificial item involved in metaphorical processes. The emphasis is on re–cognition as a form of participation in non-natural spheres, and particularly in scientific and philosophically interesting discourses. One should notice that the ability of a human subject to cover such diverse spheres is one of the basic abilities to perceive one's face as an element of fascination pertaining to the properties and capacities of the technical perfections of the digital culture. Psychological, aesthetical and other components seem to participate in the construction of the variant matrixes of cyberspace. 'Space' and 'face' just belong to them! Ultimately will *all* linguistic expressions contribute to such positions, which are in general defined and practiced as a worldwide *disembodied communication*. This character designed as 'disembodiment' and practiced at various levels of human cognition and natural languages, empowers all of us to be engaged in processes of conversion of meaning, expression, interpretation and understanding reality.

In other words: without experiencing faces, we will never be able to understand, reconstruct or practice the realities in which we unfold our lives! Do not forget, that most of what we perceive and interpret in life, is based on explanations about their facticity given to us in a natural language. The Ancient Greek already told the story of Narcissus, who once did not understand his identity when mirroring in the water surface. He had *to be told* that what he saw was him*self*! In how many educational situations are those words repeated? We often must be told about our proper life! Once told, Narcissus could not distance himself from that image. Freud classified that situation in the framework of a psychopathology and coined the term 'narcissistic identification'. One should underline the fact that Narcissus *had to be told* the truth about himself, which he did not know already himself! The key-position of language should not be underestimated, and its contribution towards intersubjectivity not diminished! Any child's cradle is made of words about him and spoken to him are to be discovered in the framework of his or her specific identity. Lacan underlined that this mirror stage, in which the child is told about being (or becoming) a self, creates a fundamental alienation in its sense of self. The most intimate lingual expressions can alienate! Emerging selves are powerfully directed towards other selves, which were before that self-identification no more or less than a potential rival. Notice, that this concerns in the first place an act of speech. And it is not evident whether the participant will be a victim of the utterance or the receiver of a creative challenge. In other words: nobody is totally alienated from the Narcist story. The predisposition of an engendering self colors the situation in which it is said to me that this mirror image is *me*, Benjamin would have recalled whilst walking a Parisian Passage!

9.4 Mondial Reach

Mondial reach? Well, *interface* is in the twenty-first century indeed one of the instruments which concretizes this reach. The term first suggested the meeting of two or more subjects and later it became a broader and in the first place digitally inspired alternative for intersubjectivity. But the spirit of the digital expanded the term through an increase of subjects made to partner and consumer in number and character. Interhuman meetings took place at lager scales thanks to new technical developments. They reached even global distances, so that the diversity of the partners also increased: not only persons but also institutions and world-wide enterprises were embraced. All these forms of interaction became possible through the unfolding of computer programs and digital techniques which engendered the multiple possibilities of a world-wide contact.

The *face* thus became in that wide field a digital expression for the *alter*. Thinking the alter always fascinates, i.e., it cannot occur without the 'face'. Each fascination (in which the face plays a constitutive linguistical role) implies a moment of recognition or appreciation of the appearance of any alter ego. Context for that importance of the face is knowledge: but the latter is no longer related to a thought pattern dynamized by a subject! Today, in what we characterized as the 'New Plural', is all knowledge the outcome of a triadic activity, including the unfolding Subject, the Self, and the self-E. They are a unity which is in certain circumstances denominated as 'face'. This triad is the elaboration of insights and suggestions concerning 'person' and 'subject' which were based on Greek and Latin etymologies of the word 'person'. They seem alienated from insights in the digital world of today as well as consequences of their role created by cyberspace and related techniques.[16]

The idea that a semiotic consideration and activity is a matter of individuality was disproved by the fact that a Self is never a self-absorbed concept nor the practice of a solo living human individual. The semiosphere of an individual is in that perspective also not restricted to the embracement of social thoughts. The Self enforces its coherence with other Selves, and the position of the Self-E delivers and reinforces in addition the digital quality of that same tendency. They all concretize the process of conversion in view of that purpose. The Mondial Reach of that conversion (which is in that context to be understood as a newly unfolded and recognized form of cognition) is therefore a deeply philosophically anchored issue. But the dominance

[16] See Paolucci (2022), p.1257 ff.

of the digital culture in the heart of the New Plural will not stop the flow of important and innermost cultural changes. The insights presented by the above chapters do not suggest such a freeze. But challenge the dynamics of the plural.

Is your *alter ego* an ego like your *Self* and of the same world, or is a deeper understanding of the difference between you and your self a necessity—that means, a difference that enlightens the cosmos in which your feelings and accents are made knowledgeable? In other words: is the *ego* of an *alter-ego* always and beyond discussion an ego of the same Plural, or at least of the same fraction of that Plural? An *alter*native is possible, but seldom reflected: the ties of the *alter* can change fundamentally, so that the exploration of alterity embraces dimensions which were hitherto not considered—because they were in fact dimensions of another world? In other words: is the expression '*alter*' unsafe and unclear? The question needs to embrace insights in another pattern of thought related with other than the classical techniques. The term' interface' confirms relationality between faces in the digital culture and cyber techniques; it nevertheless means in all regards that face-to-face situations relate to meanings and embraces signs which are developed in the process that seems basic in the New Plural.

What once was the result of intentions and attempts of a Subject is today based on processual acts between a Subject, a Self, and a Self-E in their dynamic connexity. That is the most important thesis of this book. The triad is basic in understanding and practicing of what we characterized as *the Mondial Reach of Knowledge in our days*. The latter is immediately relevant for an insight into the dynamics of interweaving knowledge and conversion. It means, that knowledge did fundamentally transform in the last decades—whilst becoming an integrated element of the world of data and belonging to databases—so that purely individual forms of knowledge do not and cannot exist. Even a personal knowledge in the sense of a private insight in a problem is part and parcel of larger and more-encompassing dimensions. That has not only to do with the creation of knowledge but also with practices and explorations of known and knowledgeable facts called 'data'.

The latter requires a specific reconsideration. There seems to be a distance between the creation and exploration of human knowledge on the one hand and the palpation of facts on the other. That split between the two layers of the human mind imports today more than ever. One of the basic issues is the difference between being a socially accepted individual and its psychological engenderment. The latter is today more than ever at distance from the first: that forms a riddle of modern thought formation. Thinking can never lead to acting as a full-fledged membership of society, although the cyber technique and the digital culture seem to suggest that there is no real borderline between the social and the cyber world. But a memory is not solely acquired by birth, education or psychological development; it seems overshadowed by social and economic, even juridical positions on the international market of facts and data. You remember? Remember the organizer of data, who produces a *database* which functions as a memory. What and what context are to be remembered?[17] Sorry to interrupt, but what is remembering today? The question is not only a matter of what can be remembered in cyberspace but—as the appeal to memory indicates—also what it means if one suggests that 'cyberspace is psychological space'.[18] The question how human psychology is entering or creating a relation with cyberspace, might be difficult to answer. Human behavior in cyberspace psychologically understood even more. Suler suggested that 'cyberspace as a whole mirrors the collective human mind, its functions, knowledge, purposes, and hopes.'[19] Notice the role and function of the epistemological task which is conferred to the often-noticed process of mirroring!

It fascinates that cyberspace is said to be partially or completely created by the human mind *through mirroring*. An important reflection is noticeable between the *database* (an organized collection of structured information, or data, typically stored electronically in a computer system) and the *managing system* that controls that base (the DBMS). The two together should be understood and function as the *cyber memory*. One of the major motivations for this statement is the often-encountered idea that cyberspace is a space 'in person'. The latter insight is, however, not sufficient to clarify how cyberspace relates to human psychological factors (such as memory) in the world of data. Memory is engrained in multiple aspects of human life, especially in interaction, without any knowledge about a beginning, a cause or a birthplace of them. So, one is attempted to conclude that there is no investigation which can make any ground understandable and acceptable for psychological anchors of today's cyberworld. Behavior *in* cyberspace differs fundamentally from cyberspace itself being a level of human behavior that is psychologically accessible for our understanding in the 'New Plural'. Our thesis is in this context, that the function and global spread of databases do not deliver any insight in the structure of a human psyche of the twenty-first century. They do, however, initiate specific behavioral patterns, as can be concluded from the development of these bases, which evolved since the early 1960s. Navigational databases which allowed only a one-to-many relationship, and the later network database that allowed multiple relationships were the original systems. They used to store and manipulate data and were foundational for how today data is collected, stored, managed, and utilized. Today's large databases can support complex queries and nearly instant responses.[20] As a result, database administrators help improve cyber performance.

These performances are in principle Mondial Reach directives because they fulfill the following functions:

1. Basic for the activity and constant unfolding of the process between the three S-components in the New Plural, and in particular the observation that there is no pause, no stop, no intermittence in the constancy of that process.

[17] Blackman (2019), p. 28ff. (A study characterized as 'focusing on a psychomediation of datafied software culture').

[18] Suler (2016), p. 22.

[19] Suler (2016), p. 54.

[20] See: https://www.guru99.com/introduction-to-database-sql.html.

2. Indicating that individual powers of the coherent presence of the S-triad are enveloped in powers at different levels which always determine the meaning of an S-triad and create that meaning in the context of sign-creation and -activity. In that framework is the digital very exclusive and determining—as is demonstrated by the special S named Self-E, which is in fact the data-managing power in the S-triad operationality.
3. No Self-E will survive or function without data management anchored in the New Plural. It means, that there exists no digital self without the power to harmonize a Self with the social practices of interface-character.
4. Consequences of those observations do all relate with the phenomenon of a newly conceived *cognition* in the New Plural. This implies:

   (a) the reinforcement of the view on the three S which relates to a Subject-directed thought, resp. cognition patterning.
   (b) the sign is only effective based on the Self-E which can be activated to know meaning. It means, that there is no level of cognition in the general New Plural without the recognition and acknowledgment of signification by of the selfie.
   (c) The latter (since inherent to the New Plural) reaches from digital data cognition resp. conversion processes to fields of Artificial Intelligence and Quantum Views, because in the New Plural is the transference of meaning encapsulated in the unified dynamics of cognition and conversion.

5. One should underline the consequences of these connections in relation with the central thesis of this book: the links between cognition and conversion. All remarks on the concept of conversion are in this regard not a concluding thesis, but elements of the continuous process of conversion as determined by the New Plural. They create a possibility to understand a plurality which transcends the discriminatory outlines of the New Plural—a step which has truly cosmic consequences. The latter remark leads to the true background philosophy of this book's central thesis.
6. The dynamics of the New Plural never halt: the digital and its anchor remembered as the analog will reach out beyond their own barriers: the cognition-question brings us to the question what will be of importance after the digit. Will it at that moment be mathematical elements, i.e., thought patterns like the Artificial Intelligence seems to suggest, or other mathematical issues that reach out to a larger comprehension which the analytical activity of the Quantum thoughts seem to embrace?

9.5 Climate and Change

Of all components which coordinate modern knowledge is 'climate change' a key issue because it forms a constitutive element of global human life in all its variations. And, what seems most fascinating and philosophically relevant, the climate change issue embraces the human Subject beyond incidental dimensions of daily life. The First-Person Singular, the 'I' or the 'Self', and even the 'Self-E', are in a deeply engraved relation with the pearl of human life called 'cognition'. Anthropology and psychology play in that context an important role as the leading study of man. But an even broader and more specific background-question remains to be answered: 'how will the human mind conceptualize its awareness and knowledge of the planet and developments in its immediate surroundings in relation with himself?' The latter—often restricted to a vision on human life and its conditions—is indeed central and most challenging in the expression 'climate change'. Cognition is basic in that regard, as the many different uses of the term: 'change', show. They tell us: 'Human Life is Part of Life of the Planet in the Cosmos'. Keep in mind, that a human being was always a center of interest in that question—the subject was always speaker and hearer at the same time: always also in issues of climate and population. But a 'Speaker – Hearer' relation seems today a complex and difficult position if the expression 'climate change' will appropriately be understood and known. It is as if the crux of understanding climate change remains hidden in a basic act of Self-understanding!

Foundational in the leading thoughts of this book and its attitude towards one of the most challenging issues of today is that climate change represents a general conceptualization of change. This insight unveils, that different types of meaning for 'change' determine our understanding and practices of the climate change. The various human positions in view of different types of cognition will thus fit our search for a more encompassing insight in that special phenomenon. A *first* observation underlines that 'climate' studies are based on a scientifically conceptualized meaning of the term 'change'. Its focus is thus on specific patterns of cognition and thought developments. One of the descriptions of climate change mentions therefore 'conditions that are changing and changeable throughout the year, averaged over a series of years'. This pattern is documented in all definitions of a climate, so that this form of cognition seems to function as a basis. One must therefore conclude and accept that the qualities of a *average changeability* as defined in this form of knowledge are belong to the basic meaning of any climate change concept wherever discussed and applied on the planet. It seems a major component of the 'climate change' concept *qua talis*.

A *second* understanding of the term change does not refer to specific patterns of interpretation and understanding but to the acquirement of relevant data. All uses of the term 'change' in the issue called 'climate change' focus primarily on the human capacity to understand and master the *changeability* in the notion 'climate change'. But the question whether all changes in the climate's changeability are indeed within the reach of human capacities to understand and eventually to manage, is seldom posed! They are the product of specific observations. The question would not be how and with what instruments thee data might be acquired, but whether such an approach fits the life and destination of a human being. The changeability is treated as an objectively considered date which founds the 'climate' concept according to the quoted definition, and that date is never considered as specifically being beyond human power in any regard. The power of the human mind is a basic issue in the strong relations between cognition and conversion as described in the preceding chapters. Is that power correctly recognized and explored?

Both approaches and perspectives are a clear circumscription of the human attitude at stake: *a 'climate change' seems only occurring when the changeability of the climate is observed and defined by a scientific activity*! It appears that this issue can only be studied or managed within the limits of human understanding, decision and enforcement.[21] No wonder, that climate change is not treated in the philosophies of Kant or Hegel, and not mentioned in the thought patterns of Husserl or Peirce! The topic was only studied during the last decades of the twentieth century, and it received only worldwide attention in the first years of the twenty-first century! In other words: during the unfolding of what we called the 'New Plural' and its Digital component became the climate change a worldwide studied issue! The difference between the two meanings of 'change' should forcefully be underlined. The criterium for their difference is the position and power of the human mind. The first meaning of 'change'—its definition—is concretized and secured as an issue which is by human definition fixated and mastered. It differs in that regard principally from the second understanding of change—its politics and management included. Moreover, it is not only another theme of human understanding, but it requires a different management of the human mind. So, the complex meaning of 'change' in the climate change (definition made by a human mind reaching out to planetary dimensions) is ultimately based on fundamental differences which are a result of a human understanding of itself!

Two viewpoints are of importance in this regard:

A *first* meaning of change in this framework accentuates its human origin thanks to the flow of scientific conceptualization. We already encountered the latter in the form of a definition which appears as a crystallization of human thought patterns. Its origin is in the course of Occidental history assigned to the human spirit in its form of Subject and/or Subjectivity. The latter reached its dominance already centuries ago in the 'Subject–Object' pattern. The question remains, whether that specific pattern can still be in effect when such themes like a climate change are considered.

A *second* meaning of change in this framework results from a growing awareness and scientific perception that human beings are not solely created in human-social, that is: environmental and thus terrestrial circumstances but also in planetary patterns. Both form the foundation of life in its generality. Within that generality plays the special foundation of human life a dominant role. It is significant how the meaning of 'change' appears to be strongly active within the thought frames of life's interpersonal relations. From what is such a meaning dependent? We have

---

[21] See Google on Climate: 'the composite or generally prevailing weather conditions of a region, as temperature, air pressure, humidity, precipitation, sunshine, cloudiness, and winds, throughout the year, averaged over a series of years'. (https://www.dictionary.com/browse/climate) + Climate change: 'a change in global or regional climate patterns, in particular a change apparent from the mid to late twentieth century onwards and attributed largely to the increased levels of atmospheric carbon dioxide produced by the use of fossil fuel' (https://www.google.be/search?q=climate+change+definition)

hardly any other answer than: *from nature in its global understanding*! This opinion was a fundamental consideration of preceding chapters in this book.[22] It means that the role of nature should be deeper understood and considered as fundamental in the case of climate changes! In other words: climate change is not a matter of the natural human being but primarily of man as a cosmic being! In all problems of climate change is the terrestrial being confronted with that planetary being! How can the homo sapiens reach out to the planetary human? How can the human subject understand the climate change without grasping the essence of himself as a Self that embraces both constituents?

Do not forget how the hand extended to the planetary ego implies and engages the *Wholeness of the Human Self*. Such a wholeness implicates the different components of any human Self in every cultural and historical as well as geographical context. That experience is fundamental for encountering the multiple dimensions of the phenomenon named climate change. It is not solely a matter of communication, as is often stated in the digital patterns of modern culture. The *plural* meaning of 'change' constitutes the term 'climate change' and breaches the duality of Subject and Object, of I and You, of Speaker and Hearer—in other words: *it challenges the inner dynamics of the Self*. That is articulated by the ego as a being which enriches its self-understanding with an awareness of being born to experience to be and to become a planetary being. The modern complexity of those attitudes determines the understanding of the human-based dimensions of climate change! The latter marked the reports of the IPCC, created in 1988. Most observations in those texts, mainly administrative and political, refer to the future of the earth among other planets. But the first decades of the twenty-first century differ again from earlier visions! Do not forget that cognition (the usual basis for a mutual understanding among the planet's inhabitants) always included ideas and pictures about a future world. But what world, what planet is at stake in our contemporary thoughts and knowledge, based on patterns of the 'New Plural'?

These final pages of the book underline again the importance and renovative tendencies of human cognition—with conversion as its most powerful influencer today. And what is most important: they also determine our planetary life. Understand the relevance of our focus on a general concretization: how will the human mind conceptualize its knowledge in this context? No wonder, that various dimensions of actual cognition and its utterances are to be considered when 'climate change' is accepted as a worldwide issue. It remains that it can be considered epistemologically in all regards. So, we must adapt a critical view to our considerations of the world-climate and the consequences of its changes if we want to understand the epistemological dimensions of the *change* concept in this cosmic issue. The latter includes a focus on patterns of human knowledge which definitively touches the barriers and restrictions of human cognition.

The tensions regarding processes of *change within knowledge* seem immense! But they are, however, seldom determined only by psychological features. It is for

[22] See Chapters VI §1, VII §1,2.

that reason difficult to fully open the human mind for its proper knowledge processes and understand how it pertains in essence to *evolutionary* processes. And what is meant by the constitutive elements of climate and its change, is difficult to identify through means of becoming, that is: the process of their constitution. Our language often tries to express that but is seldom successful. Is there a possibility to bring the nature and the character of human destiny in any coherent grip of a lingual expression? That consideration should never be forgotten in the frameworks of studies and policies concerning climate change! Even the actual coherence of cognition and conversion cannot be successful in reaching the dimensions of planetary positions which feature the modernity of mankind. Living with a climate change is therefore meaningful for all dimensions of being human, in terrestrial as well as broader contexts viewed.

Their importance became in our days reinforced by the fact that no singular type or image of man completely represents anymore a 'being a human individual on the planet'. We mentioned the 'S-triad' in the 'New Plural' in that perspective. The triad does only in approximate manners fulfill the role of the traditional concept named Subject. A fundamental difference is that a distancing from the traditional Subject implies an important *farewell to any anthropocentric attitude* in knowledge and worldview.[23] In that perspective did for instance the modern term 'indigenous people' and its profile of multiplicity, experience difficulties to unfold new profiles because it embraced a social and political understanding beyond individuality. We need momentarily to grasp meaning and sense of human existence in general forms of cognition beyond singularities; plurals are sign and symbol of a newly conceived multiplicity which embraces planet and man. Today, each humanism might ultimately lead to a political, an economic or any other form of anthropocentrism and its many forms of individualism. But we experience that the latter is a serious problem of modelling the planet's future in terms of knowledge—is that a relevant approach to the subject named climate change? An even deeper-reaching question arises: leads the actual concern with a 'climate change' to new forms of anthropocentrism? We ask that question because each language seems based upon a central positioning of human knowledge and experience. Every word needs a human self. But today, a human self which is linked to a non-anthropocentric view on reality, might not yet function in the social patterns of human life and its languages! A Self does today only function in forms of digitally enhanced communication—in words and symbols, data, behavioral and cognitive patterns.

The Jewish Torah and the Holy Bible, even the Islamic Koran, spend very few lines on the Creation of the Planet, or the Globe in the Cosmos[24] without mentioning the Human Existence as its central issue. That should be understood as an important

[23] See https://link.springer.com/article/10.1007/s10806-018-9711-1: 'Anthropocentrism, in its original connotation in environmental ethics, is the belief that value is human-centred and that all other beings are means to human ends. Environmentally concerned authors have argued that anthropocentrism is ethically wrong and at the root of ecological crises'.

[24] *Torah*: Genesis Ch.1, 2(8); *Bible*: Genesis Ch.1, 2(4); *Koran*: Soera 7, (54); 36, (81).

symbol. All major Holy Scripts share this peculiar pattern of articulation. Can we in today's critical situation of the Planet unfold an intelligent understanding of its facts and figures in a non-anthropocentric manner? This problem already received attention in earlier periods of European thinking, even in the Middle Ages. But they have never been so painfully important as in our days! We have literally no words for nature as 'nature', cosmos as 'cosmos' or planet as 'planet'. Can we therefore strengthen the various political and economic means of our thoughts, insights and formulae which are already internationally available? In other words: *is our globally recognized 'climate crisis' not a crisis of human knowledge and its expressivity?* We should read those terms in the context of our actual need to explore 'life on- and with the planet'. That insight may even differ from those of the last decades of our past century! Today do we want to circumscribe the activity of the planet as: 'life on the globe as we understand it'. However, the quality and duration of cosmic life remains an all-embracing conditional power of our human existence. We are too often enforced to regard cases we consider as climate, population, or even geographical conditions, in a non-appropriate manner. The words 'climate change' and 'climate crisis' indicate a unique semiotic issue, that is: an issue which concerns meaning.

What is at stake in such observations? We need a word, a sign, a meaning, a concept or a generally accepted lingual expression of for 'nature', 'planet's life' or 'cosmic reality'. Each word remains an element of the totality of planet and cosmos and will therefore not dissolve in any finitude. At stake is always a 'pars pro toto' being the cause for a unity of earth and planet, of planet and cosmos, of man and life. But one consideration remains important: we are always searching and thinking about an alternative *word* and thus challenge our language to grasp issues of planetary character in words or word-like expressions. Should that not inspire a final correctness, even necessity, of *anthropocentric* attitudes? In other words: do we ever succeed in managing our *Self* to acquire a correct understanding of our own specific cognitive positions?

This pertains to our *self-understanding* as an element of the processes which are mirrored by cultural traditions and languages in every setting. It seems that the strong narrative character of the human mind feeds the knowledge of cognition which should be recognized as belonging to the dynamics of being human! Is therefore the meaning of 'being-human' indeed dangerously anthropocentric, so that it cannot answer a climate crisis, or a change of the planet's face? That challenging question has various implications. A major consequence pertains to the precious awareness of a human Self in different attitudes. Climate change emphasizes two variant positions: an awareness of the *terrestrial* and an awareness of the *planetary* ego—the Subject or what is called in terms of this book: the S–triad. Modern literature on the issue demonstrates that the presence of 'climate change' problems enlarge and highlight this duality.

The great value of this accentuation in our days of the New Plural becomes clear when the expression '*planetary climate crisis'* is used. This specific terminology indicates the necessity to acknowledge the position of the knowing and socializing ego, subject or self. Perhaps remains one of the most disturbing and challenging conclusions in these days of an expanding human consciousness the question 'Who am I'? The answer is certainly no longer a matter of a single identity or a sole identification. Those concepts became old-fashioned compared to our actual need for understanding the dimensions of the human Self. The expansion which comprises my understanding and exploring reaches from earth to planet and cosmos—but what is the meaning and sense of the pronoun 'my'? Meaning and sense should indeed not lead to any form of individualism or self-centered view on oneself, the earth or the cosmos. Neither the pronouns are determinative, because they are no more than a linguistic utterance! The essence (what this book strived to indicate) is the 'me' or the 'Self' in *all* dimensions. One should seriously consider how the step from 'terrestrial' to 'planetary' *changes* the Speaker, the Subject, the Self and the Self-E together with all other first-person categories which are linguistically explored. It is important to become aware of the fact that the lingual forms of thought-formation are far more than a tool to express meanings and attitudes. Indeed, the tool is the means itself! We must consider this when we become engaged in the tensions between a terrestrial and a planetary field of action and identity. Actual climate change considerations are missing a planetary view (in the first place a 'politics') which manages and sustains such a view.

That idea is still a matter of subject-related attitudes. Most of them are characterized as individualistic—no matter what kind of individuality is at stake in the relevant segment of the planet's culture. More than any other one includes the expression (and idea) 'planetary view' a challenge to broaden the realm of human knowledge (and self-awareness) from Subject or even Nation into wider planetary dimensions related to human action. Indeed: psychology and its patterns of knowledge do belong to the issue of climate change! Planetary politics are based on insights, cognitions and politics of existing concepts of subjectivity and personal identity—but are they truly planetary? The problematic character of this issue is, that it stems directly from a Subject position which flourished in the nineteenth and twentieth century! There is *no* broadening of views and knowledges away from individual subject and nation in the direction of the planet! In other words: it is as if the often-mentioned historical transition of the Subject has no meaning or influence in cases of climate change and its need to envisage cosmic perspectives. We repeat, that cognition, psychology and other patterns of knowledge do indeed belong to climate change. But planetary politics—if actualized at all—are only explored as based on insights, cognition and politics of specific nations, in all dimensions driven by 'self'-interest. A consequence is, that the scope of a national activity in all scientific and political approaches becomes disputable. An example is when *national* actions should prevent *global* warming. A global-warming phenomenon caused by climate change is by no means an extremely large fire that went on a rampage in a national area! On the contrary, global warming inherently transcends the scope of any national and even inter-national determination as well as human action. Insight in the scope of human answering climate issues seems a matter of cognition in human lives and their history: it regards the acknowledgment and concretization of barriers and boundaries! And it shows that a simple appeal to a Subject or any other individualistic factor in life does not suffice. Why not? Simply because a human being's life is in essence by no means individual or individualistic! So, the question must be formulated again, whether our cognition is correctly applied when *global* warming is answered with *national* means—economic, technical, juridical, political means included. Note the enormous importance of the fact that all these means are basically a matter of strategic individualism. They fit the dominant patterns of power and sociality in actual life and create no link with the essence of terrestrial man, man's cosmic dimensions and his seldom fully concretized belonging to globe *and* cosmos! In other words: can a nation (solely as an individual nation) fight and extinguish the heath and threats of a global warming with technical means? Has a nation any reliable means, in other words: the correct techniques, to do so? What is more: has this question ever been posed, either in a national parliament or a multinational assignment? The turning point of those questions is by no means solely a technical issue! On the contrary, it is a seldom articulated insight in man's self-determination and position as a terrestrial *and* a planetary existence. That is for instance to conclude when national and international measures to fight certain climate-threatening issues are initiated. In many cases arises a friction because of the scale and foundation of its basic reference, which is a nation as an individual, as a subject in its traditional meaning and sense.

All that is clearly visible in forms of climate change control which lead to an in-depth of contrasting the developed against the developing world. When individual nations or groups of nations take climate-relevant measures, developed nations tend to prescribe poorer nations. This remains a copy of the very traditional Speaker–Hearer structure. An example is when developed nations unfold a political system which helps poorer nations to shift away from fossil fuels and protect these nations as well as themselves from global warming. Is such a techno-political procedure the correct and desirable form of mastering climate change in a truly planetary sense? From here might even more disputable questions unfold. Do the leaders of the developed world acquire and master full insight in their self-interest? Can there be peace and prosperity if one-third of the world prospers and the other two-third of the globe's population is living under threats? A heart-breaking conclusion can be formulated in the form of an all-encompassing question involved in today's the climate change problem: the globe remains hued by deepening international rivalries, inward-looking policies and domestic polarization. Wars and international crises do clearly show today that the globe's cognition is too self-centered.

This relatively simple conclusion is the rich fruit of the many attempts to understand the climate change and the answers formulated today. Be aware, that the national and individualistic approach, its technical qualities included, suggests that there should be a choice between various technical and economic, political and even humanitarian means to solve for instance the warming of the globe. But any insight in the tensions within the singular as well as socially acting human personality show a different issue. They are indeed steering and mastering the problems with all technical and economic means that are available within the human community of nations. But their variety threatens the positive effects: contrasts between arm and rich in every regard: institutions, governments, co-ordinations of nations, attitudes to post-colonialism etc.

The distance between today's policies and the insight in the actual cohesion between cognition and conversion is enormous—and that distance should be diminished. Indeed, there is a common knowledge and convincement that human activity changes the climate. There is no certainty about changes of the planet in conditions that reach into planetary dimensions. That insight is today classified as scientifically acknowledged. A guarantee pertaining to the planet's continued existence in its actual form cannot be given. Institutions with the task to protect and improve the actual climate conditions by means of political and scientific measures should calculate with hitherto unknown principles with equally unreliable social and economic impacts. An important dimension of such an institutional approach is its plurality: always will various nations or blocks of nations understand the necessity to decide on precious and precarious decisions based on insights which will never be positively embraced by all participants. Traditional legal, political or economical approaches must be integrated with psychological, social and behavioral sciences, effective means and studies of communication even beyond digital techniques as well as basic philosophies concerning the patterns of the human Self. An intriguing factor is, that all those changing views, interests and determining powers remain a forceful challenge to the traditional hyper-individualism of earlier centuries.[25] In that regard should a gap be created between traditional applications of economy, politics, law, or social sciences on one side and the vision on the Self as individual as well as political component—as social reality as well as thought pattern. Let us never forget, that also the 'New Plural' is just a pattern of cultural determinations which has no pretention to endure beyond time and circumstance.

Cognition, Conversion and the new *Self:*

Indeed: these are words that should not be forgotten in our days. They are key words for expressing what this book brings to the fore. And they comprise in the first place an integration of terrestrial and planetary thought patterns, which occurs by means of changing the foundational patterns of understanding ourselves. That brings us back to *conversion* as one of the most influencing powers of today. Needed is a conversion that grounds and masters our cognition by means of clarifying how terrestrial and planetary elements of human self-understanding integrate. To accept and realize that great challenge in ourselves and of our Self, we should concretely—even in its most subtly materialized form—agree with knowing and exploring the dimensions of our own situation of being a creature.

We thus conclude, all in all, that not technical, political, socio-economic or even legal measures determine the outcome of human intervention in the actual climate change. It is the position of the Human Self, created via its patterns of cognition and

[25] See.: 'non-personal' individualism, or 'structural' individualism, means beyond the grip of a person or personality on the social structure which influences life, especially social life, based on the loss or inattentiveness of the 3S-triad. In the thirties of the twentieth century was the term 'Heaven and Earth' in Chr. Protestant circles of Western Europe used to indicate terrestrial and planetary dimensions as features of human life. But in 1940, the first days of WW2, became 'heaven' the sky, which became a center of warplanes and bombardments, so that the term became meaningless until the New Plural unfolded.

conversion, which must become a key for those qualities of life—like all other qualities! Global warming, nitrogen problems and intensity of stock farming, melting icecaps, floodings and fires depend ultimately on the character and quality of human Self-determination. The period of exclusively terrestrial visions on the human Self seems outdated in the age of the 'New Plural'. These pages are thus a plea for insights and practices of humane harmony and dignity caused by an integration of cognition and conversion. A much needed and precious appraisement of human existence will be mirrored in all forms of this togetherness—and, remarkably enough, it will enrich and reform the basics of life on the planet. Human ethics should for that reason be renamed and revised.

A well understood *humanity ethics* parallels an integration of human behavior and knowledge into dimensions of terrestrial and cosmic nature. Take our school lessons in geography as an example. That topic focuses no longer on the question where wild parks, large cities, huge mountains, rivers and animals are located on earth. No, the issue should be today when and where precisely determined locations are threatened by for instance building a dam, creating frontiers, animating tourism, and what other consequences for planetary life such earthy events cause! A 'humanity ethos' does not place the human being or it's Self in the center of the globe. On the contrary, it focuses on human creations being profiled as a successful integration of terrestrial and planetary views. It asks in words of preceding pages whether the *hemisphere* can become a trustworthy component of the *semiosphere* of the Self! Notice how standpoints located on the globe have today a planetary address—for the time being without a digital address, but they are by means of a humane consciousness sustained by adequate conversion views[26]! Not only the sender but also the receiver should be highly esteemed in days when the Speaker–Hearer duality became disregarded and the Self no longer accepted as the sole Receiver! We repeat what was formulated on preceding pages: a 'Speaker – Hearer relation' seems today a complex and difficult position if the expression 'climate change' will be understood and known. It is as if the crux of understanding climate change remains hidden in the act of an appropriate Self-understanding!

The challenge of the latter reads like a renewed explanation of human origin. The terrestrial character of a human being cannot remain limited to terrestrial features but is only understandable in planetary dimensions. Fascinating parallel positions are developed in the works of the French philosopher Bruno Latour. He proposed to conclude alternative democracies in which also non-human actors (even Amazon trees) are included. Ecology should thus receive renewed attention in broader contexts. Human behaviors are often dimensioned beyond measurements and effects of the planet earth. Problems of climate change confirm that attitude and require any human being to accept, understand and practice this determination. That is the perhaps greatest challenge human cognition ever faced. Capitalist inspired travel agencies focusing on extraterrestrial views of the planet (Musk) express some of

[26] See the works of the French philosopher Bruno Latour (1947–2022), for instance at https://fr.wikipedia.org/wiki/Bruno_Latour.

those dimensions. They will in a nearby future embrace Mars, Moon and other planets, as suggested in the first chapter of this book—based on the New Plural patterning of cognition and experience. Dimensions of what occurs on the planet already reach beyond the borderlines of that celestial body. There is no flower, no animal, no earthy construction that does not claim: perceive me in my life's semiotic flow which determines the terrestrial as meaningful only if conceived in planetary dimensions! Indeed, changes do also change!

References

Blackman L (2019) Haunted data. Affect, transmedia, weird science. Bloomsbury Academic, New York

Broekman JM (1963) Phänomenologie und Egologie. Faktisches und Transzendentales Ego bei Edmund Husserl. M. Nijhoff, Den Haag

Broekman JM (2004) The virtual in E-education. IIS Publ. Cie, New York

Broekman JM (2009) Face to Face. In: International journal for the semiotics of law, Vol. 22(1). Springer, Dordrecht

Broekman JM (2010) Face to Face (II): semiotics of interactivity. In: International journal for the semiotics of law, Vol. 23(1). Springer, Dordrecht

Burks AW (1978) Review: Charles S. Peirce, the new elements of mathematics. Bull Am Math Soc 84:5

Colapietro V (1989) Peirce's approach to the self. State University of New York Press, Albany

Deleuze G, Guattari F (1984) Anti-Oedipus: Capitalism and Schizophrenia. (Transl. Eng.: Hurley R, Seem M, Lane HR, eds) Athlone, London

Hartley J, Ibrus I, Ojamaadic M (2020) In: Burks AW (ed) On the digital semiosphere: culture, media and science for the anthropocene. Bloomsbury Publishing, The Belknap Press of Harvard University Press

Kandel ER (2012) The age of insight. The quest to understand the unconscious in art, mind, and brain. Random House, New York

Kurzweil R (2005) The singularity is near. Viking/Penguin, New York

Lotman J (2005) On the semiosphere. Sign Syst Stud 33

Lotman J (2009) Culture and explosion [=Russian original 1992]. Walter de Gruyter, Berlin

Lotman J (1990) Universe of the mind: a semiotic theory of culture. Indiana University Press, Bloomington

Lotman J (1998) La Sémiosphère. PULIM, Limoges

Mangieri R (2022) Pandemics semiosphere and global network: the space turn in the Juri Lotman model. In: Biglari A (ed) Open semiotics Vol. 2: culture and society, Ch.2. L'Harmattan, Paris

Paolucci C (2022) 'Face and mask: 'Person' and 'subjectivity' in language and through signs'. In: International journal for the semiotics of law, Vol. 35(4). Springer

Peirce CS (1992) A guess at the riddle. In: Houser N, Kloesel C (eds) The essential Peirce. Selected philosophical writings, Vol. 1. Indiana University Press, Bloomington and Indianapolis

Richards IA (1971) The Philosophy of Rhetoric (1936). Oxford University Press

Singer M (1980) Signs of the self: an exploration in semiotic anthropology. In: American anthropologist, New Series, Vol. 82(3)

Stone AR (1991) Will the real body please stand up? Boundary stories about virtual cultures. In: Benedikt M (ed) Cyberspace: first steps. MIT Press, Cambridge

Suler J (2016) Psychology of the digital age. Humans becoming electric. Cambridge University Press, New York

Torop P (2005). Semiosphere and/as the research object of semiotics of culture. In: Σημειωτκή-Sign Systems Studies, Tartu Ülikooli Kirjastus, Tartu, Estland

Turkle S (1985) The second self, computers and the human Spirit. Simon & Schuster, New York